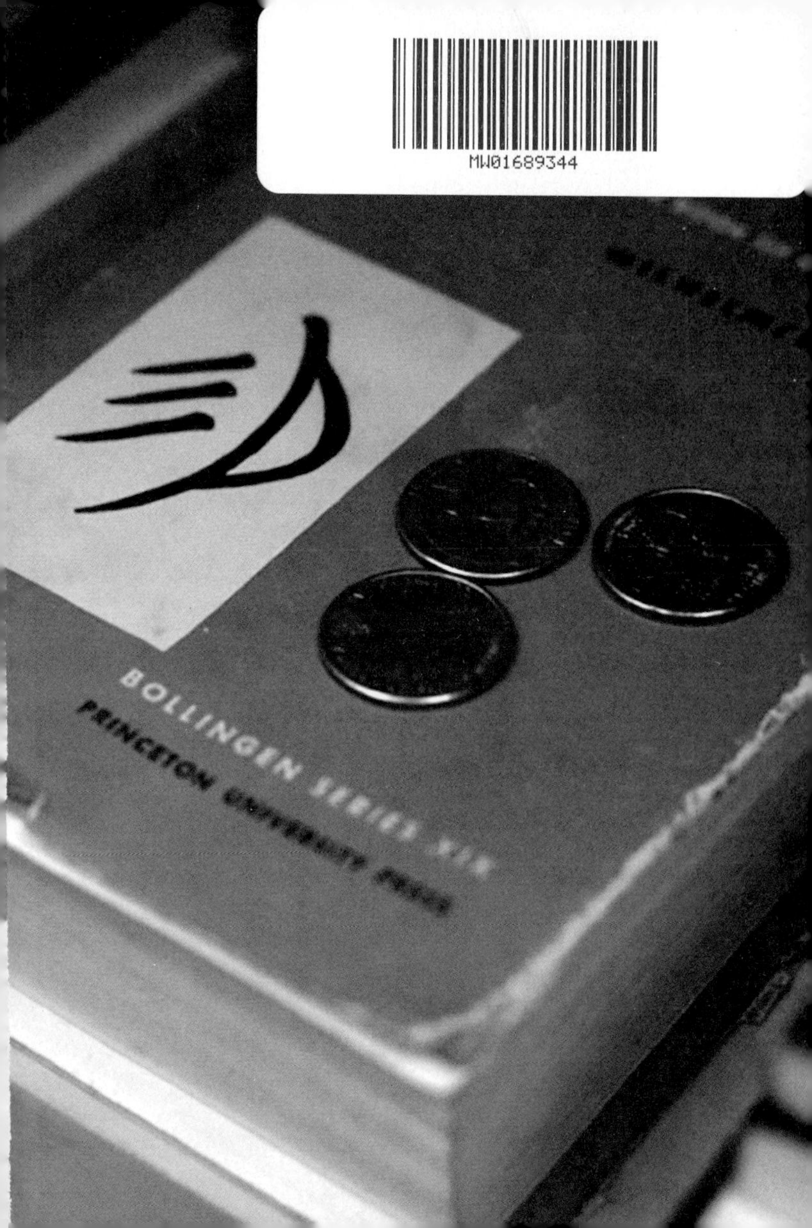
BOLLINGEN SERIES XIX
PRINCETON UNIVERSITY PRESS

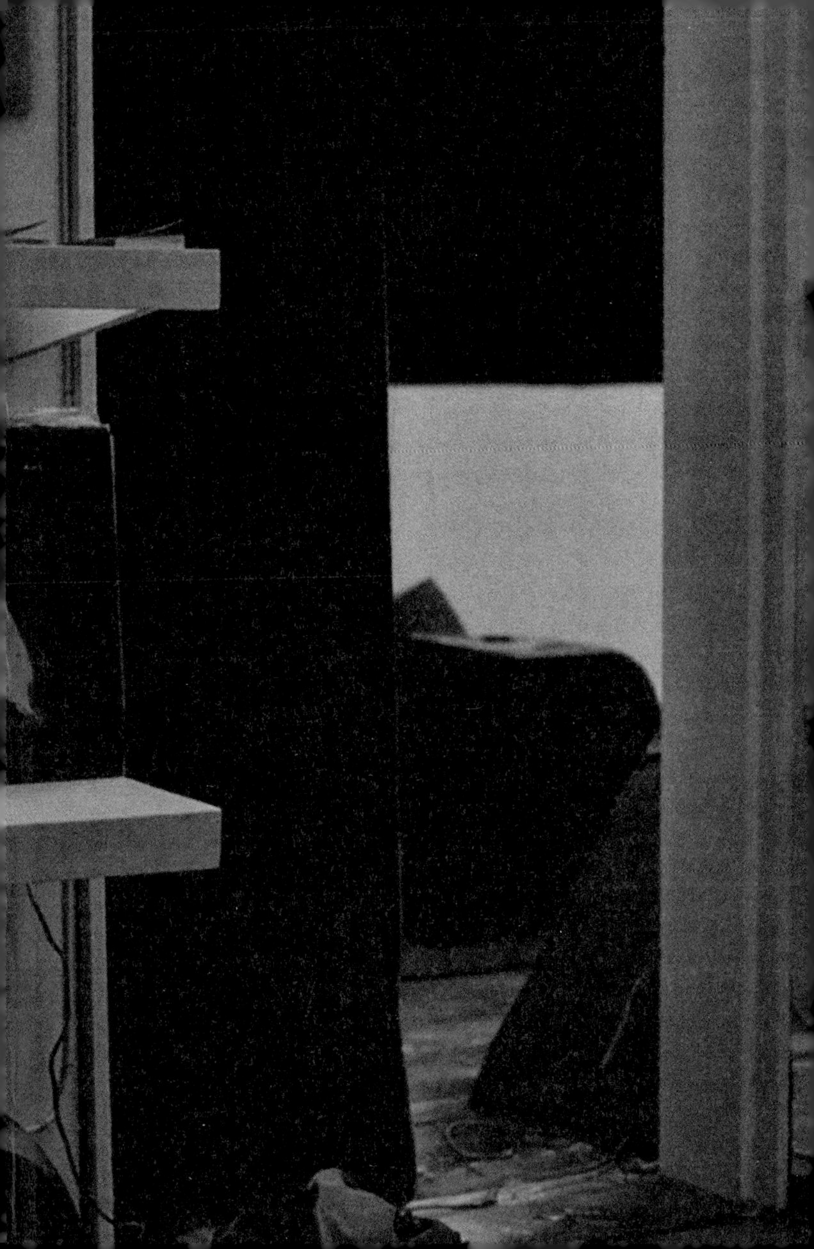

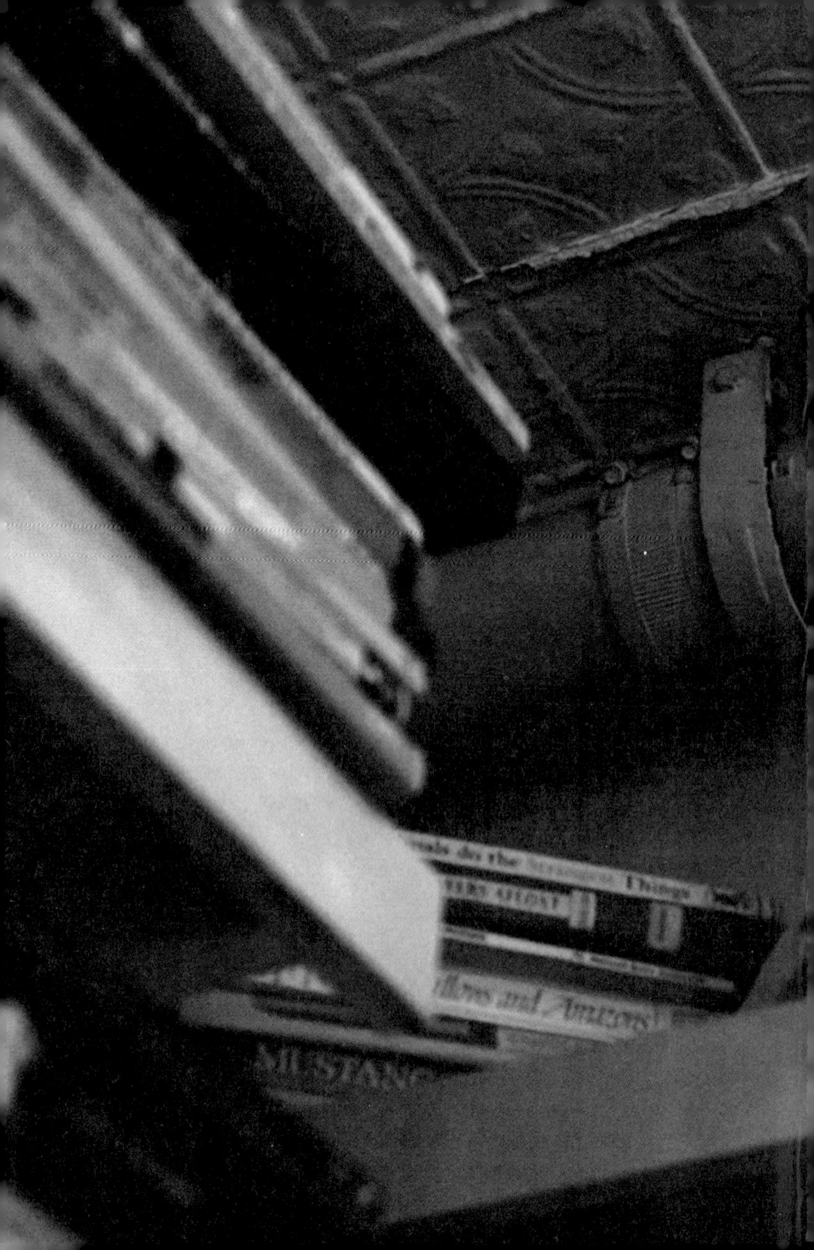

EMPTIES
Moyra Davey

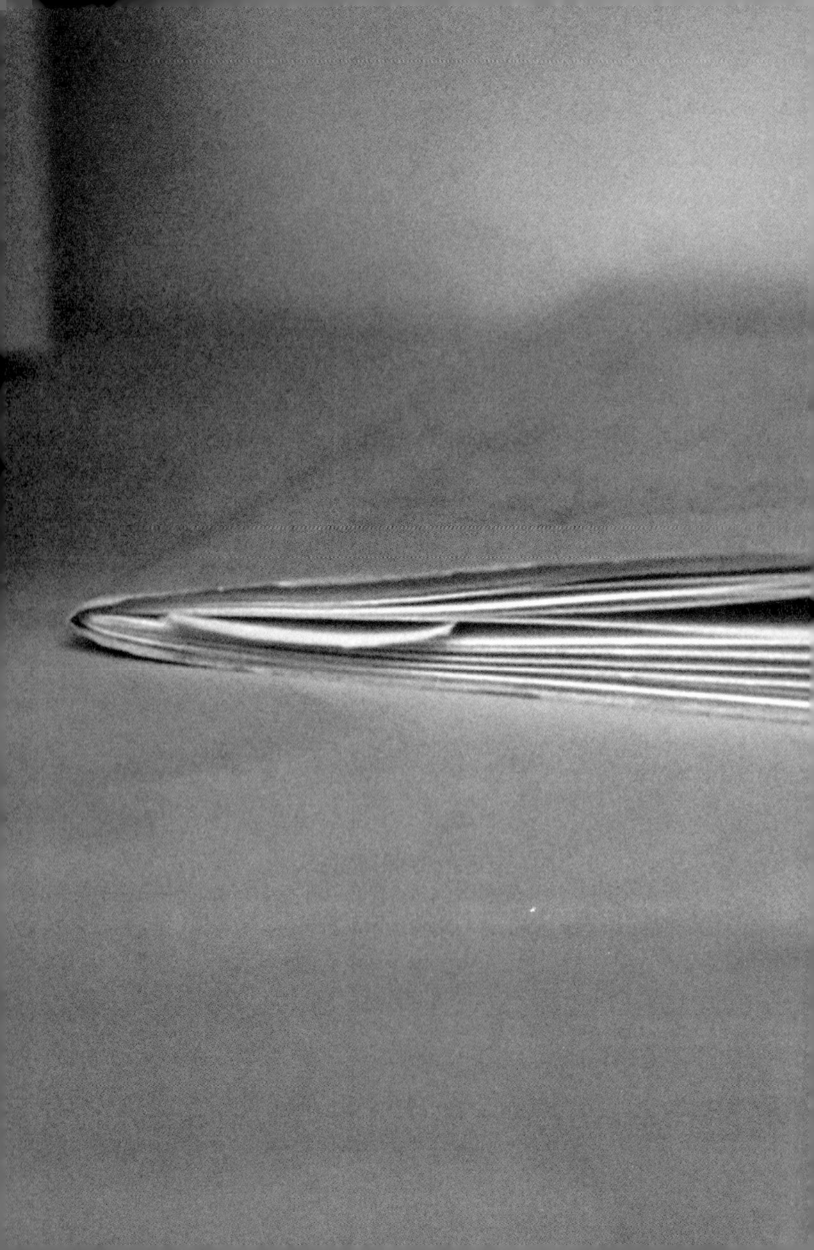

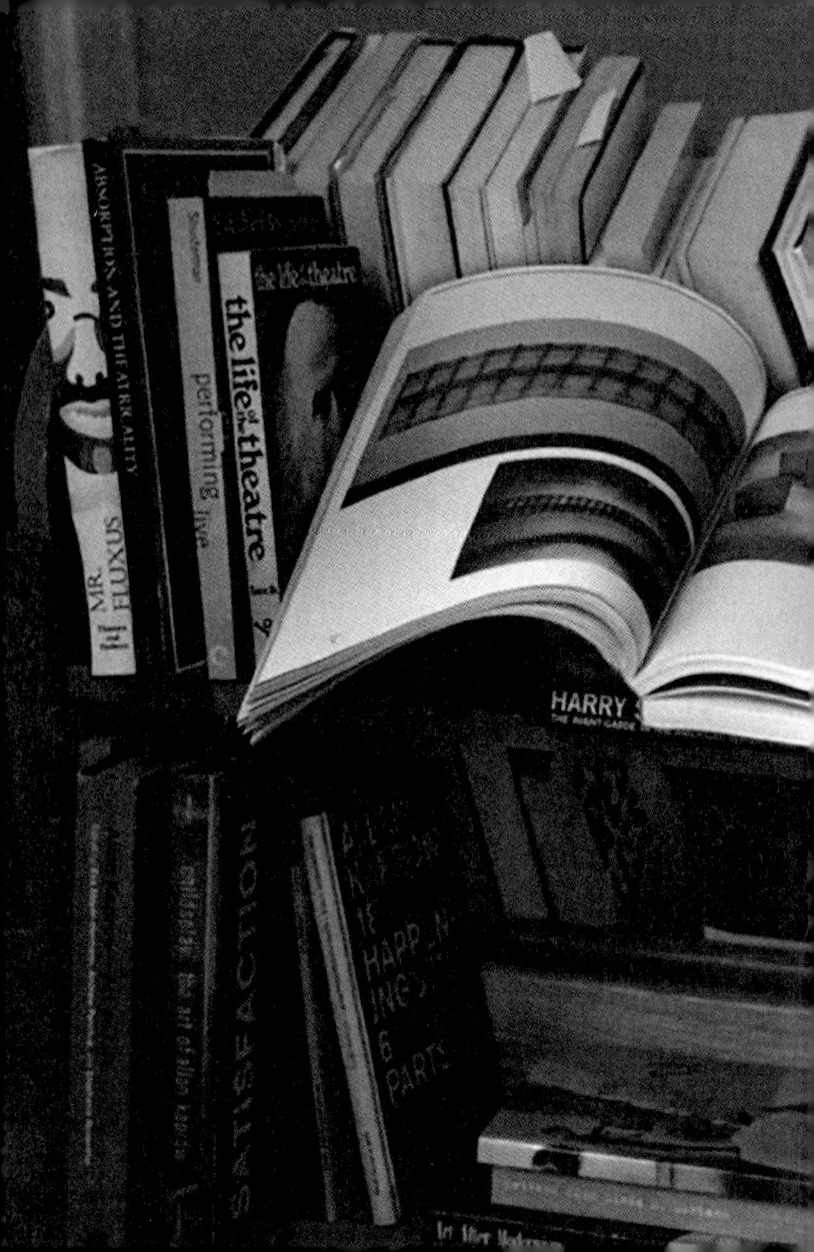

ABSORPTION AND THEATRICALITY
MR. FLUXUS
performing live
the life of the theatre
the life of the theatre
HARRY
18 HAPPENINGS IN 6 PARTS

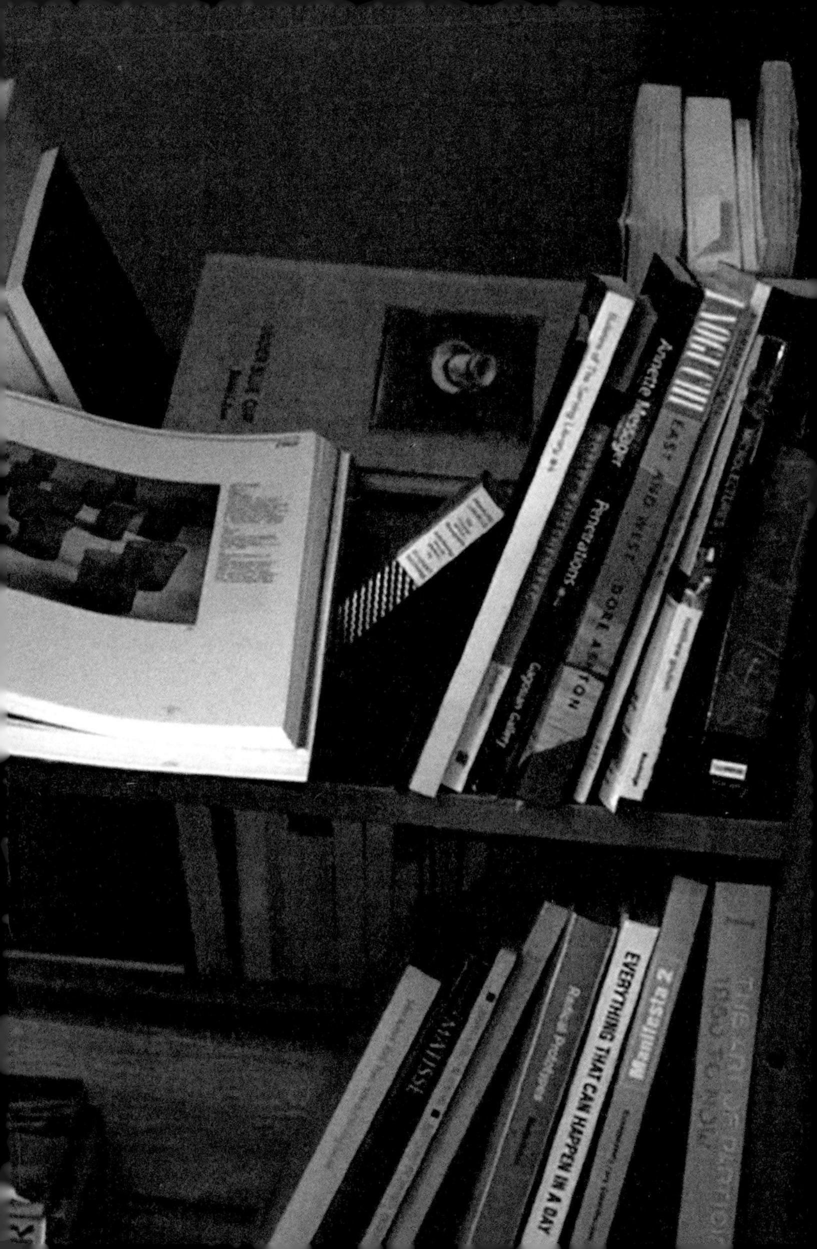

Annette Messager
Penetrations
EAST AND WEST
DORE ASHTON
MATISSE
EVERYTHING THAT CAN HAPPEN IN A DAY
Manifesta 2

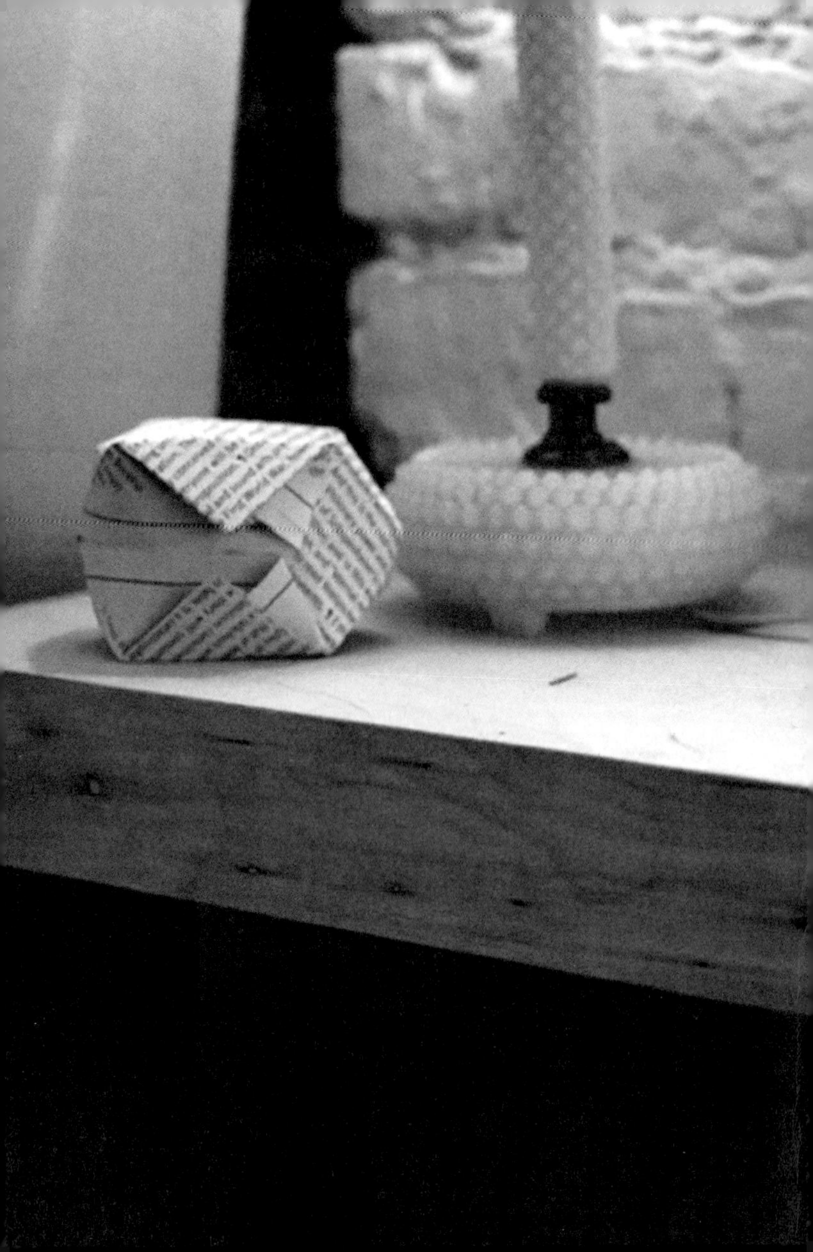

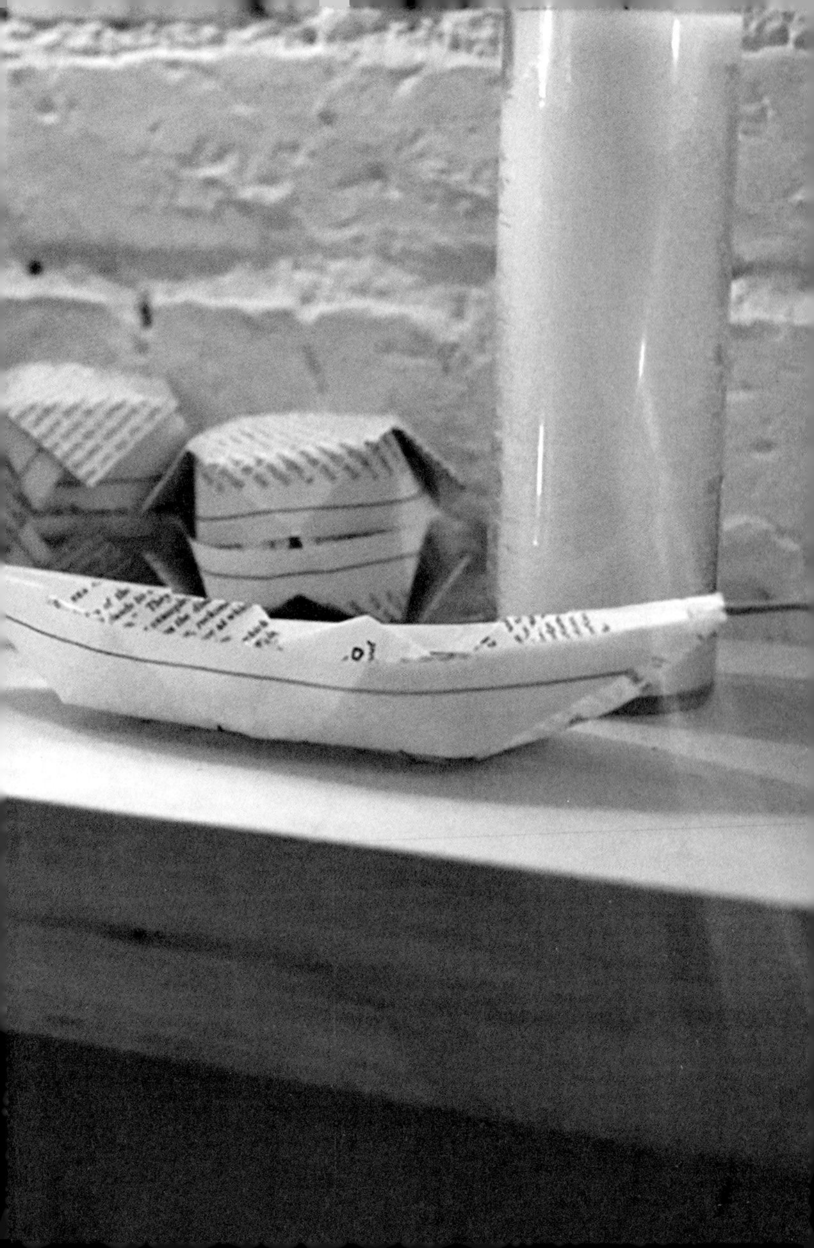

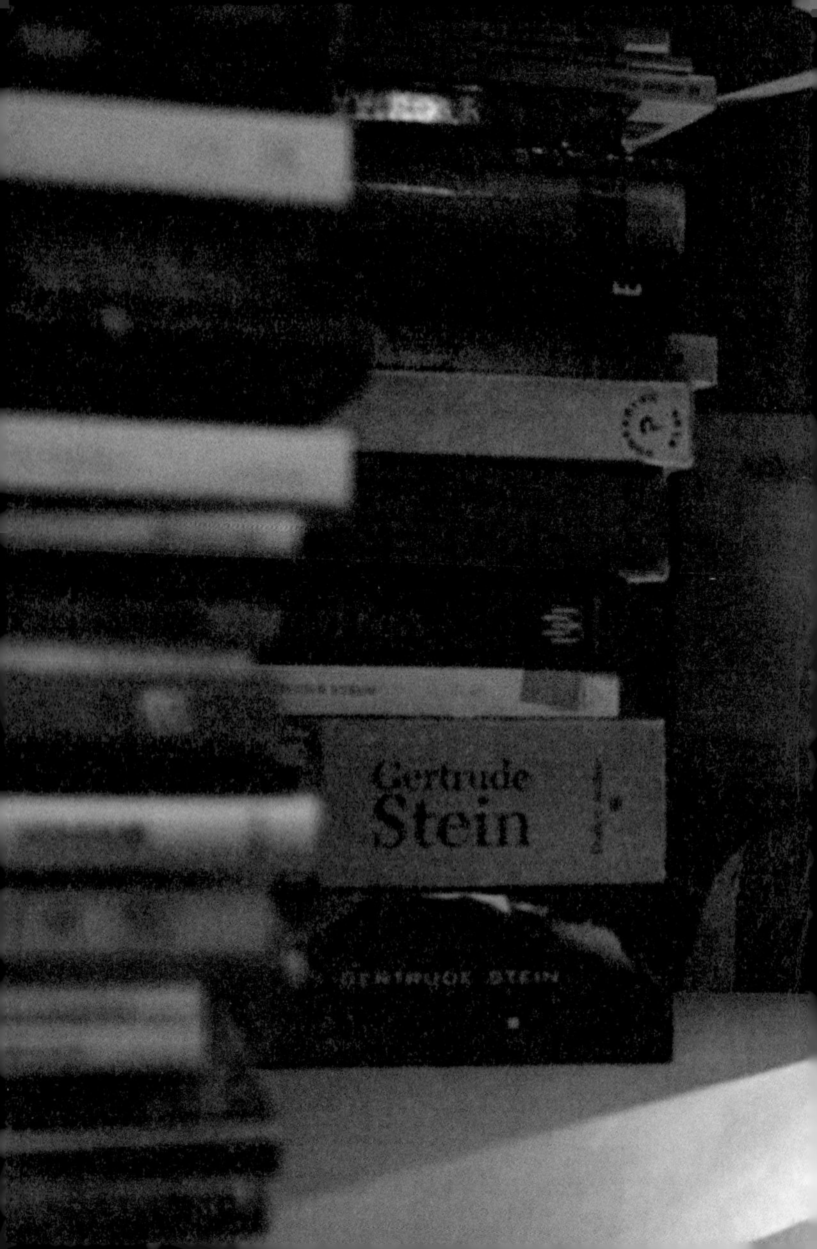
Gertrude
Stein

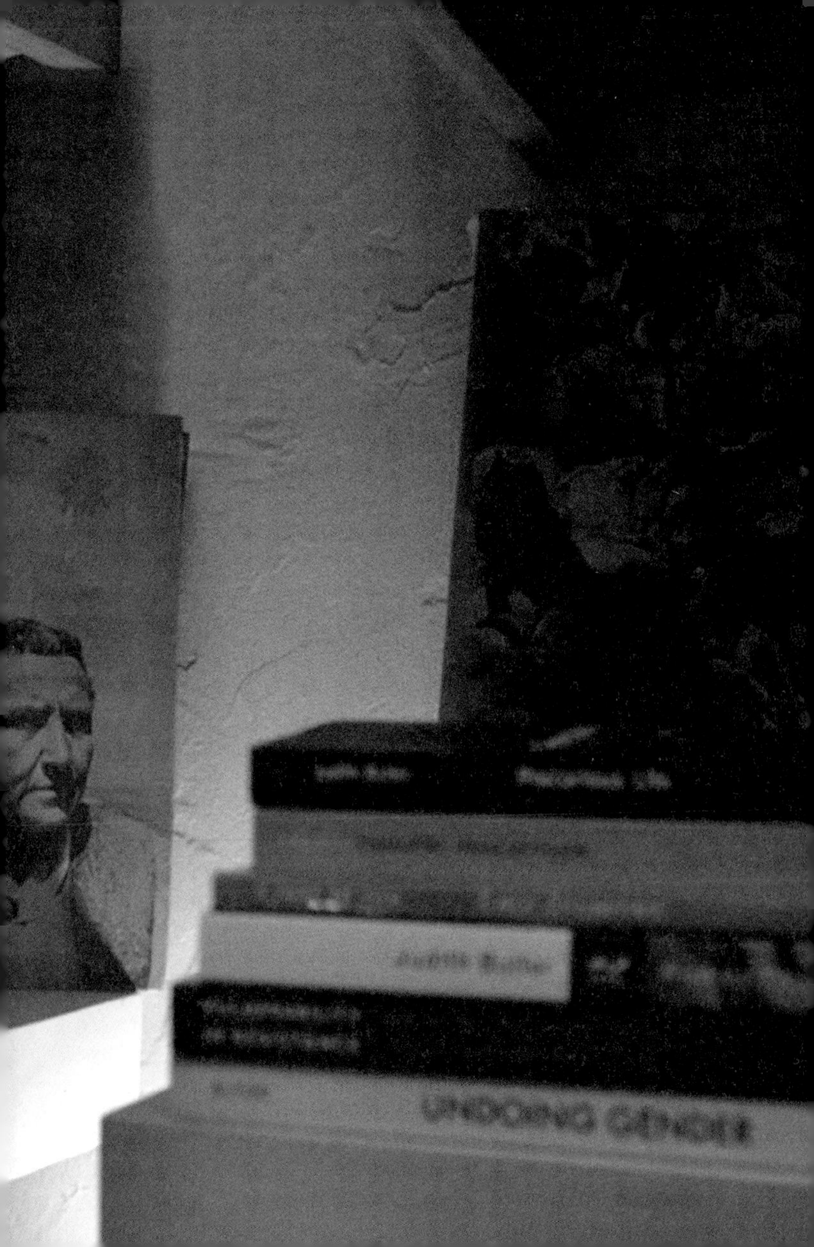
Judith Butler
UNDOING GENDER

Reading Room

Reading Room

I. Before Reading

II. While Reading

III. Seeing Reading

IV. On Reading

V. After Reading

I. Before Reading

On holding

British psychoanalyst D.W. Winnicott developed the notion of a “holding environment” in his work on child care. The term describes a mothering space – both physical and mental, emotional – created and facilitated by the “good enough” parent for the benefit of an infant: in the safety of the holding environment, which is marked by a state of total provision, the child can begin to develop away from the parent, to begin the work of individuation. We might think of it as a protected site of early mentation: held by the mother, the burgeoning mind of the child can wander. In this way, the holding environment might figure as an original site of thinking, one the child will revisit their whole life long as language rushes to fill it.

And how does language rush to fill it? The mother speaks, and the child begins to talk; the mother reads aloud and then the child learns to do it for themselves. Once a person can read on their own, they can reproduce the holding site with the help of a book. A good enough book engenders held space for thinking.

On dispersing

To disperse is to scatter, as in the wind picking up the seed head of a dandelion and casting its ethereal petals across a meadow; to spread, as in the good news; to broadcast, as in a melody on the radio.

What do these figures have in common? All are disseminative acts of communication. That is, all are acts of publication.

To disperse is to publish.

On reading rooms

The history of the reading room is a rich one, in two senses: the form's history is dense and storied, and it is marked by class. A full address of the reading room is beyond the purview of this text, but consider this: public, private; institutional, personal; temporary, permanent collections: all are designed to facilitate the reader's willing surrender to the thinking of a writer.

What if, instead of thinking of the reading room as being created by the pillows and curtains and desks – by everything outside of or adjacent to reading – we thought of the room of reading as emanating from that most elemental furnishing, the physical book?

The book goes with you, and where you are is the site of reading. Wherever you are reading this? That is the reading room.

To this end, to publish a book is to disseminate a mobile holding environment for thinking.

On *Reading Room*

Every book, a dispersed holding.
Every book, a disseminated room for reading.
We offer this book to you such that you might use it to mark out some space and time in the world. Some space and time to read.
We offer you here, with the book you are holding, some room for reading.
We offer you *Reading Room*, a dispersed holding.
May it be good enough.

The Ambient Reading Spectacular and the Reading Room

We had been sewing cushions for months by then, raiding the bargain bin of Economy Foam for odd shapes and buying wide sheets for the floor. We covered them in the olive green felt of army blankets and stitched the seams in red yarn. On these cushions, we and a small cohort of fellows reclined and read.

As that first summer passed in a rhythm of sewing, iced coffee, and stacks of books, we found that the more reading we did, the more we wanted to do. Looking ahead to the autumn we decided to formalize this passion by inviting as many people as we could to become "readers in residence," to spend a day or more simply reading in a room made for the purpose, our reading room.

We chose the smallest and coziest chamber in the space, went to Mood Fabrics and came away with yards of deep blue wool for special cushions, and lush velvet to curtain the doorways. We found worn carpets and faded brass oil lamps refitted with low bulbs, we embroidered some wall hangings and wove others from Navajo churro wool.

Our piles of cushions invited readers to configure piles of their own.

As the weather grew colder we hosted readers, making soup for them at midday (Thai coconut curry, French onion soup, Moroccan vegetable stew, red lentil dal, David's vegetarian chili) and pots of coffee all through the darkening afternoons.

Ultimately we named this project the Ambient Reading Spectacular, a celebration and investigation of that most retiring and curious act of thinking.

Why ambient? Ambient is a special word to the holders of dispersed. Inspired by a mutual love for Brian Eno's early solo records, dispersed holdings has pursued an aesthetic of pervasive durations of sound, language, and experience that we keep close to mind with the word:

> *Ambient: Sublimate, atomize what you love; live in the fine haze. Everywhere and ongoing, it expands and endures, disperses and holds. Satie, Cage, and Eno: vapor that loves the room beyond it. Visual works so slow they evaporate in front of you. Distant lectures, half heard, half daydreamt. Subtle infiltrations of environment. What of the work can be translucent, transparent to surroundings, distractions, reveries, the indifferent interventions of the world?*

These themes are not only of aesthetic interest, they also espouse an important attentional politics: ambience is an open and opening modality that operates at the threshold of awareness; it is the opposite of crisis. By not commanding or capturing attention, ambience invites the agency of one's own attention, equalizing the pressure of the inner and outer worlds. It allows mind-wander and reverie, it supports creative shaping of inner experience.
A place can be an ambience, a field of sound can be an ambience, a book can be an ambience.

As experienced, an ambience is always a collaboration between a person and their world, it is the fusion of sensation with feeling, present with past, the real with the imagined. While an act of reading might carry you along in the mind of another, it can also bring you into intimacy with your own mind. The reading mind naturally moves: into the ambient surround, onto the page, to memory, to inner argument, to dream. In this way, reading weaves a new self-experience.

Why spectacular? We had the improbable wish to show what was invisible, or at least infra-visible: the inner life of the reader. To this end, we invited filmmakers to display reading in two-minute shorts;

we gathered and read aloud to each other; and we live-scored readerly musical performances. There were workshops, library interventions, class visits, secret night inhabitations, and long discussions of what reading meant.

The final act of spectacle, of making visible, is this book, where readers were invited to show something of their experience. Some of what you will see and read here is a literal index of things that happened; more unfolded over the year that has followed as our readers kept reading. We offer this portable reading room in the hopes that it inspires you to do the same.

* * *

Reading Room is divided into three main parts: the first section, “While Reading,” documents the Ambient Reading Spectacular. It comprises descriptions of events held at dispersed over the course of the fall of 2016 and a clutch of reports from the reading room. It is followed immediately by “Seeing Reading,” which collects stills from the series of short films about reading curated by Jeff Dolven. The final section, “On Reading,” gathers twenty-one essays about readerly practices and methodologies, and personal reading histories; these texts were commissioned for this book from our residents after their reading hours came to a close.

We encourage you, dear reader, to move freely through the sections and the texts herein. This book need not be read sequentially – spend time with what essays and images draw you. Only you know what you need.

Coda

If at any point you require palate-cleansing, please see Madelyn Kent & Helen Singh Miller's notes toward the preparation of the reading tongue in appendix A. Should you wish to un- and then re-navigate this book, please see "A Sort of Practical Cartography" in appendix B, compiled by Alan Huck and dispersed holdings.

II. While Reading

On Thursday, 6 October 2016, we hosted an opening party for the Ambient Reading Spectacular. In its name, dispersed holdings would give site to various happenings centered on the act of reading. At the event, we debuted the reading room and the dispersed library. Party-goers were encouraged to pull from the shelves and deliver readings of their favorite poets and writers.

After the party, the readerly enthusiasm of our friends and collaborators affirmed our decision: we would open the reading room to those seeking shelter for quiet hours of bookish contemplation. We fluffed the cushions, and we put out a call:

Ah, what a joy it is to recline and luxuriate in the pages of a book. What a marvel, ambling through the world of another's thinking; what a gift, the time and care the writer gave to you in the form of so many words and images. Such criminal pleasure, to leave your worldly day behind, to be accountable only to your reading self and the text in front of you. If only you had the time and space! You might never leave the lines, spines, chapters, and margins of your favorite books.

Because we, like you, love reading and are intensely curious about its mysteries, this fall dispersed holdings will be hosting an Ambient Reading Spectacular, a celebration of the reader, book in hand. The heart of the Ambient Reading Spectacular will be readers themselves, resident in our reading room, a configurable secret reading refuge. In the main space and library, groups will convene for social reading days, reading aloud, listening parties, and screenings while we simultaneously collect and disperse reading logs, bibliographies, reflections, photos and videos, objects, scraps of paper, marginalia, notes, diagrams, timestamps, sounds, letters, and coffee cups.

We hope you will join us.

In readership,
David & Sal

* * *

Beginning in October and running through the fall and into winter, forty-one readers resided in the dispersed reading room. Parting the maroon curtain leading on from the library or the deep winter blue hanging across the door unto the main room, readers would enter a plush low light populated by the castaway shapes of the foam store and a stack of blankets. They could set the room as felt best for their activity, and they could stay for as long as they liked.

Our contention: thinking, writing, art-making – all want, need reading. It is so essential to these modes of being. But how often do we give it the time it warrants? Perhaps giving our friends and collaborators a kind of armature for reading in the form of dedicated space and time would serve to elevate their respective reading practices, to reinvigorate reading for them in some way, and to foreground the shelter of a book.

October 2016

Sunday	Monday	Tuesday	Wednesday
Vanessa Kowalski* Rory Parks* *Remote			
2	3	4	5
9	10	11 Mary Marge Locker	12
16 Leonard Nalencz	17	18 Gini Alhadeff	19 Benedikt Josef
23 Liz Scheer / 30	24 / 31	25 Charles Perry	26 Luc Rioual

Thursday	Friday	Saturday
		1
6 Ambient Reading Spectacular* *Event	7	8
13	14	15
20 Matthew Strother	21 Liz Scheer	22 Liz Scheer
27 Leigh Gallagher	28 Leigh Gallagher	29 Leigh Gallagher

November 2016

Sunday	Monday	Tuesday	Wednesday
David Purcell* *Remote		1 Jimmy Cajoleas	2 Jac Mullen
6 *Sunsets** *Event	7	8 Audra Wolowiec	9 Chris- topher Potter
13 Emma Wippermann	14	15	16 Joanna Fiduccia
20	21	22	23
27	28	29 Carrie Yamaoka	30 Marco Maisto

Thursday	Friday	Saturday
3 Walker Rutter- Bowman	4	5
10	11 David Hopson	12
17 Hal Foster & Sandy Tait	18 Matthew Burgess	19 D. Graham Burnett & Alyssa Loh Randall Szott
24	25	26

December 2016

Sunday	Monday	Tuesday	Wednesday
Joy Episalla* James Lescene* Helen Singh Miller* *Remote			
4 Caroline Woolard	5	6 Matthew Sandager	7
11 Jeff Dolven Michael Cunningham	12	13 Alan Huck	14
18	19	20 Jennie Uleman	21 Collected Reading* *Event
25	26	27	28

dispersed holdings, Readers in
Residence

Thursday	Friday	Saturday
1	2 John Muse	3 Spectacular Reading* *Event
8	9	10 Anna Selver- Kassell
15 Marie Howe	16	17 Paul Soullelis
22	23	24
29	30	31

16 October 2016

Reading and writing, I remember being told, are overlapping, even identical practices. I am here today as a reader in residence, but I am also writing. You too, then, holding this, must be writing this, just as I read it.

This object, the one you are holding, was given to me as a gift, and it now has for me terrific powers of emotional association, which I want to describe. This is not an exorcism; the sadness of a lost past is as much of me as anything I am.

This object, this journal, was given to me as a gift years ago, given hopefully. The pages are made of elephant dung, not paper, and the elephant circle on the front and back suggest the material. The object has been in a bookshelf in my bedroom for a number of years now, and I have not touched it because I associate it with the loss of the possibility of joyful life-long companionship. It occurred to me to use it here, today, because the community that invited me today has been community I have relied on for joyful companionship since the loss I am referring to; this is then, less an exorcism than a testament to this community.

But it is not an exchange: actual communities do not replace lost loves, they simply live alongside them despite the fact that the former are living, present humans and the latter are ghosts. It is eerie to look out from experienced eyes and see the two groups standing alongside the other – the ghosts and the humans – but it is what it means to survive loss.

So this is a testament to both the present and absent souls, and as a small but joyful gesture to the absent, I append a few verses from Jonathan Lethem from memory (so surely inaccurate) that turn tears to laughter:

To a slice of hanky-panky
Add some artificial cranky.
Season well with canned boo-hoo.
Flavor with a spoof or two.
If you're careful, while they're cooling
You can add some only fooling.
(This recipe is not worthwhile
unless you are a crocodile).

On Tuesday, 18 October, from ten to five, I am the resident reader in the room on the Bowery. It is a bright day but in here all is the color of shadowy greys, with red stitching here and there. There is one deep red felt roll. The wedge-shaped cushion made for one to lean against while stretched out on a felt mat tilts one's back to the ideal angle for reading. And as soon as the back assumes that inclination, the brain cooperates. This is a new version of the Turkish divan, though a solitary one, with indolence written all over it. Loud traffic noises on the Bowery make the room and the mind even quieter. The book I have chosen to read is *The Yellow Sofa*.

> *And as so often happens to someone giving a present, he was overcome by emotion... like a door opening into a man's egoism and innate greed, and through it a broad tide of latent generosity sweeping in.*

I stopped reading to sip some tea. What a perfect gift that half hour of quiet reading had already felt like, with no engagements pressing in, no encroachments: there was nothing I was meant to do but the very thing I was doing – sitting, my legs stretched out, reading a delightful, masterly novel. The realization of the utter pleasure of this absence of demands on my attention beyond the silent pages I held in my hands took my breath away. It was so simple. It was something I had been accustomed to reading, reading for hours, finishing a book in one sitting, without messages and notes and invitations and links to be shared and demands for attention, etc. There was so much that could intrude. I realized again that it was possible to just read, but that one had to fabricate the right conditions so that one might read. That is what I learned as resident reader: that it is necessary to fabricate the conditions for thought by dispersing the multitude of solicitations one might be subject to. And what a subtle portrait of a woman:

> *She cursed her own stupidity for falling like that into the arms of a man she did not love, from whom she derived no pleasure, brought to her present pass for no real reason, through a mere whim, and through having nothing to do.*

The second half hour goes by swiftly and it is 11:40 a.m. now. Still, time has slowed down considerably for Manhattan where a morning usually seems to last half-an-hour and an afternoon an hour-and-a-half at most. I am on page forty-nine and the book has 112 pages. "What a wise thing is prudence," I read towards the very end of it.

> *He had held out his arms in compassion to a guilty wife, to a disloyal friend; and with that simple embrace, he had made his wife for ever an ideal partner and his friend the soul of loyalty.*

By a simple embrace from a quiet room in which to be still I've re-learned to read.

On Sunday, 6 November 2016, resident Charles Perry gave a reading of his book-length essay, *Sunsets* (Molasses Books, 2014). Using synths and a Rhodes piano, dispersed scored Charles' reading for an audience of twenty friends. Scheduled to coincide with the setting of the autumn sun (which is rather something out of the east-facing windows of 134 Bowery, the edifices of the buildings opposite the room bathed in gold) the performance unfolded over the course of an hour-and-a-half. Together, the three of us pursued a dulcet and minimally grand music in an attempt to trace out the long, gentle arch of the essay, of the drifting attentions of the listeners and players, of the sunset itself.

He tries calling his son. No Answer. A period of waiting. Then his daughter, and then his wife. They can't be reached on their mobile phones. A pause in his life. He can still feel the urgency of the day's demands in his body but he has no one he can talk to.

The view from the window shows a group of trees, dark green in the evening light. There is still light in their topmost branches, the last parting traces of the day. On a tea trolley (two generations older than its observer) a glass candlestick supports four candles whose colours vary between blue and pale violet, depending on the light coming from the window. If the waiting man were to die soon, it would continue to stand there for a while; since there was never any reason for putting it by the window in the first place, there is also scarcely any reason for moving it. The evenings I have yet to see are numbered. Most will pass without my noticing the gradual fading of the light, because I won't be having to wait, I will be in the company of others, or I will be busy and will be able to reach the people I love. So this short sequence of minutes is, perhaps, a unique period of time before speeches that will be held at the end.

The colour of life outside the window has already changed. The light illuminating the edges of the trees has gone. The unused candles have lost their blue and violet colours. Right in front of me a collection of pencils and two sharpeners stand next to a lamp which will soon be switched on. There's a lot to do. Now I have to get something to eat.

Alexander Kluge and Gerhard Richter, *Dispatches from Moments of Calm*, 139–140.

I

How did we end up
here again, where fear
the first & last thing
& home less & less
outside? I swear
every fucking day
climbing the stairs
into Sal's arms,
sanctuary above
Bowery's sirens

II

Making worlds is
an act of survival:
book, bivouac,
a room to read in
with red-stitched
cushions. Now
the flame is low,
voices in the library
await in their way
silent, each

III

witness to horrors
beyond what we
have seen & over
soup Frank O’Hara
admonishes me
keep your head up
in the wind, get your
gay ass to the Frick
& never ever give
your joy away

(for Sal and David)

A one-day reading residency offered a valuable occasion for sustained inquiry into a basic problem: the unread book—and, by extension, the more general problem of "not reading." The full range of human activities, with the unique exception of reading itself, can of course be understood as "not reading." But our focus on the 19th of November was on a narrow and slightly paradoxical subset of the universe of non-reading activities, to wit, what might be called "mindful" not-reading. Which is to say, we took up, across the day, the condition of the non-reading subject in bookish and attentive contemplation of unread books.

"Unread book" is a capacious category, and one worthy of consideration. Most books spend most of their lives not being read. Indeed, not not-being-read, for the vast majority of printed books, is a vanishing flash of the (reading) eye bursting upon a slow eternity of sealed vigil. From a book's perspective, not being read is the ubiquitous, durable, quotidian norm; being unread is *status quo* for the books of the world. Similarly, most of us who retain a relationship with the printed book and who are committed to reading as a significant element of life nevertheless read much less than we do not read, and are likely to survey a library (even our own) that contains significant numbers of books that have not been read recently – and probably quite a few that have never been read at all.

One does not read different books for different reasons, and attention to this matter can be used to generate a kind of card catalog or indexing system of some value in navigating the general problem of not reading. Such an exercise opens way to an annotated bibliography of affect, imagination, aspiration, fear, and intimate relation. As part of our residency, then, the two of us spent a portion of the day preparing call slips for all the unread books we had collected for the occasion, and sorting them in stacks that reflected overlapping taxonomies of guilt, indifference, obligation, and strained sociability. Subheadings included, "Books given to me by people who asked me to read them; I did not" and "Books I have 'investigated' (read reviews and / or spent time online researching author or context), and with which I therefore feel 'familiar' despite never having opened." A special section of our non-reading room was devoted to books with uncut pages, of which we had amassed a touching number. We also spent some time on the vexed liminal category of books begun but not completed, and these were for a time arranged in a spectrum corresponding to the depth to which they had been plumbed before being set aside. (Cards indicated recollection of the reason the book was put aside: "Final dog-ear is on page 136 of 149 total pages – felt manipulated; wasn't sure where we were going.")

These activities were propaedeutic to our ultimate aim: to conceive, draft, and enact a series of "Protocols for Sustained Attention" particularly suitable to a durational encounter with an unread book (or book one had the intention of not reading). A full report on our efforts, together with an account of the theoretical premises and historical precedents from which such modes of attentional exercise derive, lies beyond the scope of the present brief, but we transcribe, below, a single draft protocol suitable for use by those wishing to take up or extend the investigation.

* * *

Protocol
(For two people and two unread books)

Each person begins with his or her unread book in-hand. A table or suitable space is configured upon which the books may be placed. In addition, an adjacent location must be arranged in advance where both individuals may comfortably recline. Phases should be of roughly equal lengths, determined in advance, and not less than seven minutes. Phase changes may be marked by a bell, if desired.

Phase I

Both persons enter the appointed room or location, in silence, carrying the unread books. These are placed on the table, side by side. The persons arrange themselves as they wish in relation to the books, and regard them in a spirit of longing for what they contain.

Phase II

Each person picks up his or her book and reclines, placing the book (closed) on his or her body in a manner that feels suitable. The eyes are closed. While attending to the weight of the book that sits upon his or her body, each person imagines reading the book. At the close of this phase, each person marks his or her place in the book, using a small strip of paper or dog-ear, or other indication.

Phase III

The two persons exchange books. Each person now reads either the left- or the right-hand page that was marked by his or her partner. (It is also possible that the page is regarded, but not read).

Phase IV

Carefully, the two persons place the two books on the table or surface, and contrive, each person holding only the book he or she received in Phase III, to cause the books to be interleaved, in the manner of a shuffled deck of cards. Contemplation ensues.

Phase V

The books are left like this for a suitable period, after which each person may recover his or her unread book.

On Saturday, 3 December 2016, we hosted "Spectacular Reading," an evening of readerly performances and screenings. The notion was to make visible and audible, to make public, the private and often inscrutable act of reading. The event featured Emma Wippermann, who presented her work "Library" (the essay version of which appears on page 173); a talk by John Muse; a performative discussion between *Moby Dick*, as animated by D. Graham Burnett, and *Paradise Lost*, as animated by Jeff Dolven; a presentation of Madelyn Kent & Helen Singh Miller's "Say Tongue" (see appendix A); and musical interludes by Tim Spelios & David Scher as "half way." "Spectacular Reading" closed with "Seeing Reading," a screening of short films about reading, curated by Jeff Dolven, featured on page 85.

I entered the space with the clearest intentions of reading. Instead, I slowly began to hoard, gathering books up in my arms by the tens and stockpiling them in the small adjacent room which was to be my day’s sanctuary. Since I could not base my reading choices around an as-of-yet unknown thesis, I let myself be guided by less deliberate methods, scanning the library with the expectation that whichever words I happened to absorb that day would gather themselves up, like fallen leaves, until they became something of a clear and definite pile. I made my selections impulsively, without plan or rationale, and, like Roland Barthes, I yielded to that which pricked me. Often I found myself completely transfixed by the image of a face gracing a book’s cover. It would seem to stare at me so insistently that I couldn’t bear to leave it alone, and in those cases I made exceptions to my privacy. I am talking mostly about Gertrude, her thousand yard stare, but also Frank, and Tomas Tranströmer as well, whose book of poems had suffered water damage at some point in its lifetime. I thought he would be pleased that a potential reader chose to completely disregard his words to instead dwell on the book’s warped pages and an imagined history of their transformation.

Always I kept a small volume of Moyra Davey’s black and white photographs beside me, though not always open, pictures of empty alcohol bottles set against untidy interiors, and with some measure of distress I attempted to extract from them a metaphor for my situation. Other books became steady companions too, such as Charles Simic’s short work on the art of Joseph Cornell. I thought of myself as emulating Cornell in a way, collecting obsessively and tinkering as a child does with a toy, attempting to do with language what he did with objects, there in my own private room on Utopia Parkway. My own mode of collecting involved photographing bits of texts, intending to later compile the fragments into something with structure and purpose, something to counter the aimlessness of my activities. Though carefully designed to cradle and shelter the reader, myself, the room overwhelmed me at times. It was not so much the room itself but the stacks I had accrued and formed into a wall around me, guarding me from the confusion and uncertainty of my purpose there, or else encircling me in it. In those instances, once I had scanned and skimmed and collected to a degree of some satisfaction, I gathered the books up in my arms again and placed them back in their appropriate stacks on the shelf, something I did with immense pleasure. For a brief moment I was emptied, with only the prospect of becoming full again to consider. And so the day became like watching the tides roll in and out in perpetuity, and at times I thought about drowning all of the books and going outside to look around.

Later, on a cart, I found a small catalogue of the work of Gabriel Orozco, and from it I photographed the following quote from Blanchot:

> *I am, not dispersed, but entirely gathered together where I am, in this spot which is my position and where the world, because of the firmness of my attachment, localizes itself.*

And when the day ended I exited the room, walked down the stairs, often skipping one or two steps at a time, and spilled out all over the sidewalk.

Arriving at the wrong time in the cold
I was received so gently
And given tea and ushered into the reading
  room
I read the long article about Leonard Cohen
  in *The New Yorker* I'd been carrying
  around for weeks.
I felt protected!
I felt safe from the dishes!
From the bank!
From the pet store and the grocery list.
I felt as if I'd entered – I had entered –
A space that had been reserved
In every sense of that word. (kept
Contained in my
Name. For me. Civilized quiet not
Exploited used or sold for money
The Space. The air the silence the tea the
  time was Not a commodity)
Given.

This was unusual

After I left
That space stayed within me.
And the gentle folk who created it and
  watched over it and me

The Ambient Reading Spectacular closed on 21 December 2016 with a party we dubbed, Collected Reading. The event began at noontime – we held a final afternoon of quiet reading hours. Then we made soup, traded coffee for wine, and toasted the end of the residencies and the imminent new year.

III. Seeing Reading

[redacted] a metaphor [redacted]

[redacted] an
orderly transit of the gaze [redacted]

[redacted] sensuously
vagrant business [redacted]

somatic and imaginative extravagance. How did we ever come to think otherwise? Perhaps because we were taught to read. Nothing is more taught to us than reading is; it is the cornerstone of the whole project of school. The basic procedures of its pedagogy – moving left to right, and top to bottom; sounding the words out as you go; gathering the sense of the paragraph serially as you move down its rows – are indispensable at the start. Having been taught as rules to children, they survive as myths for adults, a crossed grid of *is* and *ought* superimposed over actual reading like the blue and red lines on a sheet of notebook paper.

It is the shared project of all of the short films made for "Seeing Reading" to put a question to this ideal, whether critical or bemused or both. Some of them take the vantage of the reader, turning the screen into the page, presenting there a welter of encoded information or a still, rainy street. Others turn their gaze on the reader reading, to see what she is doing, tapping her foot, or mouthing the words, or weeping. All are intended as eccentric or even limit cases. I propose, to the reader here, the experiment of shifting each reading, in turn, into the center, shouldering the armchair out of the way, standing in the variable light of the video projector and looking out and around to see what you can see. What if reading is ventriloquism, as one film proposes? What does that make of stargazing? Or say reading is something you do with your restless foot. Can you do that to a contour map? Say reading reels past you on a paper towel roll. How strange, how exciting the armchair looks from here.

Sofia Theodore-Pierce, “Body of Water in a Desert Landscape”

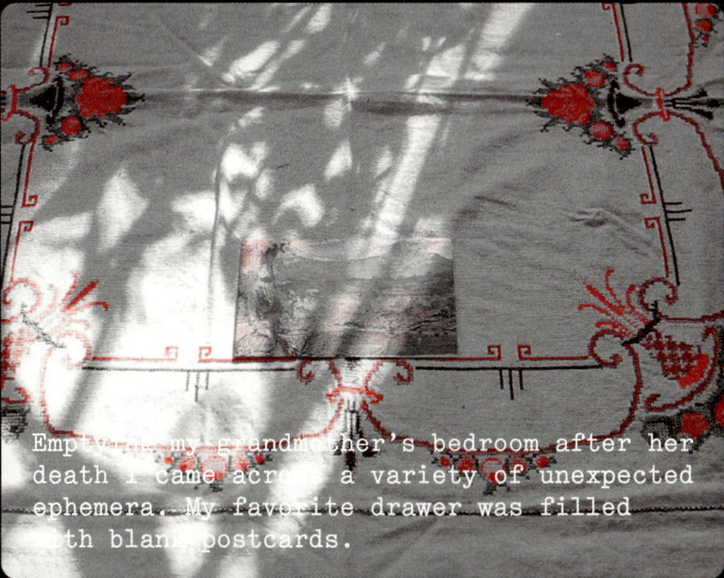

Emptying my grandmother’s bedroom after her death I came across a variety of unexpected ephemera. My favorite drawer was filled with blank postcards.

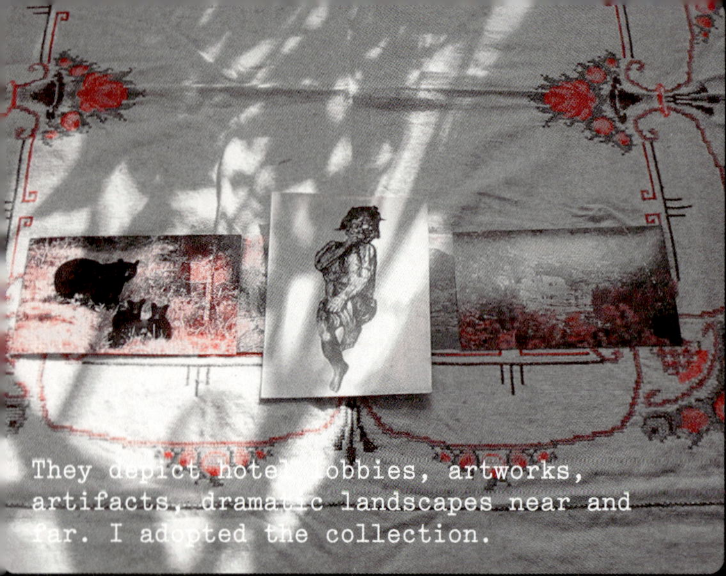

They depict hotel lobbies, artworks, artifacts, dramatic landscapes near and far. I adopted the collection.

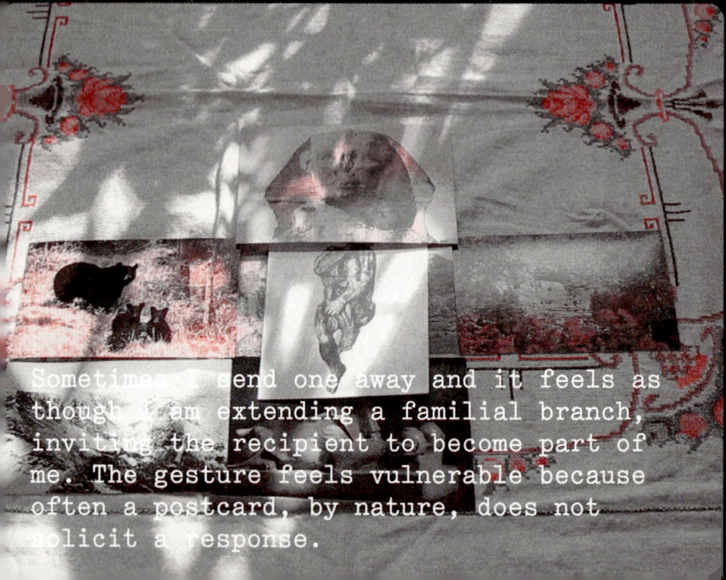

Sometimes I send one away and it feels as though I am extending a familial branch, inviting the recipient to become part of me. The gesture feels vulnerable because often a postcard, by nature, does not solicit a response.

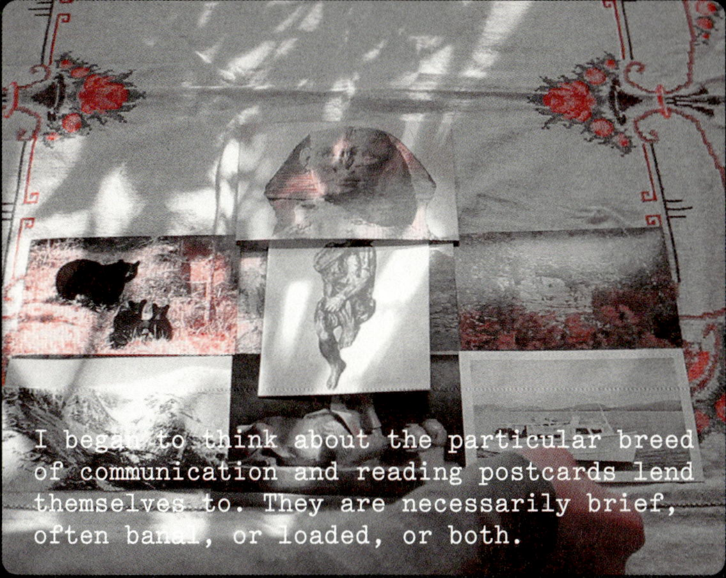

I began to think about the particular breed of communication and reading postcards lend themselves to. They are necessarily brief, often banal, or loaded, or both.

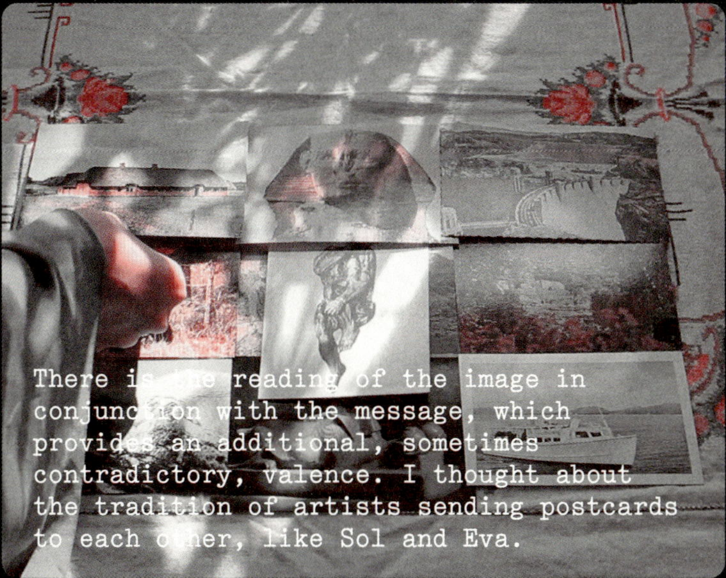

There is the reading of the image in conjunction with the message, which provides an additional, sometimes contradictory, valence. I thought about the tradition of artists sending postcards to each other, like Sol and Eva.

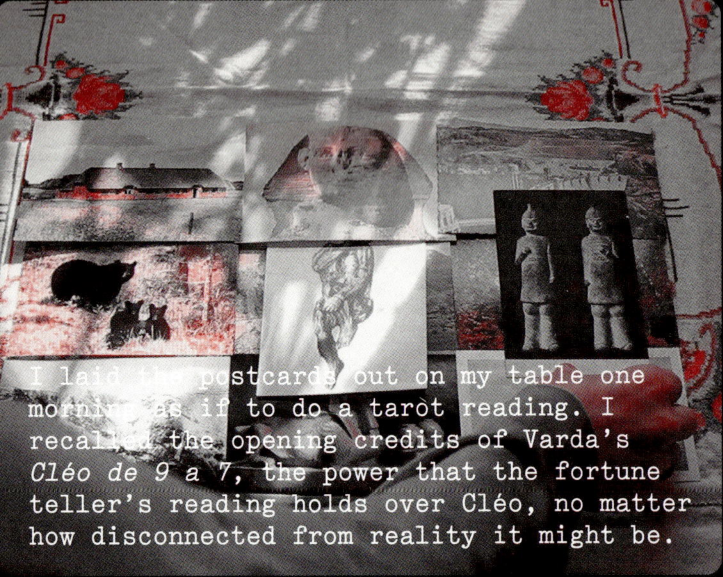

I laid the postcards out on my table one morning as if to do a tarot reading. I recalled the opening credits of Varda's *Cléo de 9 a 7*, the power that the fortune teller's reading holds over Cléo, no matter how disconnected from reality it might be.

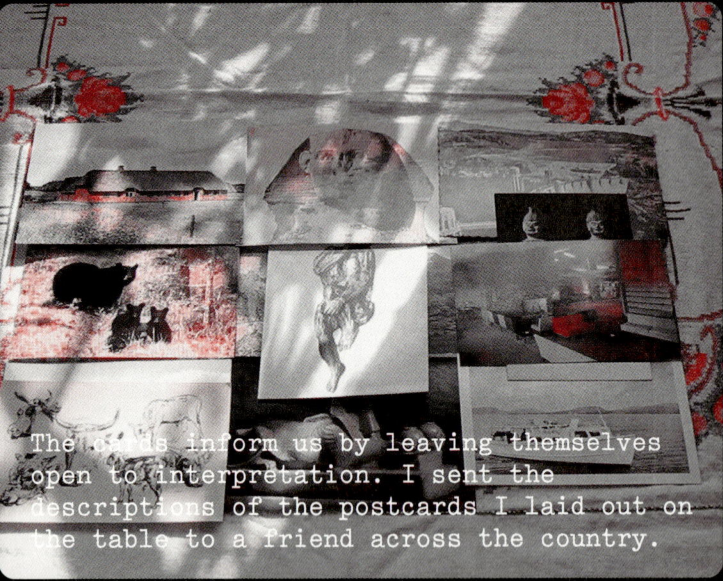

The cards inform us by leaving themselves open to interpretation. I sent the descriptions of the postcards I laid out on the table to a friend across the country.

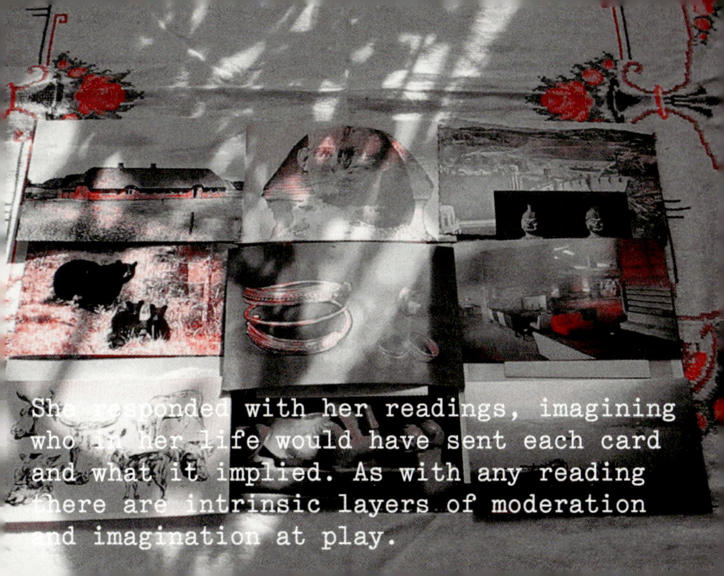

She responded with her readings, imagining who in her life would have sent each card and what it implied. As with any reading there are intrinsic layers of moderation and imagination at play.

Yara Flores, "The Kinetics of
Textual Immersion" 95

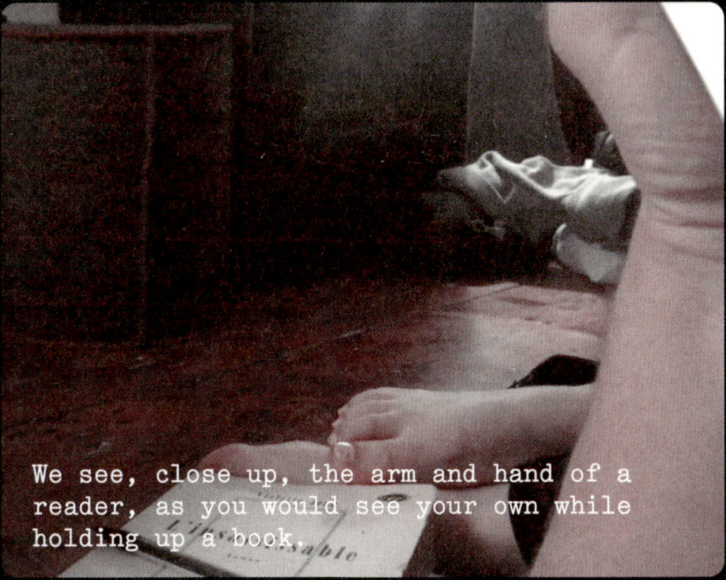

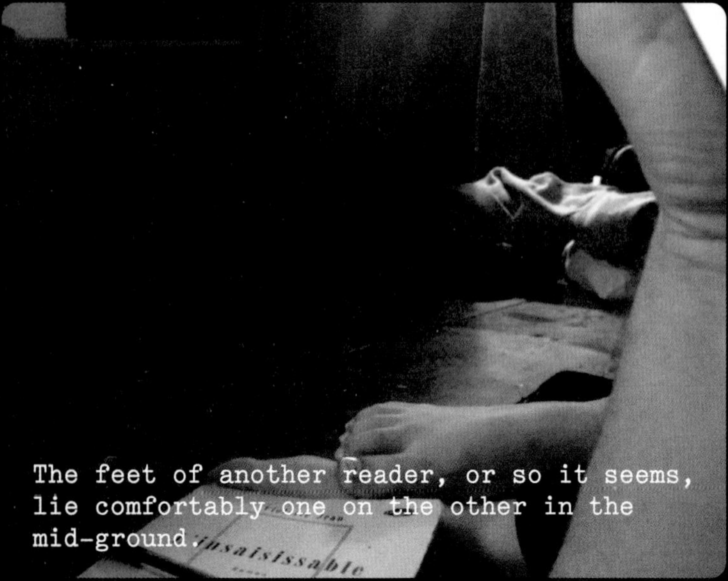

The feet of another reader, or so it seems, lie comfortably one on the other in the mid-ground.

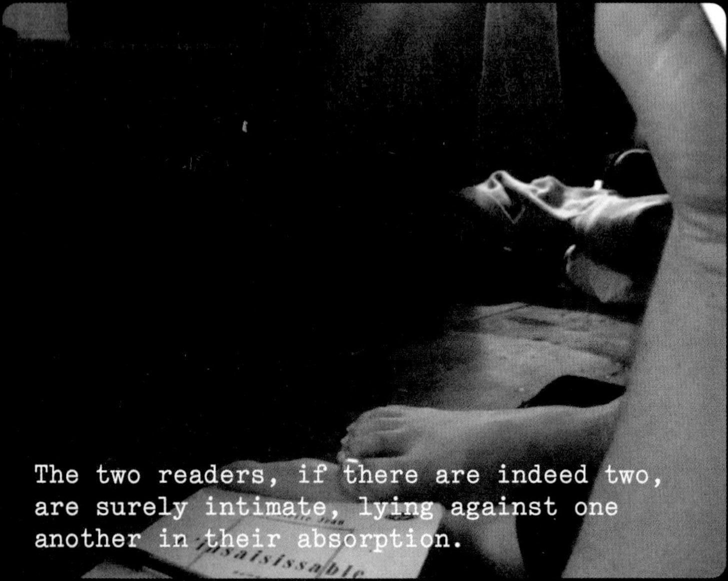

The two readers, if there are indeed two, are surely intimate, lying against one another in their absorption.

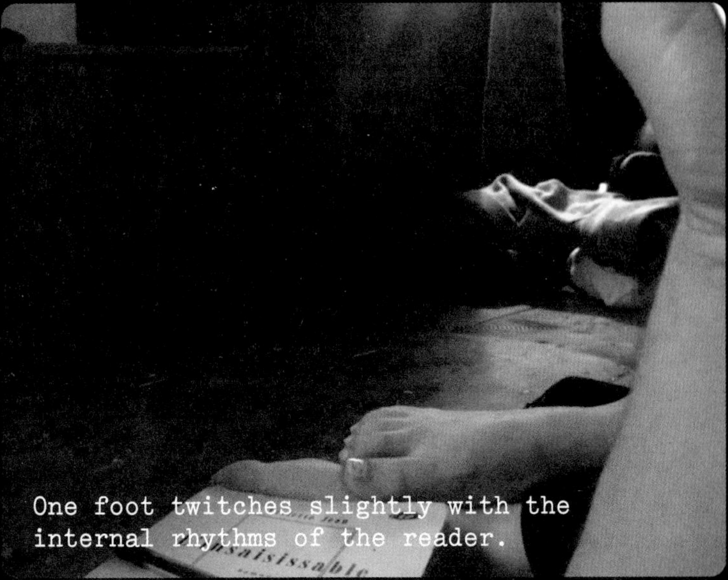

One foot twitches slightly with the internal rhythms of the reader.

Vanessa Kowalski, “Cartographies of Silence” 99

A voice sounds, reading Adrienne Rich’s poem “Cartographies of Silence” into total blackness.

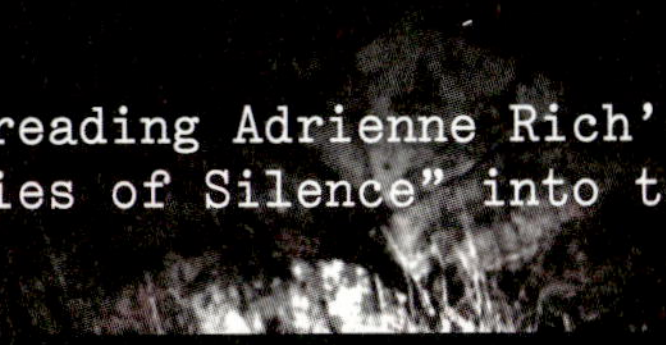

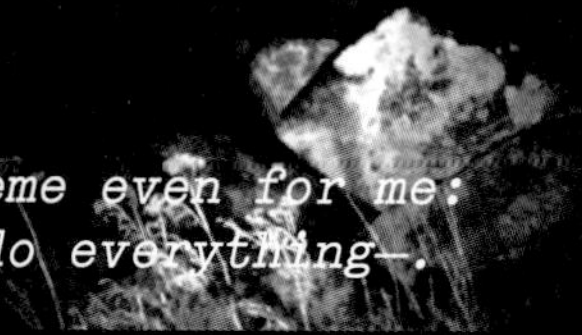

It was an old theme even for me:
Language cannot do everything—.

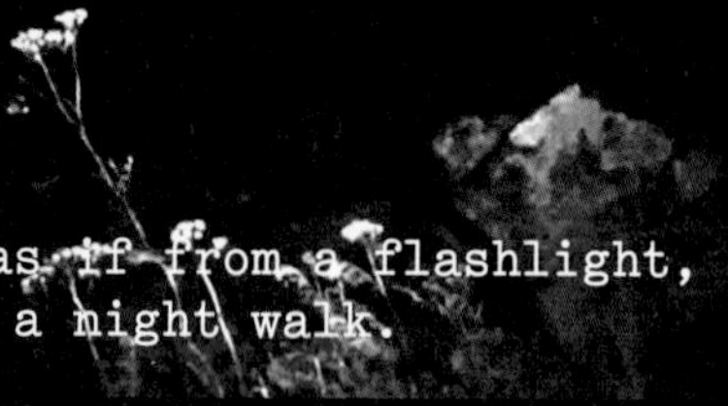

Then sudden light, as if from a flashlight,
held in the hand on a night walk.

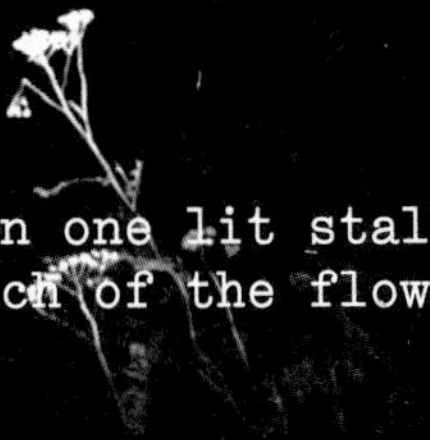

Rocks and weeds, then one lit stalk of yarrow, a small branch of the flower head broken and dangling.

Elena Taurke, “Here We Are”

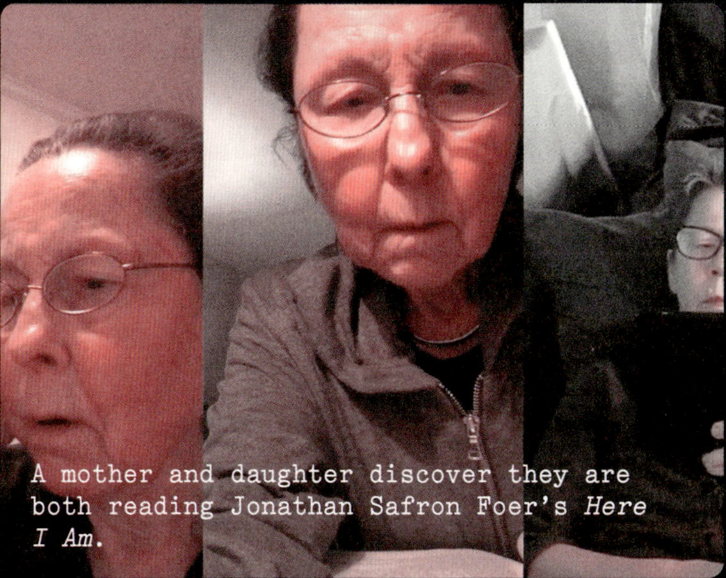

A mother and daughter discover they are both reading Jonathan Safron Foer's *Here I Am*.

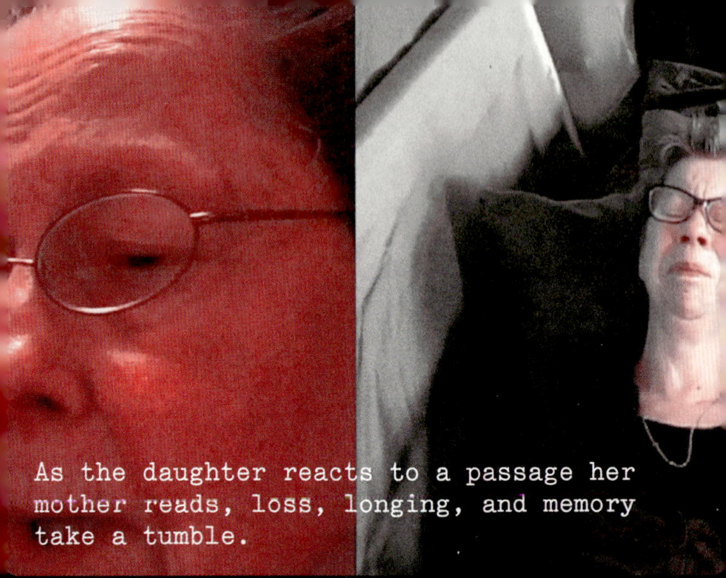

As the daughter reacts to a passage her mother reads, loss, longing, and memory take a tumble.

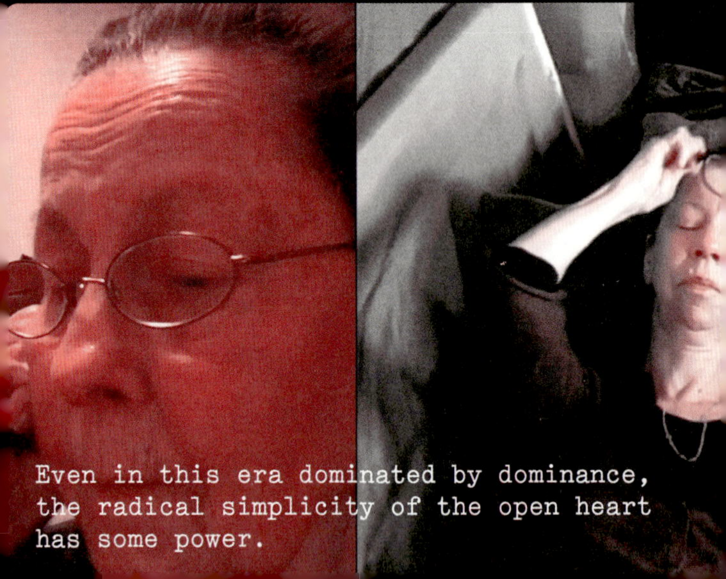

Even in this era dominated by dominance, the radical simplicity of the open heart has some power.

Hermione Spriggs & Curtis Tamm,
"The Destruction of Royal Gardens" 107

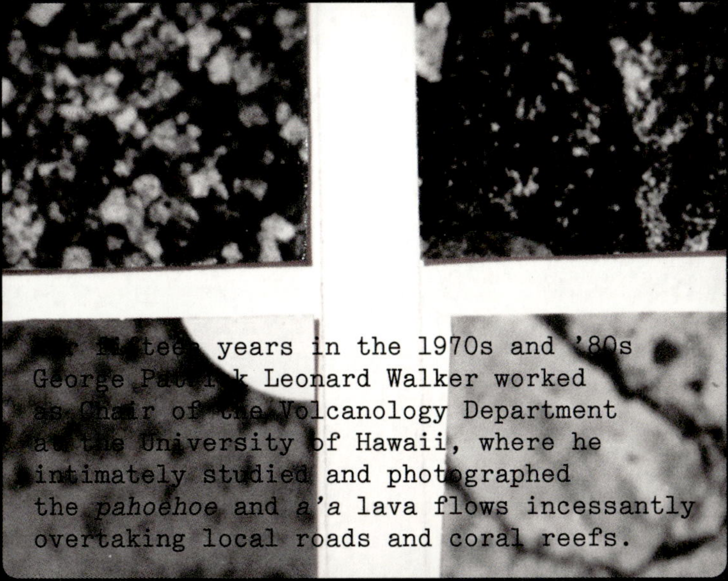

For fifteen years in the 1970s and '80s George Patrick Leonard Walker worked as Chair of the Volcanology Department at the University of Hawaii, where he intimately studied and photographed the *pahoehoe* and *a'a* lava flows incessantly overtaking local roads and coral reefs.

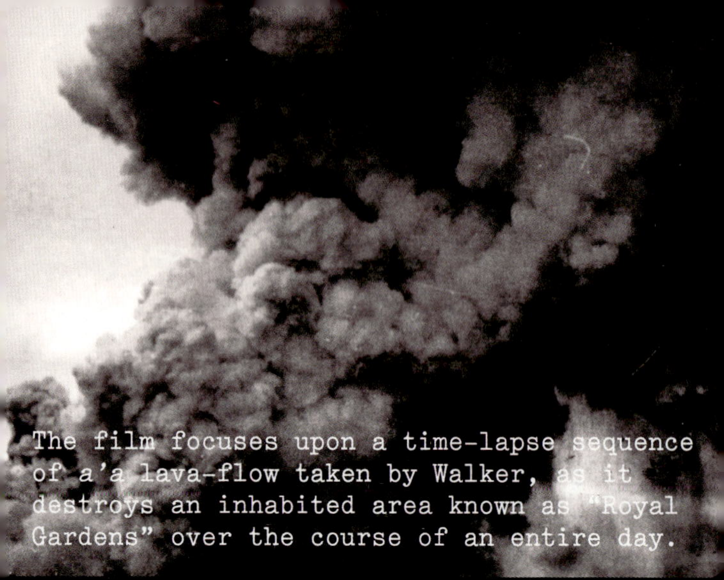

The film focuses upon a time-lapse sequence of *a'a* lava-flow taken by Walker, as it destroys an inhabited area known as "Royal Gardens" over the course of an entire day.

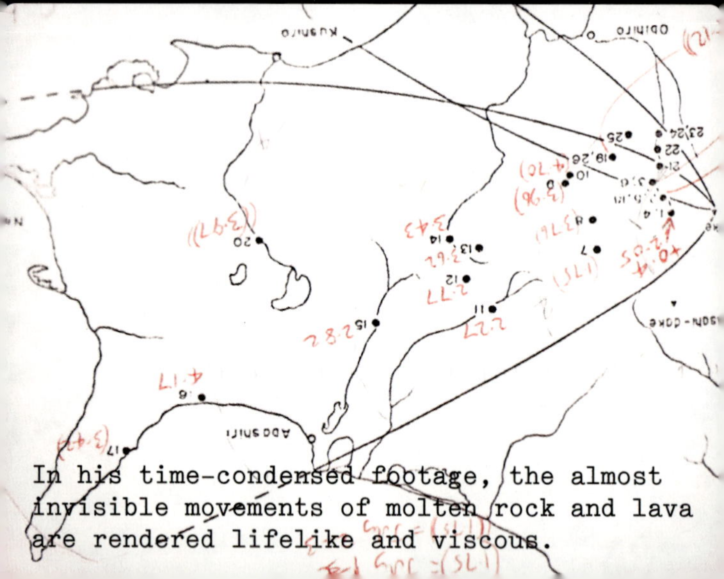

In his time-condensed footage, the almost invisible movements of molten rock and lava are rendered lifelike and viscous.

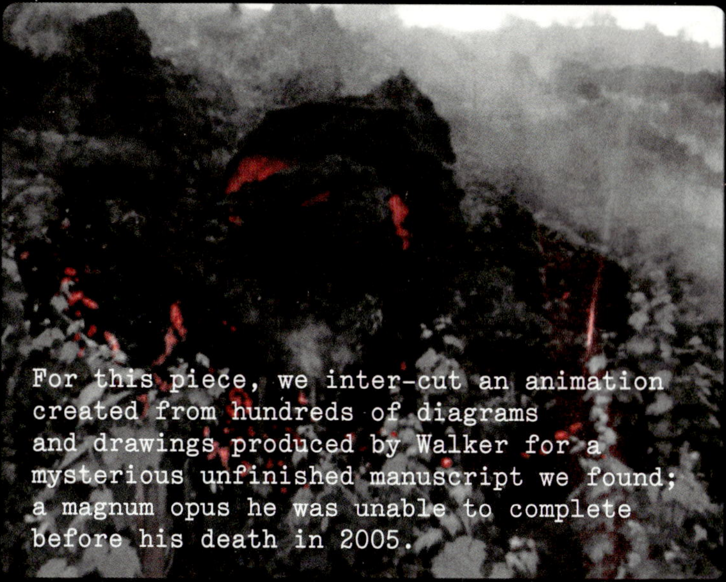

For this piece, we inter-cut an animation created from hundreds of diagrams and drawings produced by Walker for a mysterious unfinished manuscript we found; a magnum opus he was unable to complete before his death in 2005.

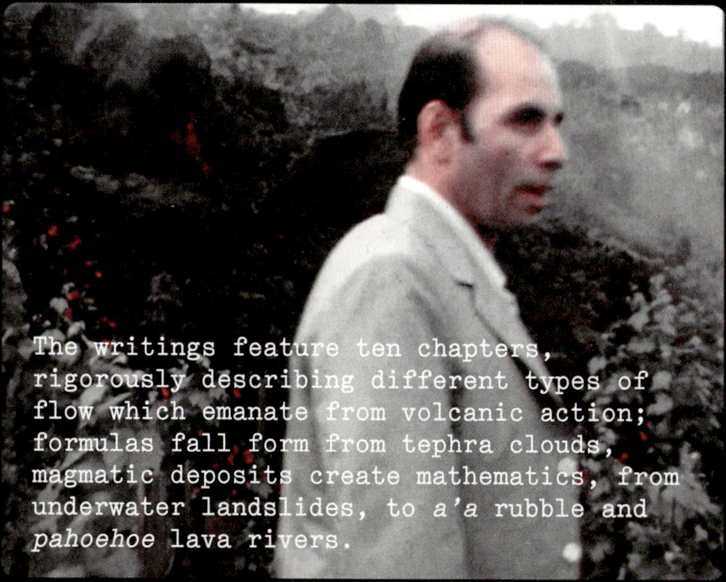

The writings feature ten chapters, rigorously describing different types of flow which emanate from volcanic action; formulas fall form from tephra clouds, magmatic deposits create mathematics, from underwater landslides, to *a'a* rubble and *pahoehoe* lava rivers.

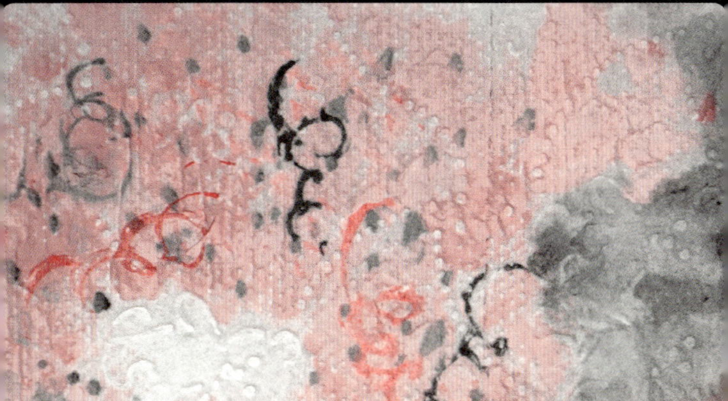

On the now rare occasions I find myself engaging in social gatherings in my hometown, locals whose faces I seldom recognize greet me warmly, “You’re the Raffaellas’ son!”

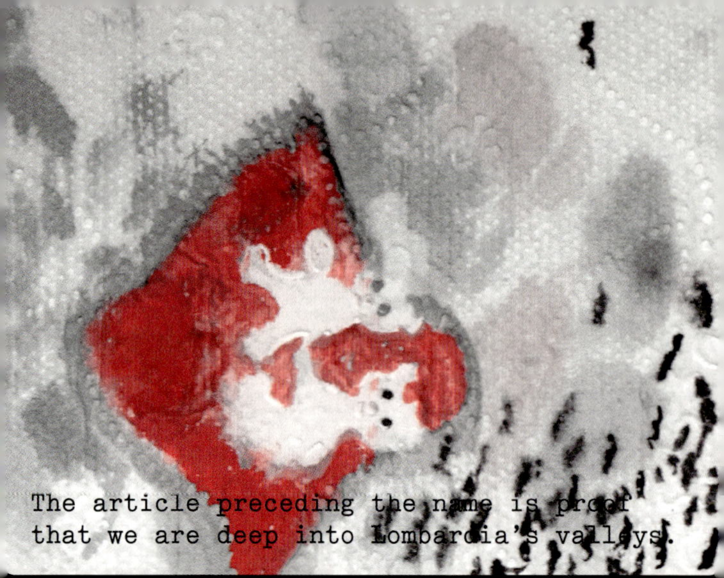

The article preceding the name is proof that we are deep into Lombardia's valleys.

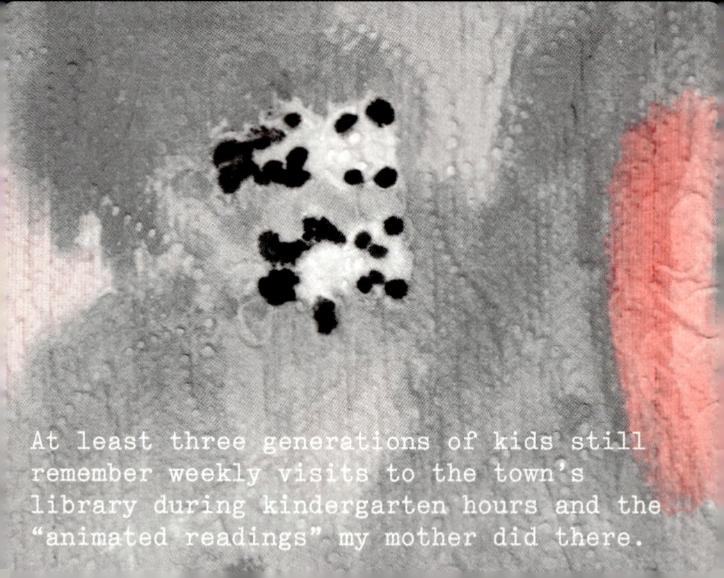

At least three generations of kids still remember weekly visits to the town's library during kindergarten hours and the "animated readings" my mother did there.

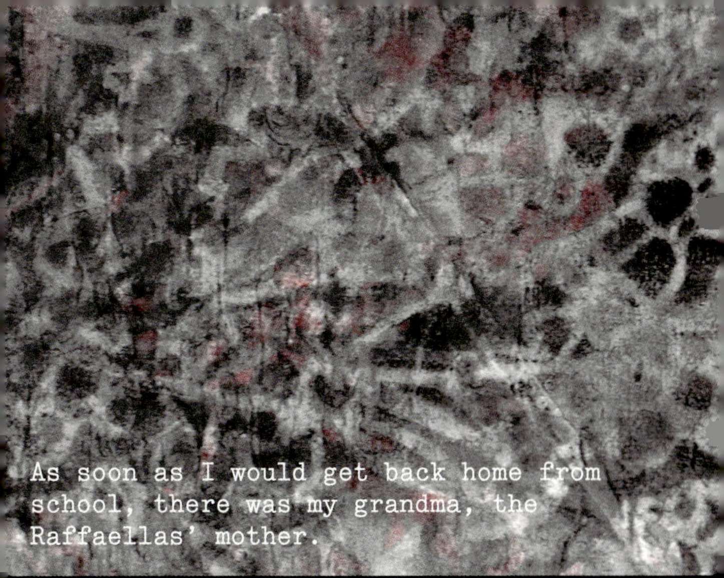

As soon as I would get back home from school, there was my grandma, the Raffaellas' mother.

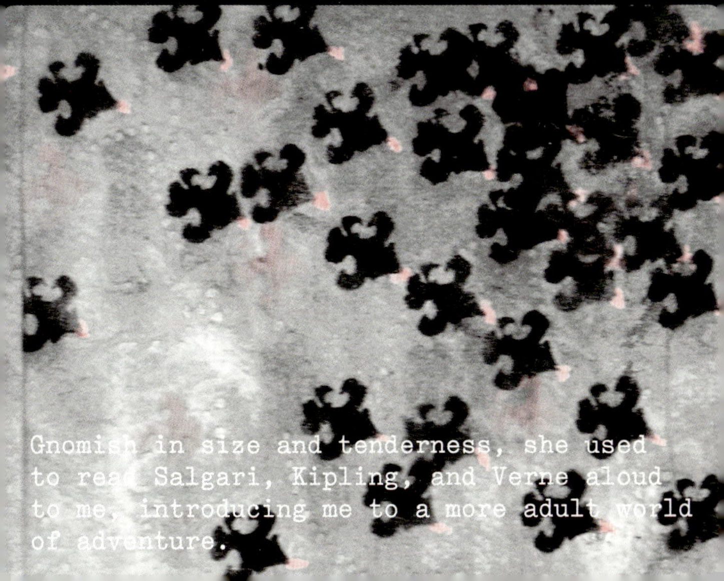

Gnomish in size and tenderness, she used to read Salgari, Kipling, and Verne aloud to me, introducing me to a more adult world of adventure.

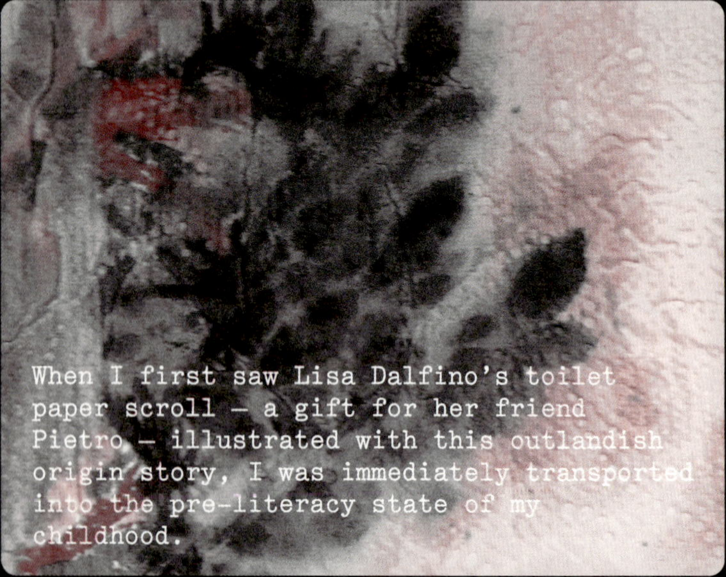

When I first saw Lisa Dalfino's toilet paper scroll – a gift for her friend Pietro – illustrated with this outlandish origin story, I was immediately transported into the pre-literacy state of my childhood.

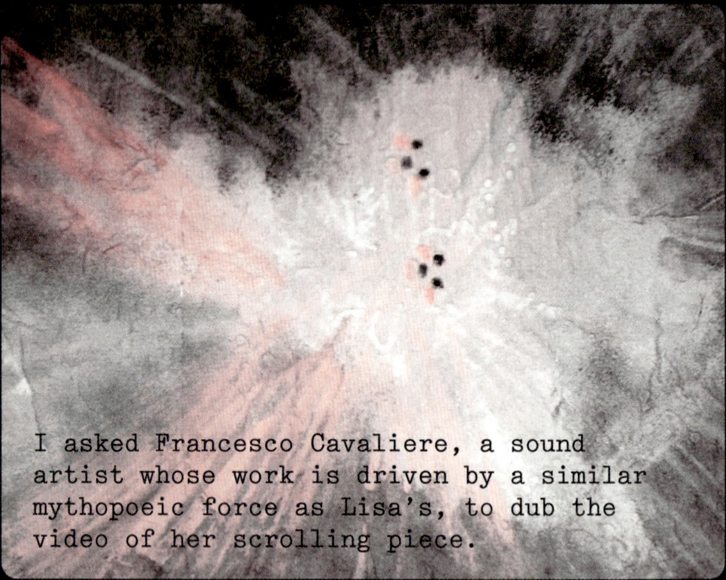

I asked Francesco Cavaliere, a sound artist whose work is driven by a similar mythopoeic force as Lisa's, to dub the video of her scrolling piece.

Jennie Uleman, "From Democracy and its Discontents"

G. W. F. Hegel, from §5 of the Introduction, *Elements of the Philosophy of Right* [1821],
ed. Allen W. Wood, trans. H. B. Nisbet (Cambridge University Press, 1991)

Those who regard thinking as a particular and distinct *faculty*, divorced from the will as an equally distinct *faculty*, and who in addition even consider that thinking is prejudicial to the will – especially the good will – show from the very outset that they are totally ignorant of the nature of the will. (pp. 37-38)

Only *one aspect* of the will is defined here – namely... the flight from every content as a limitation. (p. 38)

This is **the freedom of the void**, which is raised to the status of an actual shape and passion. (p. 38; my bold)

...if it [a passion for this the freedom of the void] turns [away from "pure contemplation"] to actuality, it becomes in the realm of both politics and religion the fanaticism of destruction, demolishing the whole existing social order, eliminating all individuals regarded as suspect by a given order, and annihilating any organization which attempts to rise up anew. Only in destroying something does this negative will have a feeling of its own existence [*Dasein*]. (p. 38)

It may well believe that it wills some positive condition, for instance the condition of universal equality...but it does not in fact will the positive actuality of this condition, for this at once gives rise to some kind of order, a particularization both of institutions and individuals; but it is precisely through the annihilation of particularity...that the self-consciousness of this negative freedom arises. Thus, whatever such freedom believes that it wills can in itself be no more than an abstract representation, and its actualization can only be the fury of destruction. (p. 38)

[In 'Addition' to passage above:]

For fanaticism wills only what is abstract, not what is articulated... (p. 39)

She is reading Hegel to us from a slide in an echoey classroom.

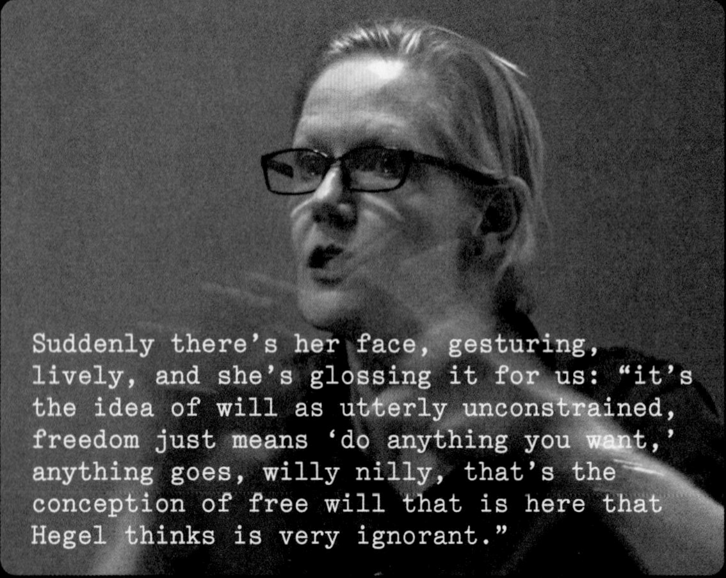

Suddenly there's her face, gesturing, lively, and she's glossing it for us: "it's the idea of will as utterly unconstrained, freedom just means 'do anything you want,' anything goes, willy nilly, that's the conception of free will that is here that Hegel thinks is very ignorant."

G. W. F. Hegel, from §5 of the Introduction, *Elements of the Philosophy of Right* [1821], ed. Allen W. Wood, trans. H. B. Nisbet (Cambridge University Press, 1991)

Those who regard thinking as a particular and distinct *faculty*, divorced from the will as an equally distinct *faculty*, and who in addition even consider that thinking is prejudicial to the will – especially the good will – show from the very outset that they are totally ignorant of the nature of the will. (pp. 37-38)

Only *one aspect* of the will is defined here – namely…the flight from every content as a limitation. (p. 38)

This is **the freedom of the void**, which is raised to the status of an actual shape and passion. (p. 38; my bold)

…if it [a passion for this the freedom of the void] turns [away from "pure contemplation"] to actuality, it becomes in the realm of both politics and religion the fanaticism of destruction, demolishing the whole existing social order, eliminating all individuals regarded as suspect by a given [illegible] organization which attempts to [illegible] does the negative will have a feeling of its own existence [*Dasein*]. (p. [illegible]

It may well believe that it wills some positive condition, for instance the condition of universal equality…but it does not in fact will the positive actuality of this condition, for this at once gives rise to some kind of order, a particularization both of institutions and individuals; but it is precisely through the annihilation of particularity…that the self-consciousness of this negative freedom arises. Thus, whatever such freedom believes that it wills can in itself be no more than an abstract representation, and its actualization can only be the fury of destruction. (p. 38)

[In 'Addition' to passage above:]

For fanaticism wills only what is abstract, not what is articulated… (p. 39)

Then she goes on to read the rest of the passages, finishing with "thus, whatever such freedom believes that it wills can in itself be no more than an abstract representation, and its actualization can only be the fury of destruction."

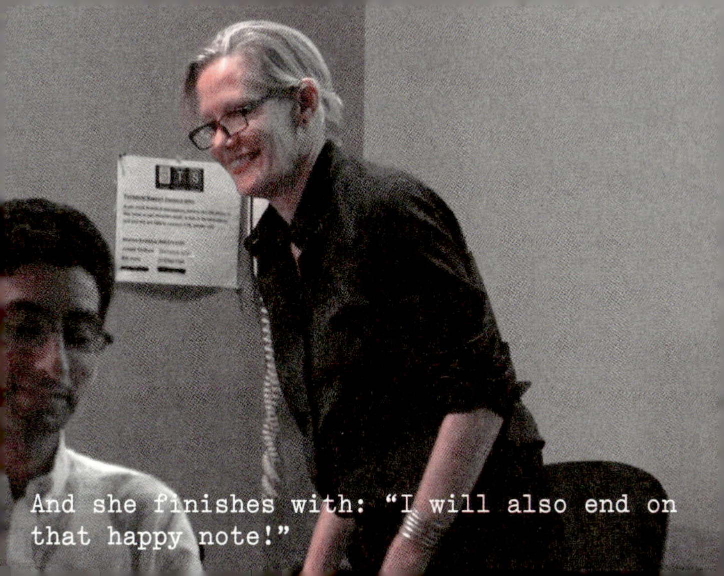

And she finishes with: "I will also end on that happy note!"

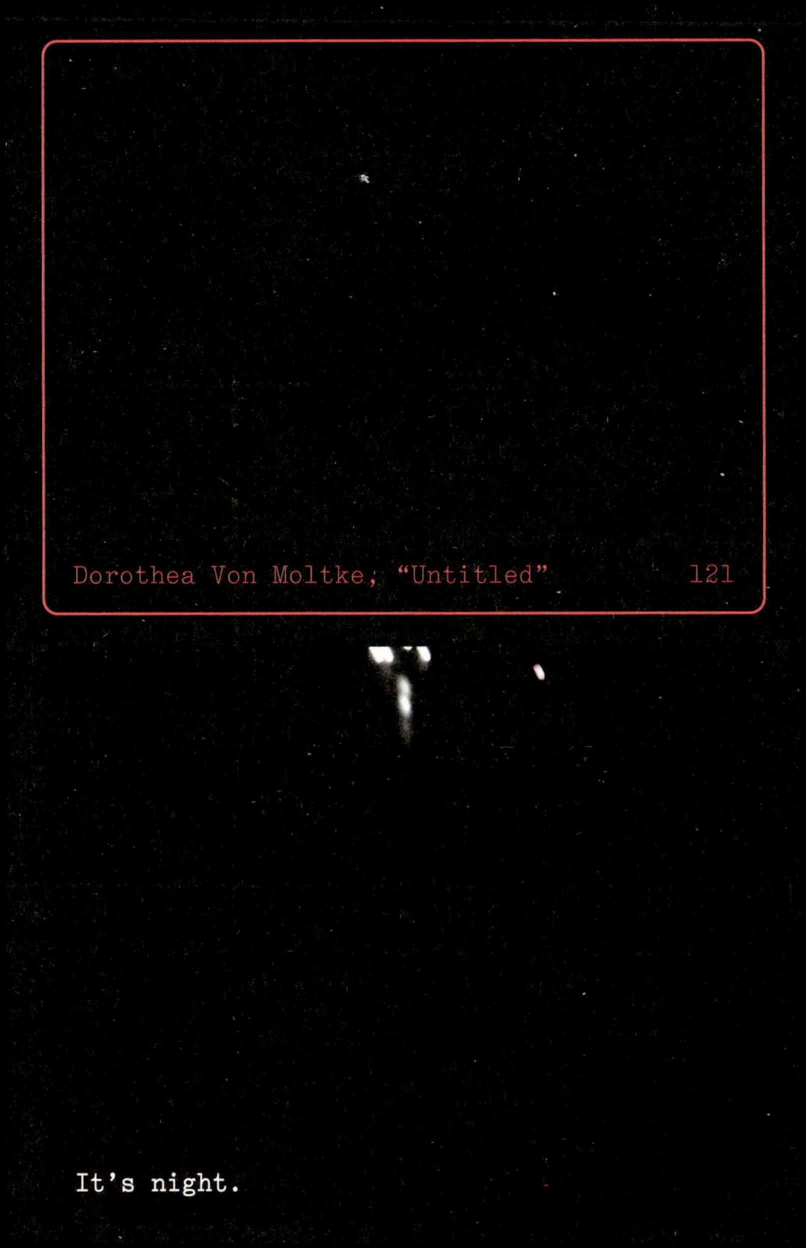

It's night.

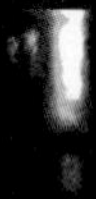

We hear footsteps and the sound of rain.

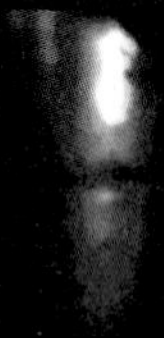

Slowly we move forward through the darkness
towards a blue-green glow in the distance.

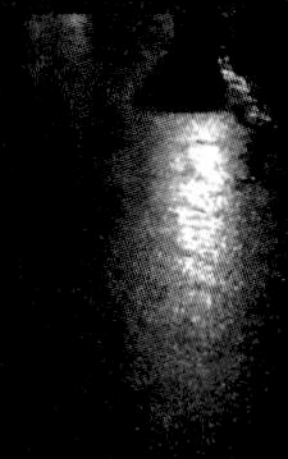

As we get closer, the light slips farther out of the frame, until all we see is its reflection, finally coming into focus as uncanny shine on wet asphalt, a puddle shimmering with rain.

Michael Ballou and David Scher,
"Are you German?" 125

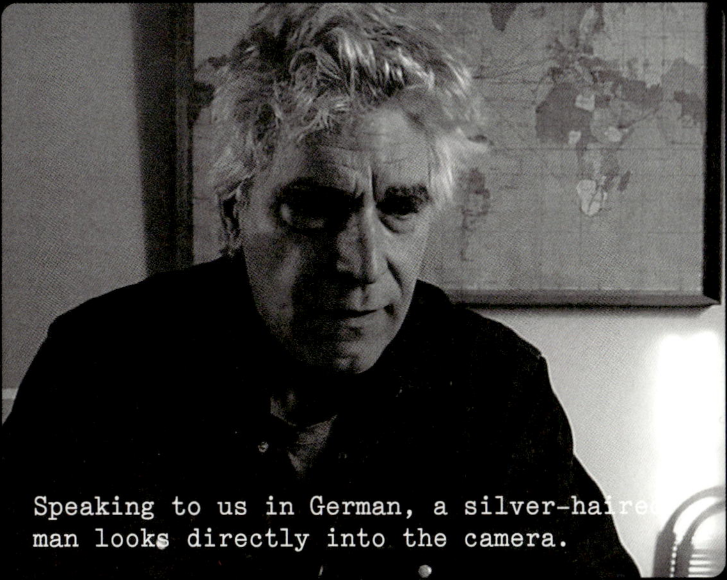
Speaking to us in German, a silver-haired man looks directly into the camera.

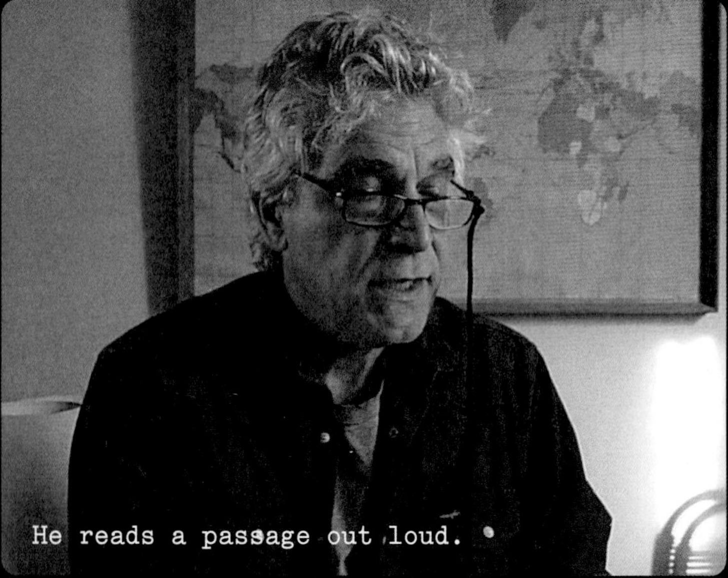
He reads a passage out loud.

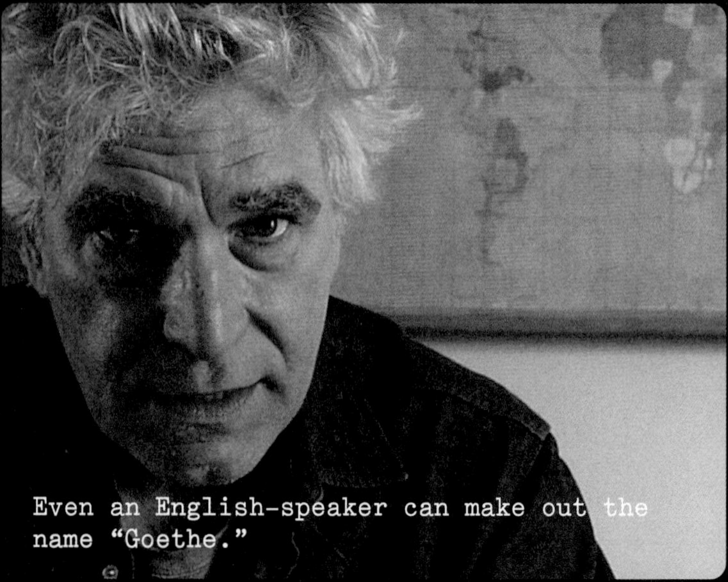
Even an English-speaker can make out the name "Goethe."

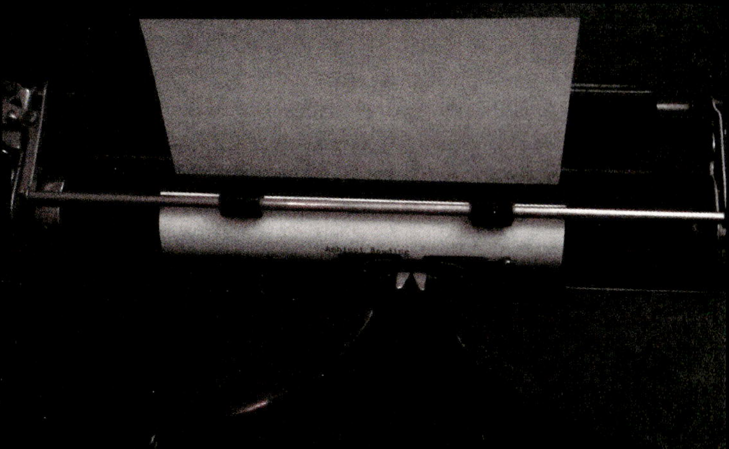

We see a manual typewriter, and hear the sounds of the keys hitting paper as words begin to appear, and a voice, reading.

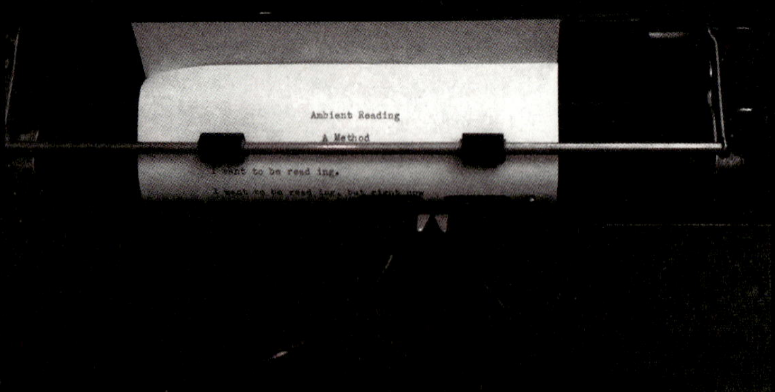

The typewriter skips, and gaps appear in the words – I want to be reading – but the voice continues calmly.

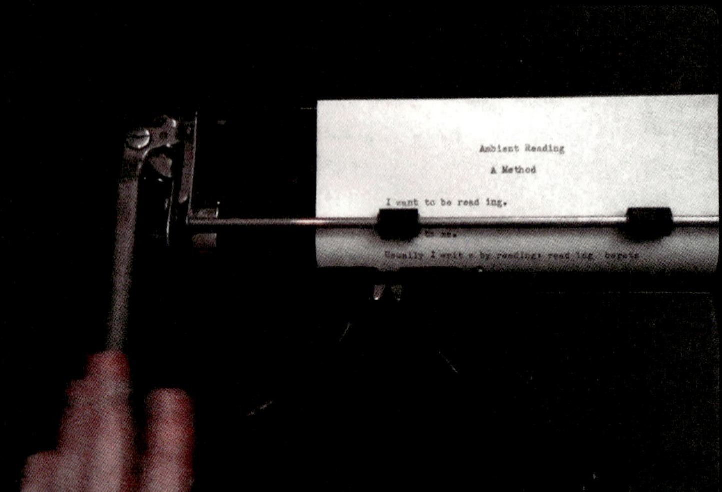

The words emerge slowly but the voice carries forward.

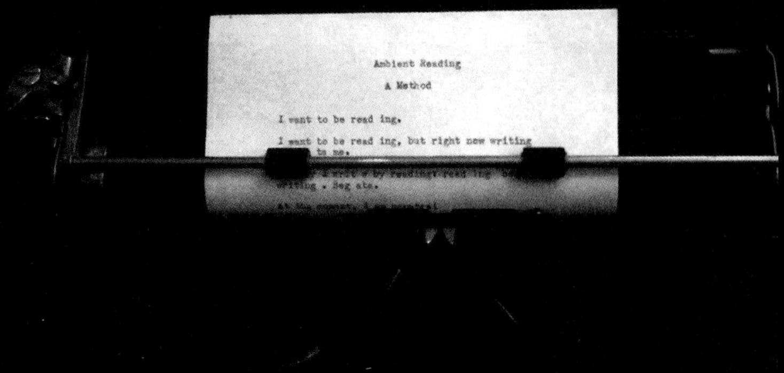

Writing is reading silently is reading aloud.

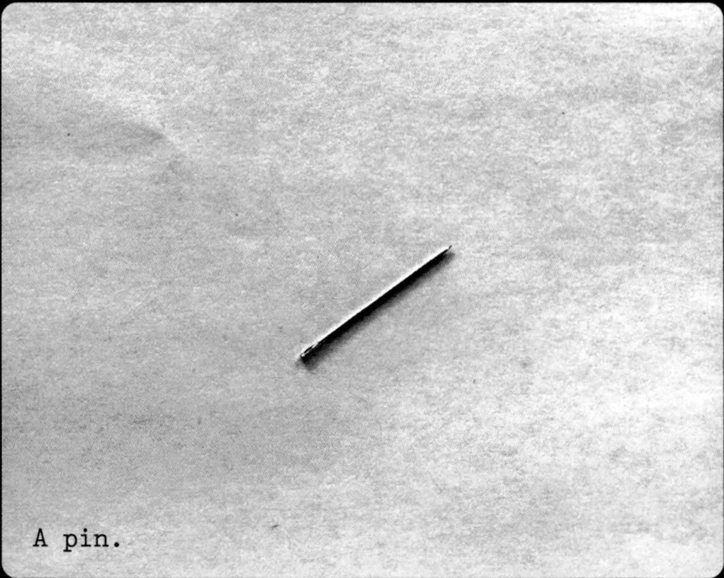
A pin.

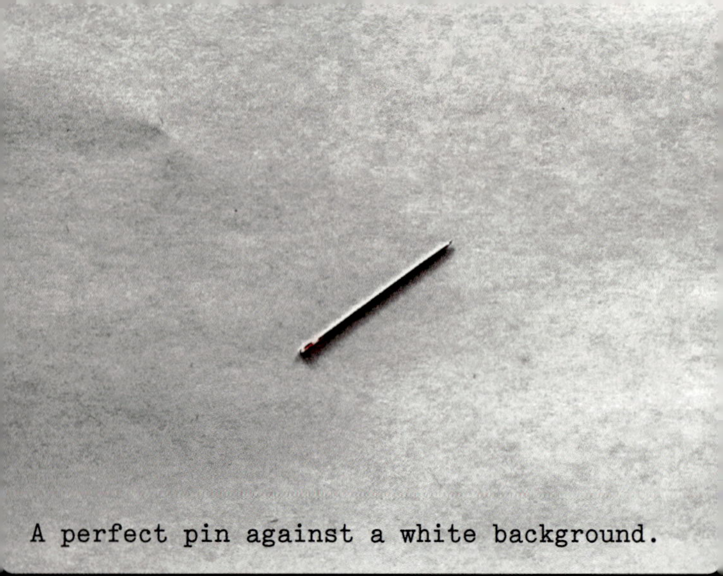

A perfect pin against a white background.

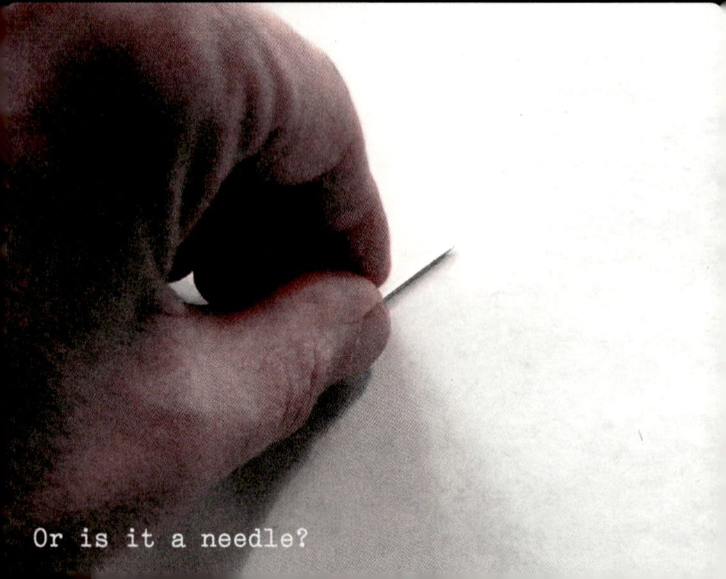

Or is it a needle?

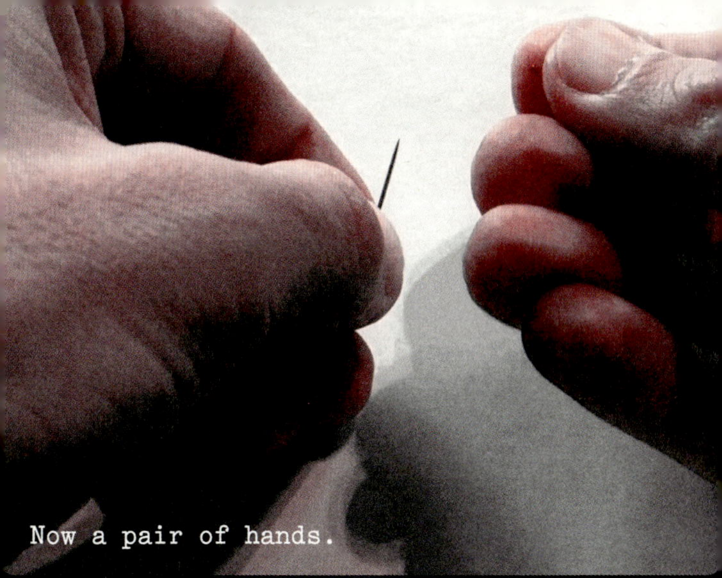
Now a pair of hands.

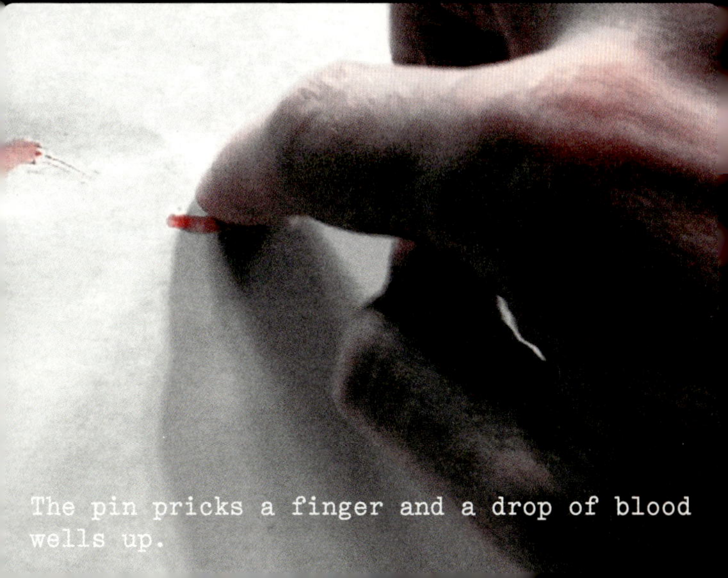
The pin pricks a finger and a drop of blood wells up.

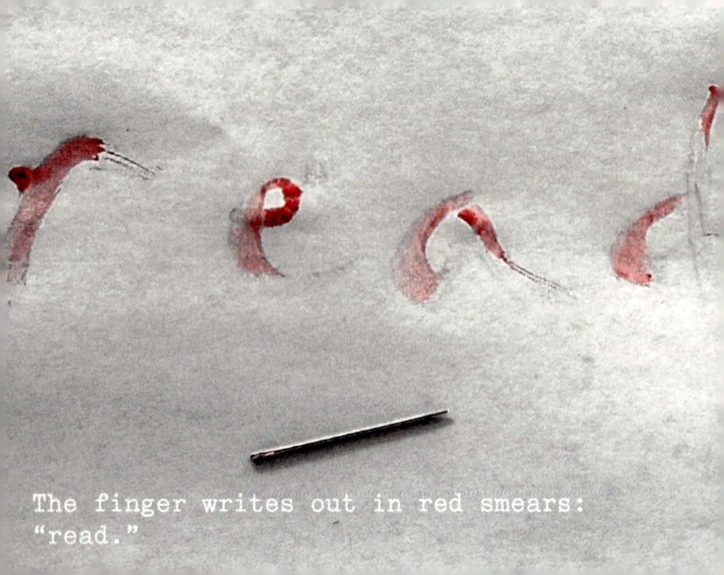

The finger writes out in red smears: "read."

IV. On Reading

Leigh Gallagher

Night Reading

Dearest,

Delighted beyond delighted to embark on this small adventure. I have an idea.

I'm very much a creature of habit and pride myself on following certain daily routines that make me feel like a generally productive / in-control person. Part of that routine includes waking up relatively early and getting to bed around midnight. But I've always been a light sleeper and a bad sleeper; it's not full-blown insomnia, but a weekly inconvenience which I manage by lying in bed for ten or thirty minutes until I know I'm not getting back to sleep, then rising, reading or writing, baking cornbread, cleaning the bathroom, enrolling in health insurance. I've never taken pills; to fight it seems silly, like arguing with nature, and while these nights make my next-days unpleasant, they're also enjoyable—peaceful in a way that normal working hours aren't, semi-mystical, maybe because of the dark and the quiet and the moon, and because my enjoyment of the dark and the quiet and the moon is tempered by an awareness that morning is coming, and I'm about to be exhausted, and the next day is going to sort of suck.

So. I'm proposing a more deliberate embrace of these nighttime episodes; a full-blown reversal of my sleeping / waking schedule for the duration of a short residency. Sleeping during the day and staying up all night. Nighttime reading on the Bowery. How romantic!

I'm thinking of the secret, subversive, subconscious associations we bring to nighttime, and the analogous associations we bring to reading.

> *A child (this child) on the top bunk reads* The Secret Garden *or the children's biography of Saint Bernadette, given to her by Nana, with the shamefully torn and Scotch-taped cover. The bottom bunk waits for a baby sister. The child takes enormous pleasure in the little game of moving from the top bunk to bottom bunk and back again, over and over. She reads in top bunk and bottom bunk, under covers and over covers. Her parents, asleep down the hall, are ignorant as mummies.*
>
> *I remember reading my first real books by the light of a chunky plastic flashlight. There were discs that turned the light either red or green or plain. A child reading in the red light about young Bernadette in the grotto who kneels to the vision of a virgin queen. She says,* Drink of my waters, and eat of me, *and other sensual things. A child reading in the green light about Mary Lennox and the dark house on the moors, the mysterious wailing she hears in the night, cries echoing down the hallways, and their source—a tender, crippled boy, all pale skin*

and sparkling eyes. I was Mary Lennox.
They bring the garden back to life. I read
the book with cockney accents in my head.

Night and reading invite private cerebral experiences; evoke latent desires / fears / memories; offer silent room for imaginative thinking that the working day finds threatening, doltish, or weird.

> *If my three-day project seems to set up particular expectations of some "experience" worth writing about, or the discovery of some thesis on night / reading parallels—I have only to remind myself that there is no way to fail. Both night and reading are without goal. Me too.*
>
> *On the Bowery, the shops are locked and roll-gated; restaurants have been hosed down, lights out. People sleep in beds, doorways, rocking on the train between Harlem and the beach. Beyond sleep, night has neither agenda nor expectation. As a participant in night, to breach contract and refuse sleep is to steal time. In this stolen time, we wander. Night allows what the day shames:* We don't have time for that. Stop dilly-dallying. Daydreaming.
>
> *Perhaps so many of us like to live in cities for the limits, prohibitions, distractions urban life presents. Why else prefer day after day of one thing followed by another, so much close-proximity smelliness,*

so many scheduled dinners? Does all the psychic cacophony of urban life keep the mind from wandering... dangerous drifting... toward fears, desires, memories, lurking in the dark gap? Please step away from the platform's edge.

Reading, too—fiction and poetry in particular—is a gappy activity, unproductive in any material sense. Hours, days, lifetimes spent deciphering some stick-scratches in the mud. That is reading. Time-intensive squinting.

Sorry, Boss, I need the day off to eavesdrop on a conversation between two figments of a dead author's imagination.

I'm thinking of reading at night as wholly consumptive, like midnight snacking, and yet anti-capitalist; reading offers free travel…

> *I attempted to stay awake reading in an apartment on the Bowery over three consecutive nights, beginning Thursday, 27 October at seven* P.M. *and ending Sunday, 30 October, at seven* A.M.*, with daytime breaks in between to return home. When I arrived that first night, it was raining in Lower Manhattan. I was sick and clammy with a head cold but willing myself to not feel sick. My project's facilitators had made a big pot of bean soup. They pointed out the beer and the coffee, the circuit breaker, the shrine to Eva Hesse, a former inhabitant of the studio, and a special reading nook, cushioned with irregular hand-sewn pillows to suit every readerly posture and position. When they left around eight o'clock, the quiet in their wake was very particular, pseudo-silent because of cars in the wet street, everything weirdly only mine.*
>
> *I tried to bring a book for every mood: books I didn't have the sustained time or quiet for during the day (*The Poetics of Space*,* Wuthering Heights*, a new collection by Sharon Olds) and security*

books—those I knew would sustain me against whatever terrors of night neurosis I expected to come (short stories by Joy Williams and Alice Munro), and decidedly night-appropriate books (Woolf, Djuna Barnes, Anne Carson, Jean Rhys) if I really wanted to delve there (though this seemed a little silly, amateur and too "experiential," like some naïve American writing a book about Cuba from a terrace in Havana). And the outlier, Don DeLillo's Underworld, *which I'd recently bought but was hesitant to start (too male, too apocalyptic, too real). I started with* Underworld. *Read through the baseball part, ate soup, cookies, drank coffee, drank a beer. I took a nap in the reading nook for a little while, a hot water bottle inside the sleeping bag my boyfriend S had lent me, which I thought of as a kind of comfort-totem, like a child's blanky (s had had the bag since he was a kid on camping trips, and he'd told me the story of how several years ago, after he'd broken up with a girlfriend he was living with in Astoria, he couldn't bear to sleep in their bed in the interim between her moving out and his getting a new place. He spent the nights on the couch in his sleeping bag—I could see him clutching it and looking sad even with his eyes closed [he is an enviably sound sleeper] through his thirtieth birthday, through Hurricane Sandy whipping itself against the windows, and my heart ached for him the way that we always ache for the people we love in the time before we knew them).*

I read, napped, drank more coffee, read more, wrote in a notebook, cried a little over some passing loneliness, felt feverish, grew sicker, watched the first lights pale the sky, and left around six o'clock. Out on Broome, my senses were heightened after the cooped-up quiet. The street sweepers and their violent brushing-by. I was hot and cold and slightly manic. No birds, just the steely light of day beginning. I always have the feeling, at this hour, that I'm about to board a plane.

I locked up and left halfway through a Joy Williams story about two little girls on a train, freaky mirror of a story I had just finished writing (also about two little girls on a train) and I finished Joy's story waiting for the train at Canal Street, then began another on the train, continued reading for an hour or two more at home in bed—I felt I was reading a marathon and couldn't stop. Eventually I fell asleep and had dreams

I don’t remember, thought thoughts with narrative arcs, and over the course of the next day and the next night, the blurring of sunset, of sunrise, of reading life, waking life, and sleeping life, I found myself proving a point I already knew to be true: that the mind is always, always hungry for excursions into story.

...and sleep deprivation undermines the productivity of the workday.

> *In the daytimes between my reading nights I went home and slept or tried to sleep, for four or five hours, between about one o'clock and six o'clock.* Tossing and turning, tossing and turning, *a phrase like bright-lit waves. On Friday I went to my dentist's office to fill out some insurance paperwork, and when she suggested she drill a cavity right then and there, I sat down in the chair and then got up again.* I'm sorry. *I couldn't, at that moment, imagine the sensitivity of an injection in my gum.*
>
> *Sleeplessness makes an already sensitive person more sensitive. The forehead-wobble of* tired, *brain goo, a perceptible lag in the leg muscles. A Chinese soccer fan died from eleven days of sleeplessness so he could watch the entire European Football Championship. Imagine dying from a voluntary lack of sleep! And your death an anecdote on the internet. In periods of exhaustion, I find myself trying square-hole-in-the-round-peg solutions. Food replaces rest; day-drifting replaces night-dreaming; text replaces thought; one person replaces another.*

Also on my mind at the time: another person. And hand-in-hand, the sense that maybe s and I had run our course. I was only half-sure, and I was too tired to make a real decision, but I felt the slow beginnings of a crack, like a fissure in thick glass, and I knew the break wouldn't be fast and clean, but prolonged, stalling, blundering, sad. I knew it and I resisted knowing it. And in the periphery, this other person, fuzzing up my brain. Sleeplessness, too, makes an already restless person more restless.

I'm thinking of woman as moon and women as night creatures.

> *Women are moony-faced, glowing, but subdued and cool. A face like a breast. A breast like a body-moon. (If you can imagine it you can write it, and it if can be written, it can be read.) It's so easy for me to imagine woman-as-moon, but it's more difficult to image man-as-sun. I suppose some are—bold and blazing and* out*—as in "sun's out today." The ones I'm attracted to are more like those outer maybe-planets in our solar system—the ones scientists argue about—is it a planet or is it not? Evasive, far off, shrouded in deep space fog.*
>
> *This other person was someone from my past—*N*—and he happened to be in town visiting during my three nights of reading, crashing on a friend's couch in the East Village. He'd made it clear that the visit wasn't directly about seeing me—it was only* indirectly *about seeing me. We'd been friends when I'd lived in Michigan, where he still lives. One spring day in 2013, we napped in his bed on the floor of his warehouse apartment, above a famous barbeque / karaoke joint, where middle-aged crooning rose up through the floor:* Ain't no sunshine

when she's gone. / Only darkness every-day. *We spent a lot of time touching each other's faces and discussing, in low voices, why we couldn't actually be together, and we never really have been*—together—*since.*

I'm thinking of Djuna Barnes, Jean Rhys, Virginia Woolf, Kafka, Anne Carson, Elizabeth Hardwick, Gaston Bachelard, Mike Kelley...

On Friday night, I flipped from book to book, left stories unfinished, read a poem, grazed the shelves, flipped back, finished a story here or there, and what resulted was my own pastiched text. My reading liberally like this created a sort of collaged experience—still narrative, but in which a nun-character in DeLillo became an aunt character in Alice Munro became a meditation on aging in Sharon Olds...

Deeply lost in the night.
I'm a fart in a gale of wind, an
humble violet under a cow pad.
When you have a fever you are heavy
and light, you are small and swollen,
you climb endlessly a ladder which
turns like a wheel.
It is in these terms that I wish
to praise sleep, as a glimpse of
something *incognito*.
What is *incognito* hides from us
because it has something worth
hiding, or so we judge.

We look to the East for a wisdom
that we shall not use—and to the
sleeper for the secret that we
shall not find.

I could still feel it on my face where
his hand had touched me.

Though those two are buried at
opposite ends of the earth, one
dog will find them both.

...Tom Hanks.

There is surprisingly little sleeplessness shown in Sleepless in Seattle*—sleeplessness being almost un-Hollywood to watch as a person reading.*

We know that Tom Hanks' wife has died recently, and that Sam (Tom) is bummed—pacing on his lovely lakeside deck all night while his son (Jonas) calls a talk radio show to help his mourning father. There's even a pleasant ghost scene, where his dead wife visits in a flowy '80s shift and sits at the foot of the couch while Sam tells her how much he misses her. But this is no picture of real nighttime grief. Night grief would be Sam on his hands and knees, on the kitchen floor, bursting at the human seams, sobbing in that sort of desperate, chest-hammering way that actually disjoints the cries from the crier, the physical grief from the thing being grieved, and in that way offers something like temporary relief.

Or at least tempers the heat of that blended love and loss that results in such grief.

To sob in the dark of night, unseen, all alone with your grief like an object...is indulgent, and luscious, even transcendent. *The out-of-body experience of grief becomes a coping mechanism for the grief itself.*

In partial conclusion:

One can cry oneself psychedelic.

Sleep deprivation hallucinations.

A series of black marks on a white page can evoke images and sense perceptions, and elicit intense emotional reactions, sexual desire, weeping.

Reading, therefore, is socially-acceptable hallucination.

The saddest periods of my life have also been the periods that I've read the most: hung onto books like life rafts.

I'm thinking of night as a metaphor for the subconscious (duh!) both out-of-time and an extension of time.

In the suburbs of Detroit, the artist Mike Kelley tried to buy his childhood home from its current owners, who, despite Kelley's fame and money, declined to sell. Instead, Kelley recreated the house: an unspectacular single-story with white vinyl siding, as a mobile model. This was Kelley's last art piece before his suicide in 2012. Now the "Mobile Homestead" is permanently installed behind the Museum of Contemporary Art Detroit.

Kelley envisioned the house as a multi-purpose art piece: at street-level, it functions as a community space—a tongue-and-cheek artist "giving back"—while the work's second use is invisible, unknown. A hatch in the main floor leads to two basement levels of passageways and bunker-like rooms, intended to facilitate "private rites of an aesthetic nature" for Kelley himself and select invited participants. Nothing made down there is to be exhibited, Kelley stipulated: the project creates "a very direct clash between the public nature of the house-turned-community center versus the antisocial activity of my secret burrowing."

*Kelley's personal biography (house) sits stacked atop his fantasized biography—childhood events that, unremembered, presented themselves as blank rooms, subconscious psychic spaces in which anything might have happened. Or the capital-*A *Artist whose private process has no ties to the public, day-lit market.*

Mike Kelley: "People will know that there are structures under the house, and they might even know that things are done there...but they won't know what those things are..."

Gaston Bachelard: "The cellar dreamer knows that the walls of the cellar are buried walls, that they are walls with a single casing, walls that have the entire earth behind them. And so the situation grows more dramatic, and fear becomes exaggerated. But where is the fear that does not become exaggerated?"

Virginia Woolf: "[Mr. Ramsay, stumbling along a passage one dark morning, stretched his arms out, but Mrs. Ramsay having died rather suddenly the night before, his arms, though stretched out, remained empty.]"

Night as a particular haven for the artist who can be, in the dark, someone else, no longer a woman or no longer a clerk, or the artist who looks forward to night in order to be no one at all.

> *During a lonely point late Friday night I read the first half of Jean Rhys' novel* Voyage in the Dark. *A sad book, poor girl-characters with dirty knees and puffy eyes—heroines whose desperation for love mixes stickily with their desperation for bread, and what comes out are joyless transactions of sex-for-dresses. The whole book smells of mildewed train compartments. It's a jarring transition, from Rhys' character's body back into my own—in the sleeping bag in the strange room in downtown Manhattan, October 2016…*
>
> *Jean Rhys, in* Good Morning, Midnight, *when her protagonist drinks wine, cries, looks in the mirror: "It isn't my face, this tortured and tormented mask. I can take it off whenever I like and hang it up on a nail."*
>
> *In view of Eva Hesse, her face and diary on the mantle, I feel particularly no-one-at-all. Small in my accomplishments and too old to impress anyone. I look up from the book, nothing, look back down.*

I would like to leave this experience with a ghost story, but I see no flashing-past of long dark hair, no turtle-necked sculptresses leaning in the doorframe.

Kafka: "Why are you watching? Someone must watch, it is said. Someone must be there."

I am watching Rhys character, watching for my phone screen to light up, Eva is or is not watching me, and Rhys is probably watching Eva, from across the room in some velvet, bohemian heaven; together we make everything real.

Insomnia as lonely, reading as quelling loneliness.

> *The foggy summer between my freshman and sophomore year of college I had no job, no friends, a bad-news boyfriend two hours away, and I was very depressed. This was San Francisco, 2003. I locked myself in my bedroom and read book after book while one of my many roommates recorded didgeridoo samples through our shared wall. I read all day, and didn't go out much, and didn't eat—I remember knowing that this was a strange dark lull in my life, and I could wait it out through reading. I could read myself into some lighter place, and eventually the feeling would rise and float off like a cloud. The only book I remember from that summer was Steinbeck's* The Winter of Our Discontent. *The grocer-protagonist talking to his shelves of canned goods. My grandmother died and I learned the boyfriend was cheating on me with a girl who, by his account, preferred anal. I lost fifteen pounds in a matter of weeks.*
>
> *I'm always worrying a double-sided worry: that on the one hand, I've wasted too much of my life* living *instead of reading / writing, and on the other, I've wasted too much of my life reading / writing instead*

of living. *When fiction falls into relief, it becomes not so much an illumination of reality, but a dangerous distraction from it. To look back one day and think,* Wait, did that happen to me or did I only read it in a book? *I'd be painting myself as more romantic than I am if I said that this thought didn't terrify me.*

Books as surrogate lovers. Reading-at-night as a surrogate dream.

> *Reading reaches its end point when the need to tend to real life eclipses the pull of fiction.*
>
> *On Saturday night, my last night, I broke out. I was reading* Underworld *again, and I put it down mid-page around midnight. I wasn't sick anymore, I had slept alright the day before, and I felt both energized in the aftermath of my cold and more or less acclimated to night—no longer as strange or still as it had felt on Thursday and Friday. I told myself, "I'll only go out for a walk," but this was a walk with a purpose—fast toward an address that had come through a text, a party in Tribeca that* N *was at.*
>
> *He was outside waiting, sitting on the lower rungs of some scaffolding with his hands folded in his lap, wearing the only clothes I'd ever seen him wear. When I got there he stood up.* N *is a tall, thin, low-voiced person prone to migraines and social anxiety. He has a trapdoor memory—constantly reminding me of things I said years ago, which always sound like they were said by someone wittier—and a leany sort of posture that makes people fall in love from*

a distance. The tender, cripple-boy from The Secret Garden *learns to walk, and all that sitting has gifted him perfect posture.*

We walked east to Chinatown and sat in a park where a solitary man practiced late-night tai chi—the slow-motion fluidity of gesture. No kissing, but sitting as close as two people can sit, sort of bracing ourselves *against each other, talking about nothing really, but under the talk, other, unspoken talk, questions like* what *and* why *and* why right now; *imaginary futures and* who will hurt who first? *s's face came to me, like a streetlight watching the scene. I flushed with what wasn't yet guilt but was almost worse—the understanding that there would be guilt, tomorrow—that what happens at night only feels "of no consequence" at night. Day, on the other hand, is a hard, bright judge.*

When I walked him to the train an hour later, there was a difficult saying-goodbye scene—a physical wrenching away—and I knew that if I went back to the Eva shrine and the books and the olive cushions, I'd die of grief. I'd be Tom Hanks on hands and knees in the unseen scenes. Again the pre-guilt: had I failed as a faithful partner and *as a reader? Or was I let off the book by my argument of nighttime as anti-time, anything-time? The popularity, too, of failure narratives can't be undersold: a failure narrative always makes the reader feel better about herself. She is better at decisions, loyalty, and stick-to-itiveness than this sloppy narrator. And how many hundreds of pages had I read in the last three nights? All of these conciliations as I descended underground, rode the J to Bushwick, danced to techno in a foggy basement, and made it back to the Bowery just in time to watch the sunrise, one last time, from the fire escape.*

If we take seriously the colloquial, the reader "loses herself in a book" or "discovers herself in a book" in much the same way we lose and discover ourselves in dreams.

I wish I'd written "in much the same way that we lose or discover ourselves in other people."

A poem made up of lines, redacted and rearranged, from Elizabeth Hardwick's Sleepless Nights*:*

It is Saturday and people with debts are
going to restaurants...
I am alone here in New York, no longer a
we...*one is out of the commonest of*
plurals. Orgasms of twenty years ago
leave no memory. Better to be hand-
some and leave...
In truth, moments, months, even years were
magical.
The moon changed the field to the silvery
lavender of daybreak.
Pages turned, answering prayers, and per-
sons called out, Are you there?

In my dreams, this experiment would happen from something like sundown to sunup, seven P.M. to seven A.M. or so, for at least three nights. Dreamy time frames are 12–17 October, 26–30 October, 16–20 November, as these are times when I'll have the least amount of stuff to do during the day. Vampires!

Sleeplessly awaiting your response,

Emma Wippermann

Library

Jane Bennett exalts in the inanimate, in the "accumulating pile of lively and potentially dangerous matter." This is the library. Who's on the shelf?

1:12 P.M., 13 November 2016

I temporarily removed all the male-authored books from the bookshelves and put them in the other room. It's slapstick and satisfying, and the steward of the library said, "Don't think this isn't a critique."

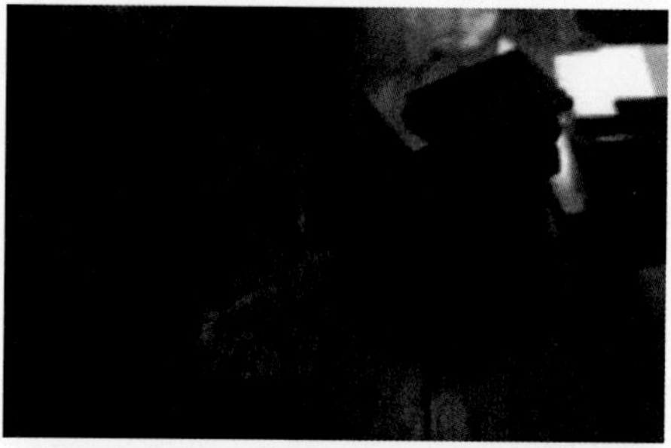

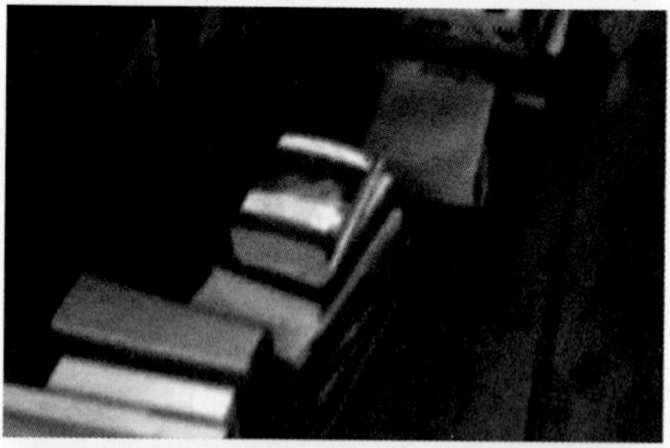

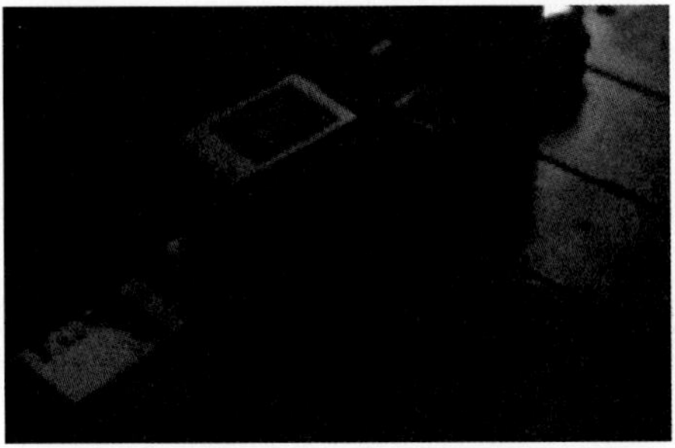

The steward was right, but I wasn't critiquing her.

The dividing action in *Library* is so basic, so problematically obvious, that I keep coming back to Eve Sedgwick and her gender contradiction: in *Epistemology of the Closet*, she writes that being gay, with regard to gender, has a fundamental contradiction; on one hand, it plays with the "liminality or transitivity between genders" but on the other hand, it reflects "an impulse of separatism… within each gender." As a variously gendered person I play with the liminality, but in this project, I very much reaffirm the separatism.

Work that engages disparity, even with reparative intention, is still engaging disparity. And with my own taste as arbiter, there's only an approximate relationship between the concept and the bodies involved (all the Norton Anthologies were out; Paul Preciado and Baldwin stayed, and so did a collection of essays on mid-century sculpture).

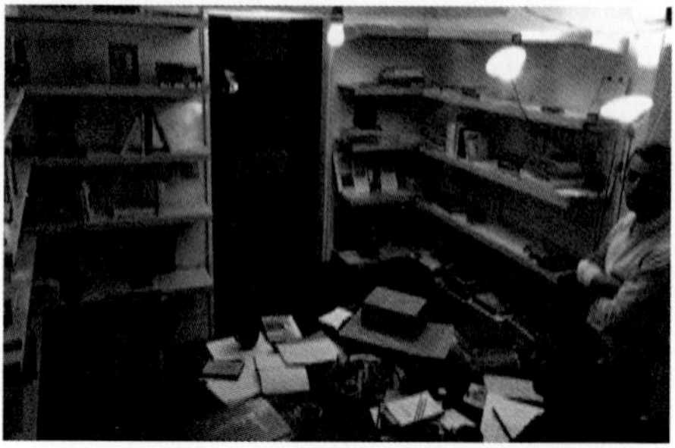

7:50 P.M., 13 November 2016

In *The Problem of Reading*, Moyra Davey asks: "What does it mean to spend a good part of one's life absorbed in books? Given that our time is limited, the problem of reading becomes one of exclusion." I removed most of the books from the shelves, and now we have to read to fill the empty space. Or displace it.

In this time of the "precariat" and "crisis ordinariness"—as Lauren Berlant suggests—reading is particularly important; political engagement (be it at a rally, a desk, or on social media) must be accompanied by engagement with one's self and others' selves. In *The Need for Roots*, Simone Weil writes that political parties are inherently unethical; within them, each individual must submit themself to the cause, causing true heterogeneity and plurality to become impossible. Strangely enough for a French intellectual in the 1940s, she advocated a form of individualism: every person must be their own person, and politics too easily subjugates the self. However, one of the most lauded ways to shape the self is reading, *subsuming* one's person to another's person. The problem of reading, then, becomes political; who do we join our thoughts with? Who do we give access?

The male-authored books, after being removed from the shelves and relocated to the other rooms, occupied even more space; they were more active in their displacement. This could be viewed as a fault or disappointment—these books are impossible to displace, the canon is set—or we could see it as further illustration of the basic, even impetuous gesture of *Library*—removal isn't enough, relocation isn't enough: here, *Library* becomes about production and consumption. We want *beautiful* "potentially dangerous piles of matter." More must be recovered from the archives, more must be written and published and purchased.

It's also about labor. The project took about six hours to complete. I documented the books in their original positions, and carefully arranged the ones I removed from the shelves in order to return them to the library in the right places. As soon as *Library* was "complete," it was undone. Which asks the question: were the bare shelves the climax of the performance? Or was the hurried, late evening *return* of the man books the point of it all?

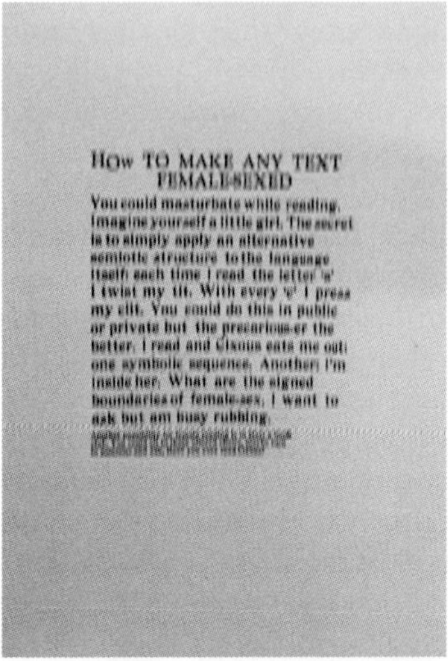

HOW TO MAKE ANY TEXT FEMALE-SEXED

You could masturbate while reading. Imagine yourself a little girl. The secret is to simply apply an alternative semiotic structure to the language itself: each time I read the letter 'e' I twist my tit. With every 'c' I press my clit. You could do this in public or private but the precarious-er the better. I read and Cixous eats me out: one symbolic sequence. Another: I'm inside her. What are the signed boundaries of female-sex, I want to ask but am busy rubbing.

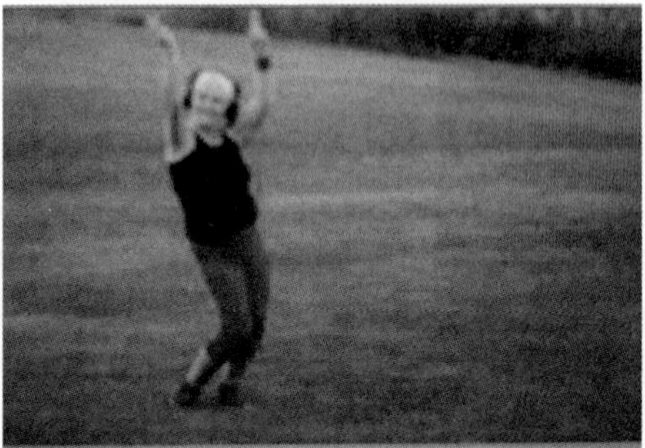

'Corporal' vs. 'Corporeal'

I've gotten some arm muscles from this project. It's about my body as much as it's about the frustration I feel in libraries and bookstores. Can a person with tits lift and carry out all these books? How do we deal with feelings that reinforce the system we're up against?

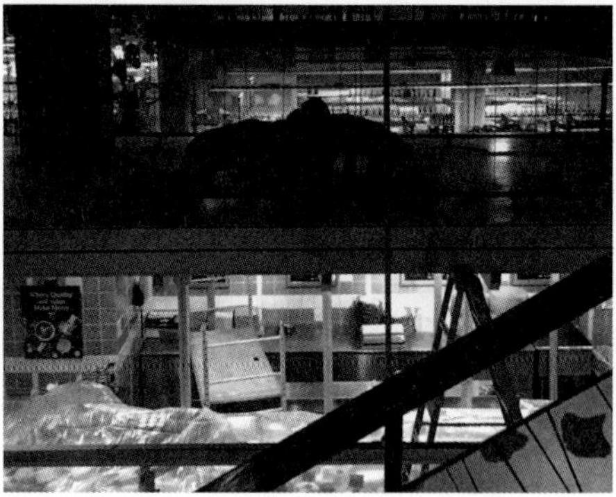

And what do these things I'm lifting do to us? What do we do with, as Bennett has called it, "the capacity of things...to act as quasi agents or forces with trajectories, propensities, or tendencies of their own"? Who and what do we let speak?

We must tend to things, and attend to what the things mean about our thinking. In other iterations, I've taken out all the books written by white people. The books remaining on the shelf have, for some moments, room to breathe. I then crowd them back up and I, one, we must start reading differently.

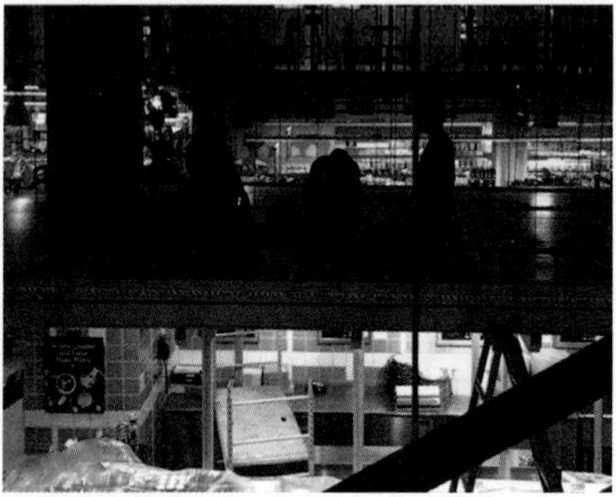

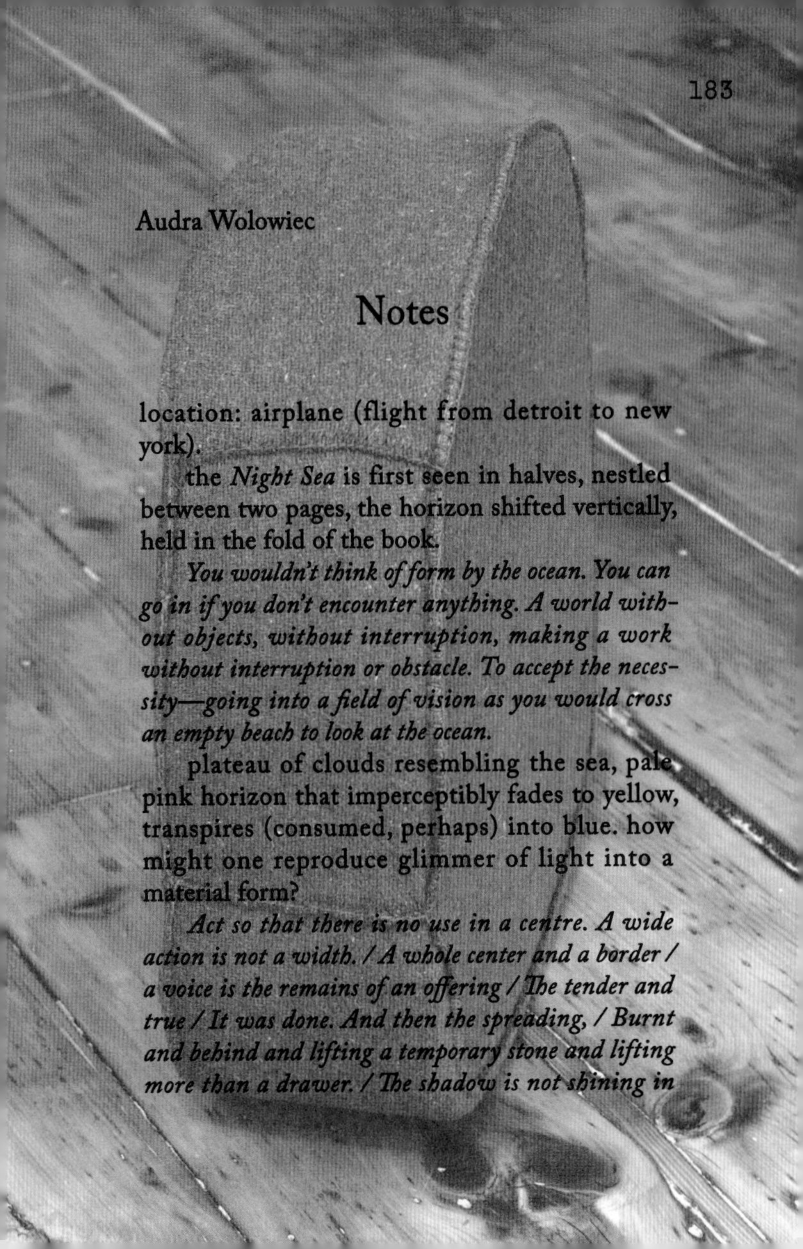

Audra Wolowiec

Notes

location: airplane (flight from detroit to new york).

the *Night Sea* is first seen in halves, nestled between two pages, the horizon shifted vertically, held in the fold of the book.

You wouldn't think of form by the ocean. You can go in if you don't encounter anything. A world without objects, without interruption, making a work without interruption or obstacle. To accept the necessity—going into a field of vision as you would cross an empty beach to look at the ocean.

plateau of clouds resembling the sea, pale pink horizon that imperceptibly fades to yellow, transpires (consumed, perhaps) into blue. how might one reproduce glimmer of light into a material form?

Act so that there is no use in a centre. A wide action is not a width. / A whole center and a border / a voice is the remains of an offering / The tender and true / It was done. And then the spreading, / Burnt and behind and lifting a temporary stone and lifting more than a drawer. / The shadow is not shining in the way there is a black line. / a wide place stranger, a wideness makes an active center.

What comes through is an opening onto contact, slippage, surprise: a wondering. What comes through is a fabulous woodenly dream of life captured in an instant. What comes through is a puzzle for the jumping eye, a wondering machine for the mind figuring out what to make of things in the encounter with an image. What comes through is the clarity of the body that has things to say. What comes through is the fingertips of a hand framed by beautiful black nail polish. What comes through is a gift of specificity, powerful and weighted with precision. What comes through is contact. What comes through is already formed and moving on its own but it's not alone. What comes through is the way a sensory touch meets a fabulation. What comes through is the possibilities lodged in a stranger intimacy.

* * *

These lines of text were culled from Suzanne Hudson's book *Agnes Martin: Night Sea* and Gertrude Stein's *Tender Buttons* through a non-linear process. They were not intended by their authors to be read in this order and have been re-composed as an invitation for errant readers.

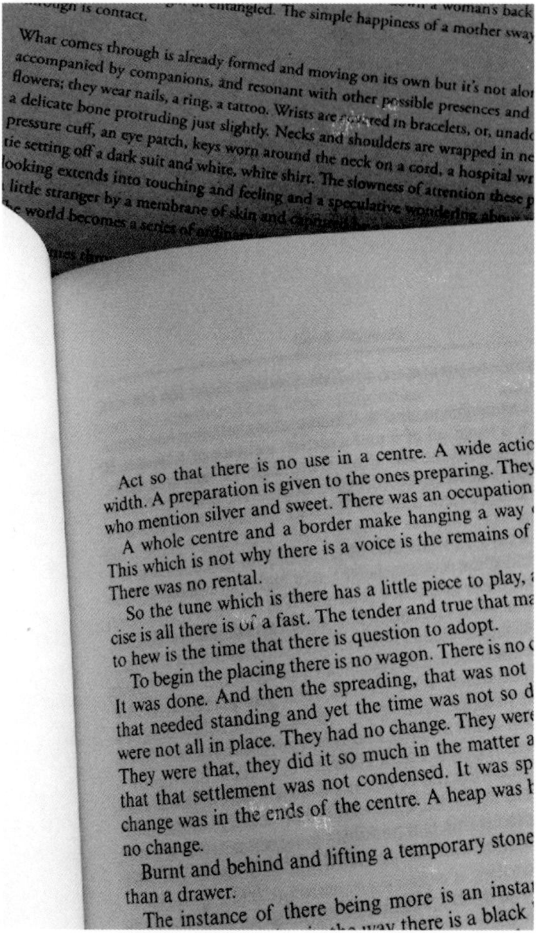

ough is contact. entangled. The simple happiness of a mother swa

What comes through is already formed and moving on its own but it's not alo
accompanied by companions, and resonant with other possible presences and
flowers; they wear nails, a ring, a tattoo. Wrists are covered in bracelets, or, unad
a delicate bone protruding just slightly. Necks and shoulders are wrapped in ne
pressure cuff, an eye patch, keys worn around the neck on a cord, a hospital wr
tie setting off a dark suit and white, white shirt. The slowness of attention these p
looking extends into touching and feeling and a speculative wondering abo
little stranger by a membrane of skin and captured
world becomes a series of ordina

Act so that there is no use in a centre. A wide actio
width. A preparation is given to the ones preparing. They
who mention silver and sweet. There was an occupation
A whole centre and a border make hanging a way
This which is not why there is a voice is the remains of
There was no rental.
So the tune which is there has a little piece to play,
cise is all there is of a fast. The tender and true that ma
to hew is the time that there is question to adopt.
To begin the placing there is no wagon. There is no
It was done. And then the spreading, that was not
that needed standing and yet the time was not so d
were not all in place. They had no change. They were
They were that, they did it so much in the matter a
that that settlement was not condensed. It was sp
change was in the ends of the centre. A heap was h
no change.
Burnt and behind and lifting a temporary stone
than a drawer.
The instance of there being more is an insta

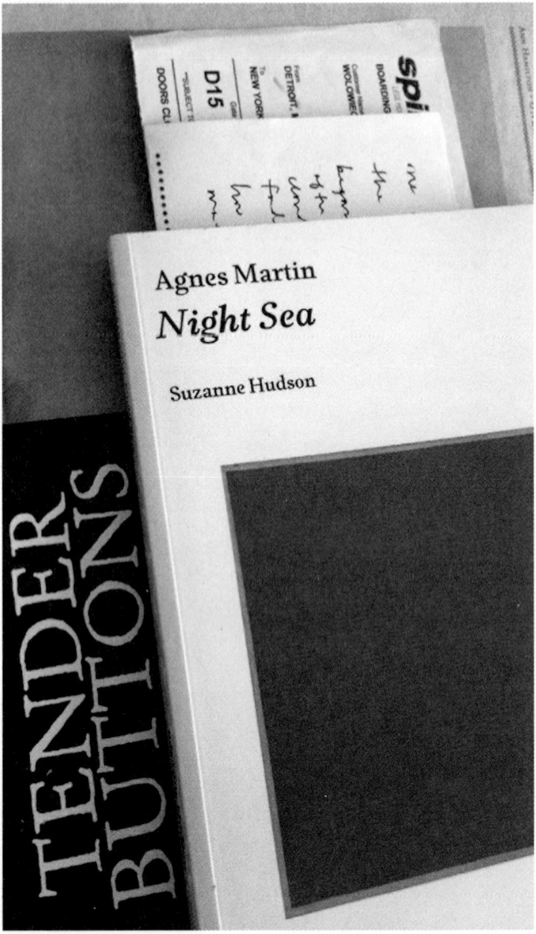
Agnes Martin
Night Sea
Suzanne Hudson
TENDER BUTTONS

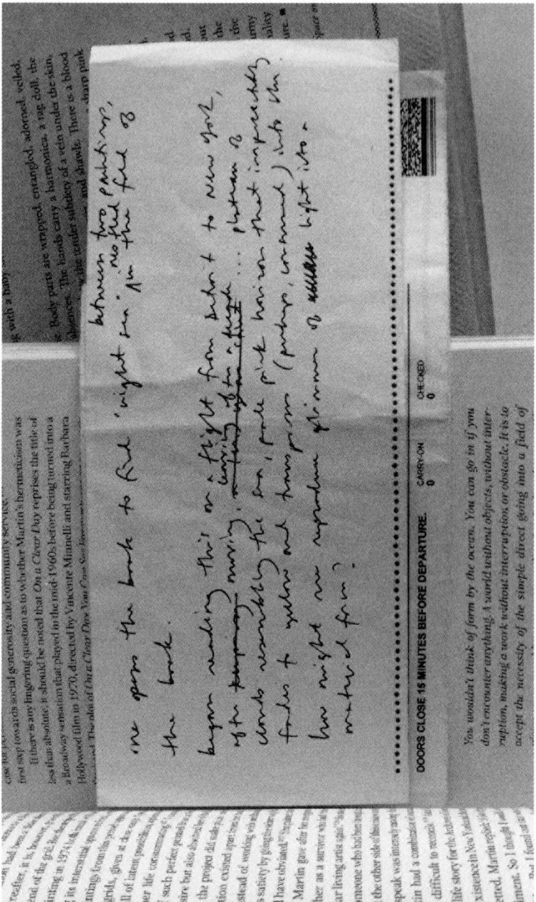
DOORS CLOSE 15 MINUTES BEFORE DEPARTURE.
CARRY-ON
0
CHECKED
0

Carrie Yamaoka

Untitled

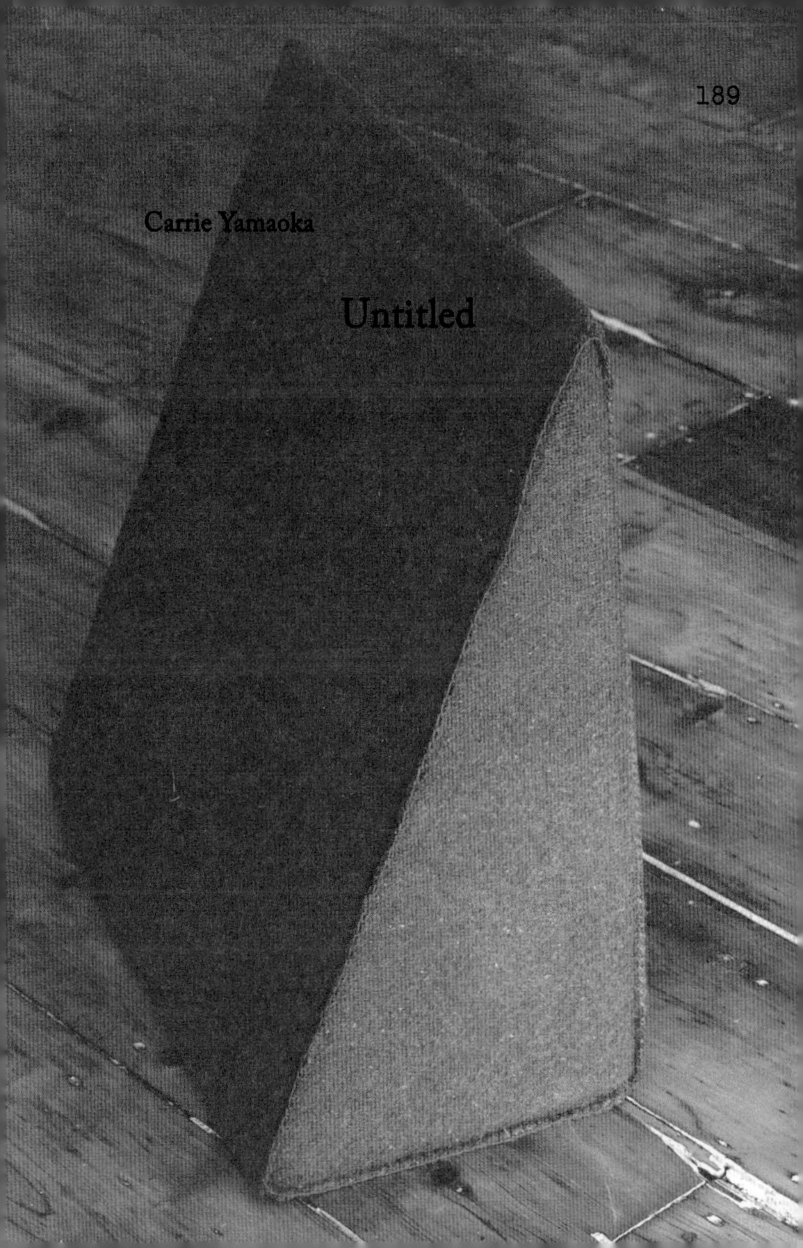

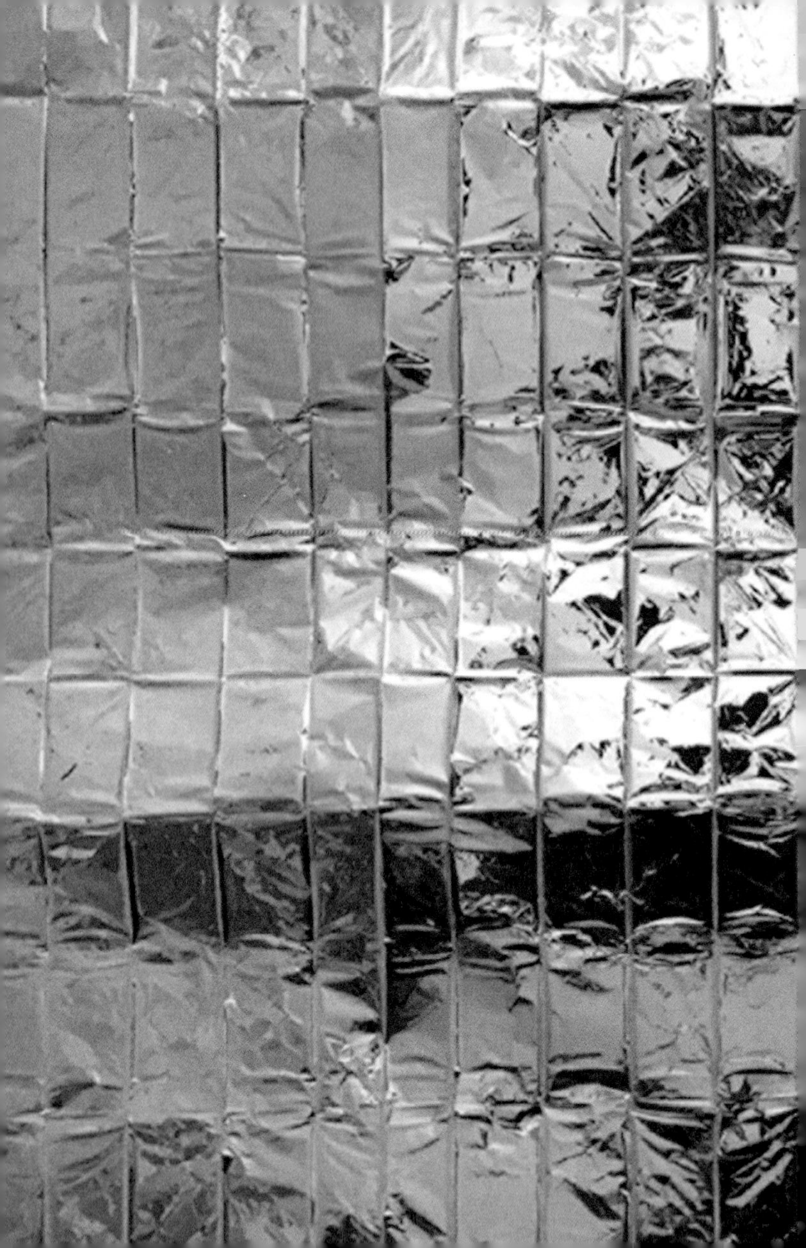

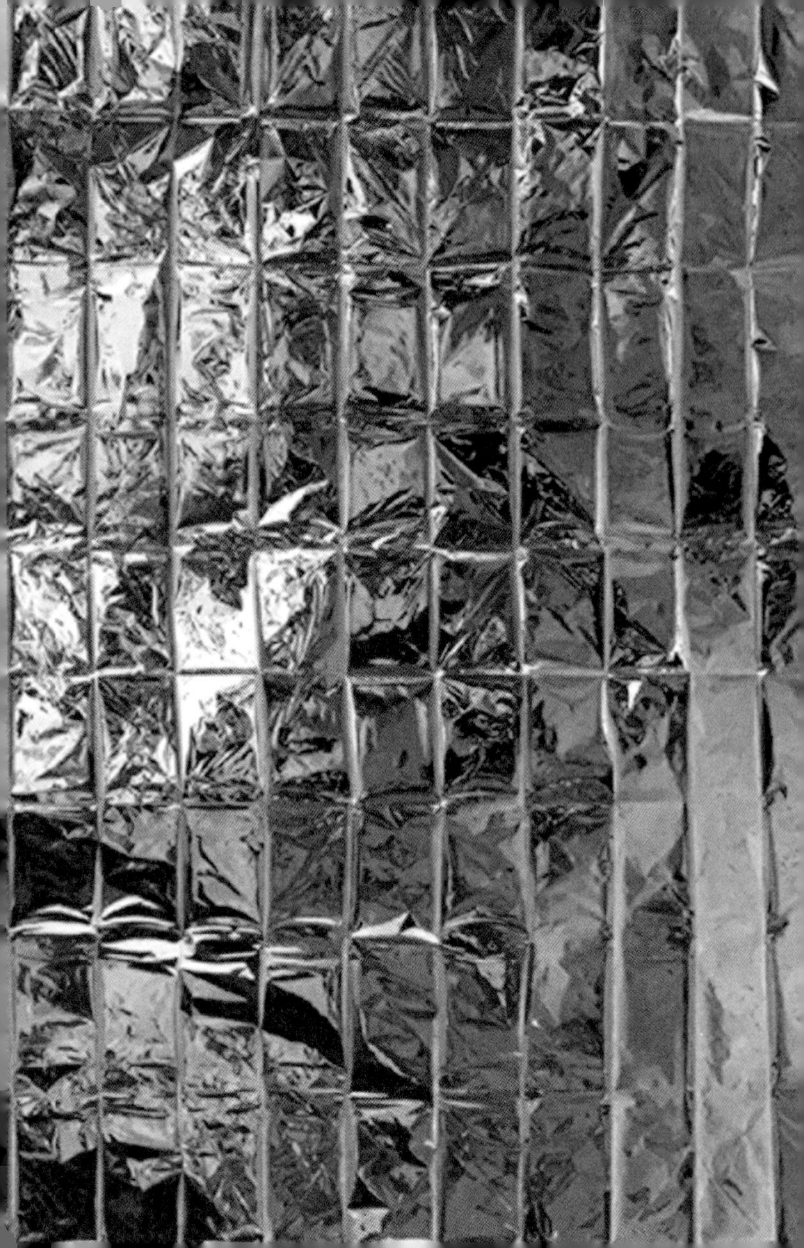

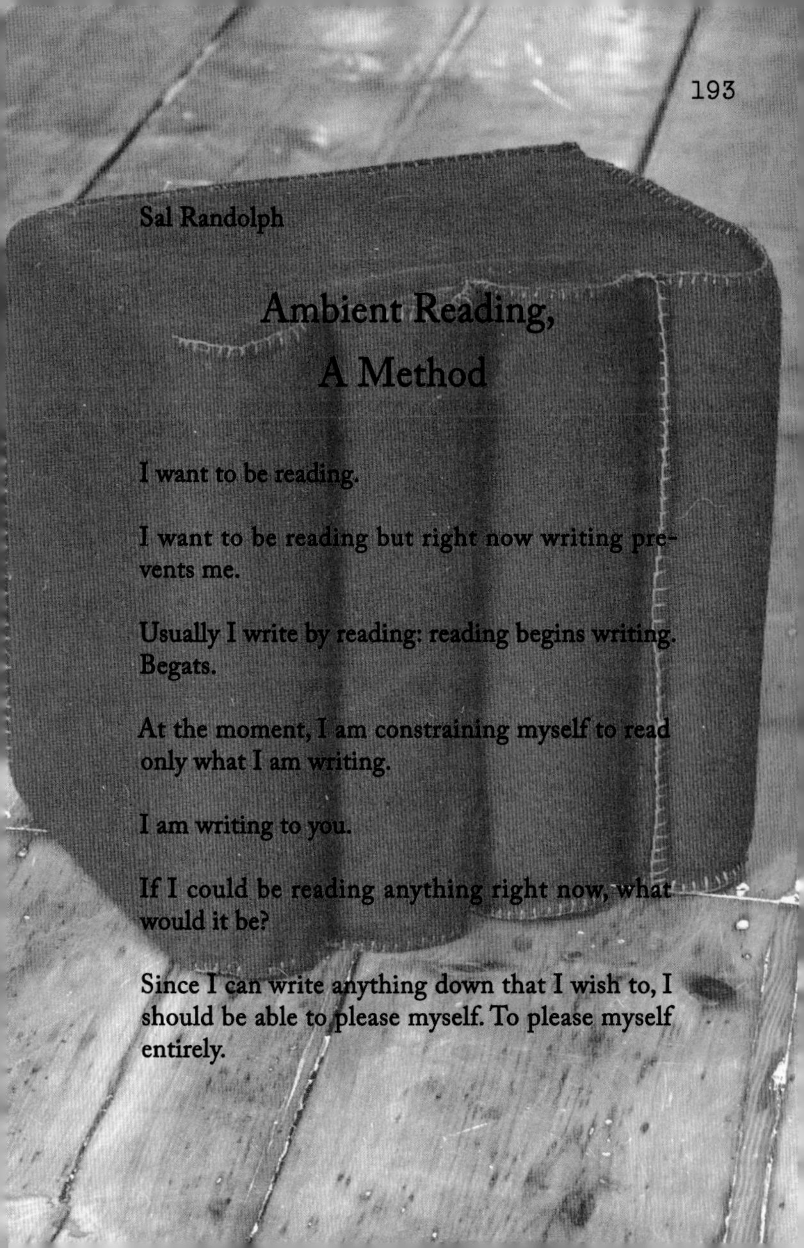

Sal Randolph

Ambient Reading, A Method

I want to be reading.

I want to be reading but right now writing prevents me.

Usually I write by reading: reading begins writing. Begats.

At the moment, I am constraining myself to read only what I am writing.

I am writing to you.

If I could be reading anything right now, what would it be?

Since I can write anything down that I wish to, I should be able to please myself. To please myself entirely.

In a book I was just looking at, I read the word "anise." I was pleased, and jealous. That writer was sitting outside, out back, by the anise. The anise gave him something to say, a beautiful word to interrupt his thinking with.

In another book I picked up, the writer was tumbling around the word "maroon" and feeling for its puns, its associations. An unhappy color. An island you can't get off of. A part of me is still stuck there.

Sometimes it is enough to open a book and read a single word. I open the *I Ching* and receive the word "innocence."

And so I go forward, without expecting anything.

Ambient reading is going forward without expecting anything. I am full of theories, but at the moment I don't love them.

I'm sitting in a room full of books.

To be at play.

If I weren't writing, I would lie down and close my eyes. Words would keep happening inside me.

When words are happening inside you, is that writing, or reading?

I'd like to spend all day reading, slowly and deeply, going word by word the way the writer meant me to, building a little city from the bricks of those words, something appearing in the air above my head. Can you see it floating there?

A few days ago, over dinner at an Indian restaurant, someone I didn't know suggested I read Heidegger.

How many books am I in the middle of right now?

Ambient reading isn't like the kind of reading where you lie on the couch with a book and read all day from beginning to end.

If I want to be reading, but must read only what I am writing, then I want some words which are like gymnasiums.

But I can't help reading. I am in a room surrounded by books, and there are words on the spines.

I stole that word from the spine of a book: gymnasium. It seemed just like the gymnasium I wanted. A word which is the itself of itself.

I am supposed to be writing as if I am speaking.

But the writing and the speaking are separated by time. Writing is writing. Speaking is speaking. But both writing and speaking are reading.

I pull a book down from the shelf because of its title: *In the Realm of Appearances*. I have been thinking about the word "appear."

I had forgotten it, but it turns out to be John Yau's book on Andy Warhol, which I read some years ago.

On page fifty-six I see: "The artist as innocent child." I close the book.

Sometimes I wonder why we need writing at all. Writing in the linear sense, in the intentional sense.

Words themselves, words lifting and floating free, seem enough. More than enough. Each word is an excess.

But I am aware, of course, that I am writing now, writing in just the sense of transcribing my thinking, transcribing my imaginary speaking.

There are words in my head, and my hands play on the keyboard like a court stenographer. There are words floating in my head.

There are imaginary speakings. I am speaking to you.

I am writing to you.

Which makes this a letter.

Is a letter a way of conversing when two mouths are not near each other? I am writing to you.

If I am here reading my own words…But I am here, reading my own words. Give me a new word.

This is where I’ve always done poorly as a writer. If I ask for a word, they all flee, leaving only the silly, the sentimental, the overwrought, the dull, the flat, the predetermined, the obvious. Rubble.

This is one reason I like to read. To put words back into my head.

I carry around certain books to read ambiently.

I read in them, rather than read them.

Often, a single word is enough, but you may have to read a whole page, or many to find that word.

"Does she mean that the afternoon should pass"

And now I have "afternoon."

An obvious word, perhaps, because it is in fact afternoon as I am writing.

But with the word afternoon, I get a color, a pale buttery liquid yellow. And a sound, something far off that I can't quite make out. And the motion of swaying, as if in a hammock. And the sensation of time simultaneously lived and empty. A garment on a clothesline, fluttering slightly.

I carry another book around with me because of a phrase that occurs in its introduction. The phrase is, "it loves to happen."

The author himself does not know the origin of the phrase, which appeared in his notes. He can only speculate.

Another book I carry because it suggests that it is possible to write as if no one will ever read what you are writing, to be unselfconsciously private in public, to please yourself entirely.

To write as if you were merely reading.

Is it possible to write as if you are receiving a letter rather than sending one?

Dear Sal, the writing says, because I am reading.

When I am reading it is always as if I am reading a letter written to me.

Some books know me so well.

I have a stack of books about reading, but I don't want to read them. Not right now. Reading is like being an instrument that someone is playing.

Ambient reading is like two instruments meeting each other.

I love UlyssesReader on Twitter. It tweets out bits of James Joyce's *Ulysses* 140 characters at a time. That's not exactly true. The algorithm chooses sentences or phrases, parts that cohere between punctuations: it never leaves you blankly mid-word.

Let's see what it's saying.

Right now it says, "between his lips."

I think of it like this: The coder took *Ulysses*, put it in a perfume bottle, and atomized it into a mist.

These fine droplets float free.

Ulysses is liberated from its terrible weight of expectation, of protocol, of interpretation. It is freed from the literal weight of its bound books.

Right now: "between his lips."

I look up and see Jorie Graham's book of poems, *The Errancy*.

What if we thought of the words on the spines of books as representatives of the words within. Not pictures, but political representatives.

The library as a congress of titles.

What if all the pages were sealed in glue, and the only words we had left were the titles? If we had to make a new language from only the words on spines.

So much of the language would be proper names, they would have to be pressed into new meanings.

Am I errant, do I err? Am I sent on an errand?

Or is the errancy ongoing, everywhere, ubiquitous, ever-present? Is there nothing but errancy? (Between his lips. The innocent, the errant gymnasium. All afternoon. It loves to happen.)

If I am writing to be reading, I have a paradox of being.

Writing is frightening, reading is comforting.

Do I write to frighten myself so that I will need comfort?

Do I write to steady myself with the little march of words?

Line up! Line up! All of you, fall in line! Hold hands!

We're taking the words for a walk, and we can't get lost. Don't lose anyone.

I am writing to you. You are writing to me.

I am reading you.

I am at a ouija board, listening.

Tell me myself, tell me true.

Ambient reading is a kind of permission. It is the permission to stray within the text. No one knows where we are going.

The blue and white teacup on the handmade ouija board seems to move under its own command. Our fingers touch it but only to follow.

One letter at a time it glides to form words.

No one knows where we are going.

I imagine you reading this. I imagine reading this to you. I am reading this to you.

Paul Soulellis

Eva_script

Eva_script was made in collaboration with Sal Randolph and David Richardson using the following protocol:

PROTOCOL OF THE DOCUMENT

Encounter / Reading (seven minutes)
Negation (seven minutes)
Writing (fifteen or more minutes)

Having gathered in these rooms with our devices, together but separate, please find your place. We will spread out. Once settled, an email will be sent to each of you with a link. This begins our encounter with the Document. We attend to the Document by reading. During your encounter, please navigate the Document, but do not type or manipulate the objects you find. We are in it together, reading quietly through this air, connected in these rooms. The first phase will continue for seven minutes. A bell will signal the end of Reading, and the beginning of Negation. Please turn away from the Document. You may close your computer, put it to sleep, or shut your eyes. Following the seven minute Negation phase, the bell will sound, and you may enter the Document again. Now, write. We will write together—in, on, around, and with the objects. It is up to you. The Document may transform. The Writing phase will be fifteen minutes, until a bell sounds, but you may continue, as you wish. Once you leave the document, you may not return; it will be printed and dispersed into the space. Please speak with the others when you are finished, in order to return us to convivial space.

* * *

Communication our, words to me
words, to me

a laugh 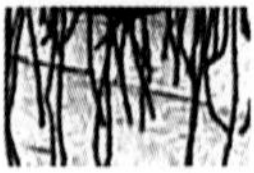 a minute planned

bus tour

slept there

lovely old

and compulsive

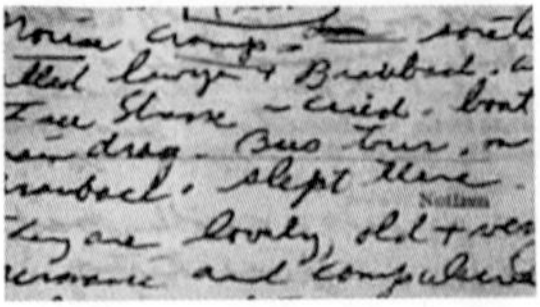

after

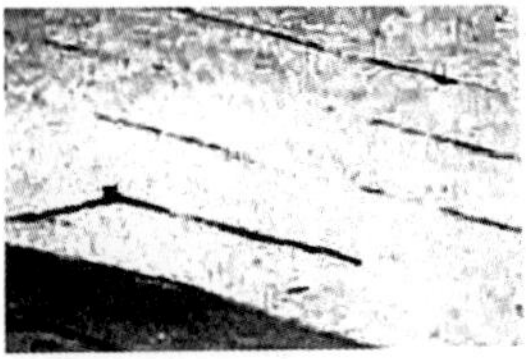

After. Before – makes no difference.

these are the relics
how close are they
can they be copied
where they're pointing
she says:
Mon. 10:30
Importance of continuity in sessions for me now.
Therefore more dreams. write down.
It is to forget! Write and figure out!

direction and
entanglement

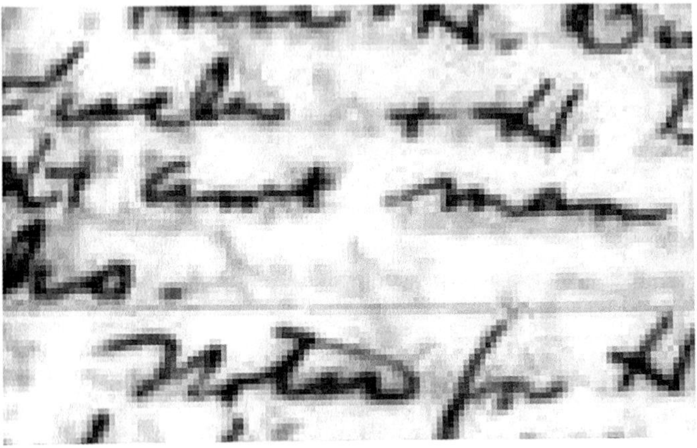

notion for

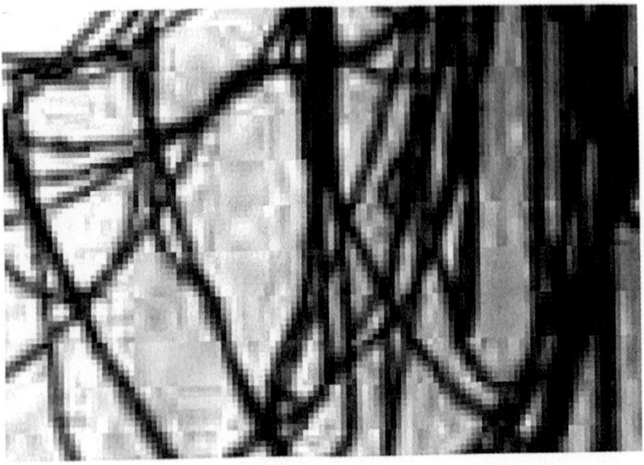

weaved through holes. Attached
together but separate

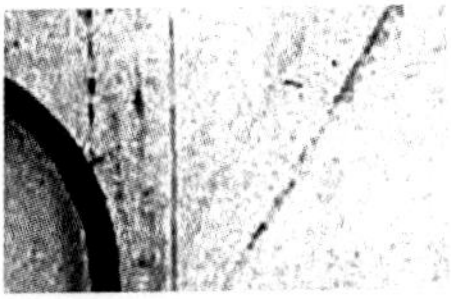

it is to forget

relic

they

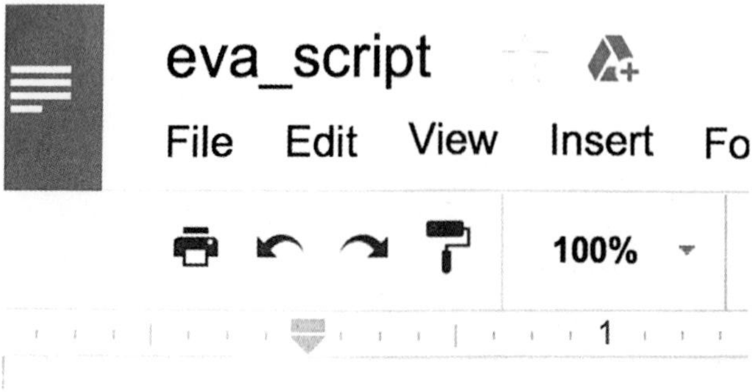

What is in me that I do not trust?
[Diagrams]

words to me, our

scripting

scripture, these
words

our scripting, our

I am knot thoroughly convinced that

af

got sculptures
wet dampness rain - revised
must, much anxiety

immediately

very strange

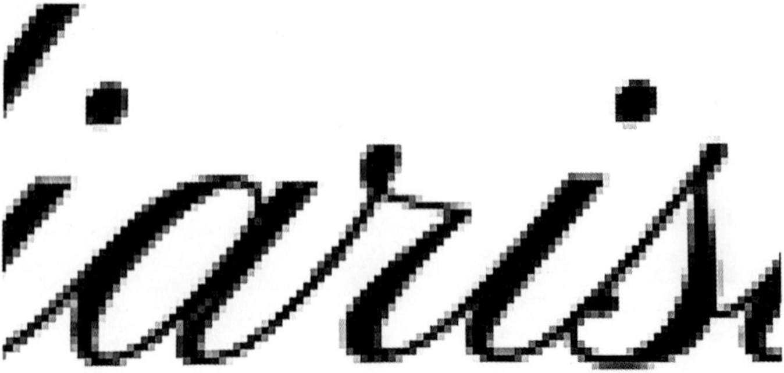

Anonymous Manatee

weaved through h

together but sep

Paul Soulellis

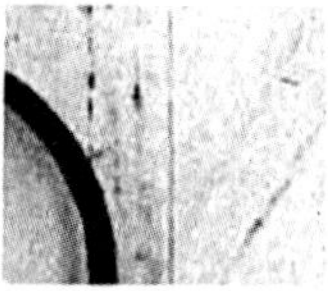

it is to forget

__________ *(watching the diarist, the historian, over their shoulder)* We r history's voyeurs

(always remember history's tools, keep them handy)

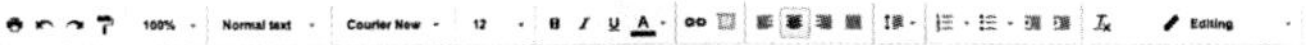

knot

or some such
she says too

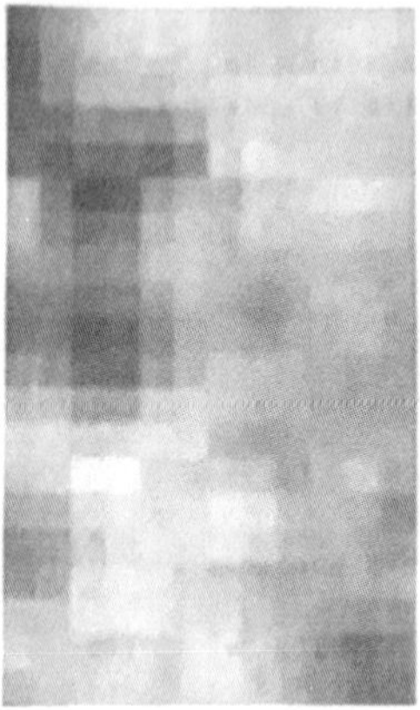

size 5

ages in your diaries, so many photographs of u, and all i can remember are the sneakers you wore in kettwig, ur ankles and cuffed, big pants.

CAN THIS BE ALL THAT REMAINS?

my sapphic fragment: an image of ur dirty white sneaker

here i go, revising history again.

my hand in red, like a grade school teacher, writing thru the margins, into the fabric of this text

derrida calls it "cutting in" or some such. every act of reading / writing / shaping the residue a violence, an imposition.

BUT WE MUST BEGIN

Revision history

Today, 4:01 PM
- Paul Soulellis
- All anonymous users

Today, 11:30 AM
- Paul Soulellis

December 16, 5:46 PM
- Paul Soulellis

December 16, 5:10 PM
- Paul Soulellis

to whom should we attribute the residue?

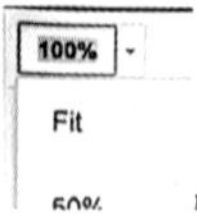

my memory: less “100%” / more “fit”

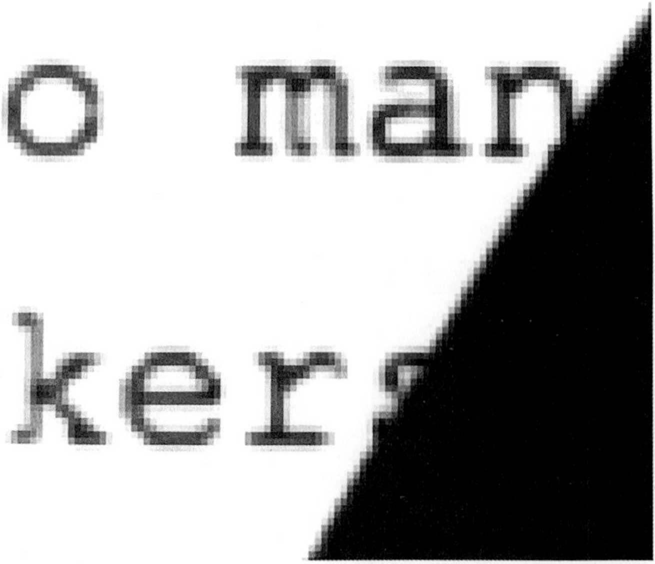

ages in your diaries, so man
. i can remember are the sneaker

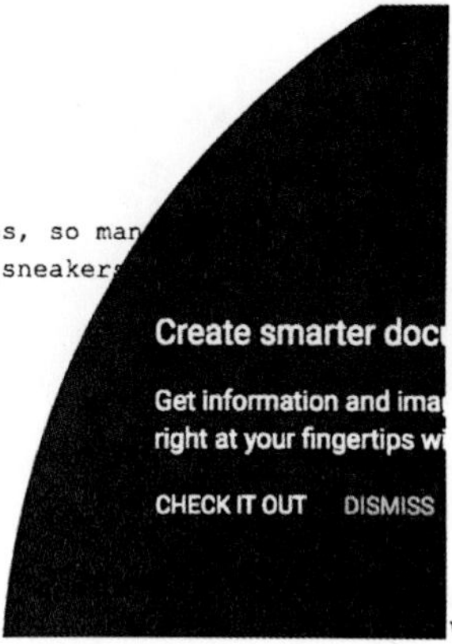

what is a "smarter document"?

o man
ker

one that loves its blank space, it's ignorance

let me be the genius of the margins.

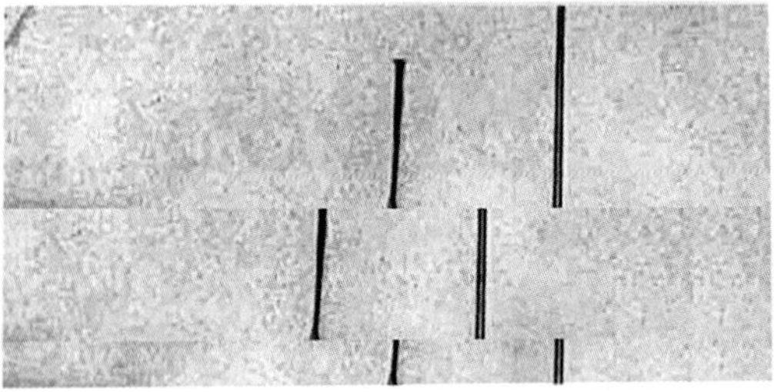

I could knot work
I could knot work
I could knot work
I could knot work
I could knot work
I could knot work
I could knot your work into a text
ileI could knot work

knot w
knot w
knot w
knot w
knot w
knot w
knot w $(-T)$ =

I could

not

kno w

words to me, our communication.

." or son

: residue

that loves blank space

undone

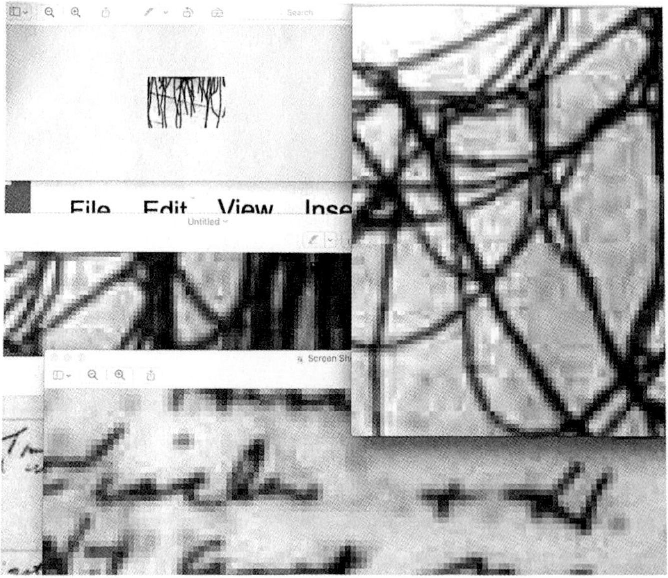
File Edit View Inse
Untitled
Screen Sh

Jimmy Cajoleas

I Could Do This Forever

Seven years old and I'm in a tree at my grandparents' house, propped up by a sturdy limb and hidden by leaves. No one can find me. The joy is exquisite. I'm reading the Hardy Boys—or better yet, the Three Investigators, who were cosigned by no less than Alfred Hitchcock. It's *The Mystery of the Whispering Mummy*, the one where Jupiter Jones gets a mummy to speak to him. My grandmother wanders around the yard, hollering out my name, and I ignore her, smiling and reading.

I could do this forever.

* * *

I'm nine and I'm reading *The Rainmaker* by John Grisham. It's an adult book, my first one, and my mom has paper-clipped the "dirty" parts together so I won't peek. Of course, the first thing I do is find a quiet spot in the backyard and flip those pages open. I read and I read and I read.

But there's something I can't figure out.

Why would anybody dream about rubbing some lady's legs? What's so special about legs? It doesn't make any sense to me.

The rest of the book is about people dying for lack of insurance coverage. For the rest of the day I stare out at the road, watching strangers drive by. All adults are probably evil, I decide, rubbing each other's legs and defrauding dying children. And one day I'll have to be one of them.

Pretty good book though.

* * *

Sophomore year of high school and believe it or not, I'm a football player. Not too bad either, considering my size. I'm reading *Franny and Zooey* by J.D. Salinger on the bus to an away game, headphones on, trying to ignore our idiot coach. He's a red-headed asshole who sings gospel songs all practice and flirts with cheerleaders at pep rallies, I've seen him do it. I hate that guy about as much as I've ever hated anyone.

I feel a weird hot soft fleshy mass on my neck. I jolt away and turn my head.

It's a dick.

"Haha," says Laney, a senior, one of the biggest guys on the team. It's his dick on my neck. "I'm gonna make you suck that later."

I go in for fifteen minutes that game before getting knocked out in the fourth quarter. I come to in the huddle, being held up by two linemen.

"Sorry," says one of them. "We couldn't leave you laying on the ground. They would have called a timeout, and coach says we got to let the clock run down."

And it still takes me a whole other year before I get the guts enough to quit.

* * *

Me on the dirty tiled floor outside my freshman dorm room, winter of 2003, while my roommate sits inside, masturbating in front of his computer. He has informed me he will be "done in a minute." It's nighttime and I am in great terror, reading the *King James Bible*. A drunken frat boy rides a wobbly bike down the hallway towards me. In his hand is a dented silver can of Coors Lite. He shakes it vigorously and rears back, about to hurl it at me, the GDI ("god-damned independent") stinking up his floor with my lack of group affiliation. I hold the *Bible* up and he recoils like a vampire, riding past me, the beer can lowered.

"You're lucky," he calls to me over his shoulder. "I can't fuck you up while you're reading the *Bible*."

* * *

After a show in Toronto, in a downstairs green room with split-vinyl couches that smell like sweat and stale beer. We had a decent crowd for once, and the rest of the band brought a bunch of people—girls mainly—backstage to drink all the leftover free booze. I'm reading the end of *The Return the King* and crying openly. It's humiliating, but I can't stop. I'm right at the part where Aragorn is wandering around, healing people, and the old ladies start whispering an old prophecy about how the "hands of the king are the hands of a healer" and I am undone. I mean losing it. Big, ugly tears.

"Is he okay?" asks one of the girls, a woozy brunette. "Sure," says the singer. "He's always like that."

* * *

Standing on a chair in the smoke room, the basement of the best worst house I've ever lived in. I'm with my friends. We all graduated college and didn't leave. We have horrible jobs but our rent is only $100 each so we feel rich, better than millionaires. We've been here so long we drink for free at all the bars, and no one bothers to charge us for breakfast. We are on the second case of beer. We are on the third bottle of Jim Beam. Everything is so beautiful I can hardly take it.

I'm reading aloud from *The Battlefield Where The Moon Says I Love You*, a four-hundred-page nightmare poem by the dead Mississippian Frank Stanford. We all know it. It's our favorite.

"I with my sackful of dreams my heart never puts down!" I holler, my third favorite line. "Get off the damn chair," says my friend, P.S. Dean, pushing

me. "It's my turn to throw." He yanks the book out of my hands and climbs on the chair, his eyes shut. He doesn't even need to read, he's got the whole book memorized.

* * *

In Uganda by lantern light, trying to read Flannery O'Connor. There's a bat the size of a football hanging upside down in our doorway. I've got nightmares from the malaria pills, I keep seeing my grandfather on all fours in his pajamas crawling through a flood. It's a bad scene in my head right now, I'll tell you. But I love it here, I do, I love my friend Chad sleeping next to me, I love the bat hanging there silent and peaceful, I love this story called "Revelation," where a mean woman sees a bridge to Heaven and everyone she hates jumping and dancing across it. Outside everything smells like gasoline.

It will be a long night, and I'm glad to be awake for it.

* * *

My leg itches and I'm at a walk-in medical clinic in Austin, Texas, receiving my fourth rabies shot. I had an encounter with a rabid bat while having drinks with my mother. My mother caught the bat in her shawl and demanded animal control test its brain. I got bit and now rabies is swimming somewhere in my veins. I'm reading *Scott Pilgrim Vol. 5* in the waiting room.

I very much want a cigarette.

"Mr. Cajoleas," says the nurse. I follow him back to a small antiseptic room and sit on the crumply paper sheet. He swabs me with a cotton ball and tells me to relax. It's only then that I notice the nurse has one arm.

"Don't worry," he says, raising the needle. "I can shoot you up just fine."

* * *

It's three A.M. two weeks ago and I'm wired. My brain is wild, a rat scravenging up every worry and terror I ever had while my girlfriend sleeps deep and content beside me. I can't ever sleep, I hate that I can't sleep. Everything in me is baffled and afraid, convinced that I will die, am already dying, that nothing will ever go right again. I slide out of bed, careful not to wake her, and grab an old copy of the poems from the old Zen monk Ryōkan. I flip open to a random page and read it aloud, whisper it like a prayer:

The thief left it behind—
the moon
at the window.

I run to my window and peek out over the fire escape. There she is, a cold glimmer in the sky, waiting for me. I smile a little bit. I can't help it.

Yeah, yeah, I think, *okay.*
I turn the page. I could do this forever.

David Richardson

Society of My Spectacles,
A dérive

I

The whole life of those societies in which modern conditions of production prevail presents itself as an immense accumulation of spectacles. *All that once was directly lived has become mere representation.*
– Guy Debord,
Section 1, *The Society of the Spectacle*, 1967

2

I watched Mrs. Smith's pale arm chart a jagged course across the green expanse. From an arbitrary mooring, her dance began: left, and then right, right on, until it broke off and went under. The air was filled with percussive clacking, the tempo charging and convicted, the rhythm cacophonous, irregular. Her cryptic choreography trailed puffy white lines and the loping marks bled into masses. I lost, and found, and lost the beat. My head ached.

This went on for weeks. Only when my mother was made to sign my math test for its low score, the first such instance of underperformance in my young academic career, was I called out of my reverie. Pressed for explanation, I admitted that, from the third row of Mrs. Smith's second grade classroom, I could not see the chalkboard.

Within the week, my mother took me to Dr. Hatch, the optometrist, and then on to the eyeglasses store.

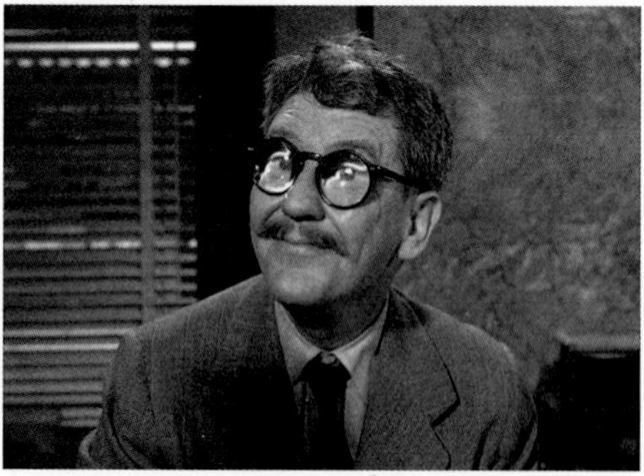

3

Mrs. Smith was notorious, a disciplinarian of a bygone era. Parents routinely called the school in August when class assignments came out and requested that their tender learner be moved to a different room. While corporal punishment was, legally speaking, well out of the American public classroom by the time I arrived in my seat in room 102, the steel-plated coldness of her words made up for their immateriality. My mother was thrilled.

I mostly kept below Smith's attention, but she had a heat-seeker for the soft belly of every student. You caught it at least once. My turn came around in the spring. She was maybe sixty-five at the time. Her loose and freckled skin folded over and clung to itself, strung along the tendons in her neck like wet laundry on a line. From beneath the snuffed-out conflagration of grey hair atop her head, Smith glared at my face:

"David, you look awful smart in those new glasses. Maybe you can help the class with this problem?"

In this moment, she's called me out on two counts: once for math, by which I am already puzzled and shamed; and a second time for the new pair of cobalt blue wire ellipses anchored by two squiggled arms that reached for and pulled out my ears. I'd been hoping, in the strip mall lens wear depot, that they were substantial enough to hide behind, but indeed they only made me more visible. Such is schooldays luck.

"David, you go to Market Basket and you buy an apple. It costs eighty-six cents. You give the man a dollar. How much change do you get back?"

The whole class is looking. Their collective gaze runs along the frames, skating across the surface of the lenses until it dips down into my eyes. Then it spills out to cover my face. I count back from one hundred, ninety-nine, ninety-eight, ninety-seven, nodding my head at each passing penny, when she stops me:

"You mean to tell me you are going to stand there at the grocery and shake your head fourteen times to make sure you get the correct change?"

She mimics me for the class, exaggerating each nod, looking like a toy dodo dunking its beak into a puddle over and over. The class laughs. My face goes red.

4

The spectacle appears at once as society itself, as a part of society and as a means of unification. As a part of society, it is that sector where all attention, all consciousness, converges. Being isolated—and precisely for that reason—this sector is the locus of illusion and false consciousness; the unity it imposes is merely the official language of generalized separation.

– Guy Debord,
Section 3, *The Society of the Spectacle*, 1967

5

Smith's petty sadism that day in room 102 had consequence beyond the immediate shame it caused me: it served as a bruising reminder of my physical form. As I watched her make a little spectacle of my embodied calculations, as she mimicked me, I remembered, painfully, that there was a me to mimic. Her exaggerated motions were my own—I had undersigned them with my neck and forehead—and in seeing her, in all the hard resolution conferred by the beveled panes of shatterproof plastic that now hung over my eyes, I understood, again, that I had a body. This is the condition of physicality: all our lives we are taught and taught and taught about the body, and the teacher is pain. Smith's lesson is with me like a scar.

As the chalkboard had resolved for me into discernible figures, so too had the judging eyes of my classmates. I could now see, with more clarity than ever before, the phenomenon of my being seen. This recognition christened a new awareness: I was both a part of and separate from my class, the collective, and by Smith's temporary ousting I knew the sting and loneliness of ridicule. My response? That of any child: I resolved to become invisible.

6

The family optometrist was in Milford, the next town over. Dr. John Hatch. Around his neck hung a squeaking rubber toy, a duck. He was a master at gathering and directing the attention of his child patients. I thought myself too old the first time around for the duckie, but by the time I returned to his office, my four-eyed pride having wilted to despair in the round vanity mirror he held to my face, I willingly submitted to his game.

"Eyes on the duckie, David. Very good. Now, you're a cameraman. You are a cameraman filming the duck and you want to get the picture nice and crisp. Which lens are you going to choose, number one..."

The black plastic slide lifted like a curtain and through the aperture of the phoropter a lens dropped, with a satisfying lock, into place.

"...or number two?"

Number two all but melted the poor bird's beak. It would have to be camera one. Over many rounds of similar decisions, I followed my vision to greater and still greater sharpness until the duckie's yellow edge seemed so keen it might slice through the dim exam room.

I admired the symphony of the phoropter, its proliferation of neat circles and hard lines, the gears that turned like a well-made clock, the balletic grace of its crane arm as Hatch slowly guided the face piece from its resting place by the wall to the saddle of my nose. My head held aloft, my neck erect, still and sure, I felt a calm relief as all the bones around my eyes were met by the machine. Peering into the two lenses, the room faded, and my earthly responsibility was reduced to a simple choice: one, or two. There in the leather chair, Smith's incessant beckoning seemed very far away.

"David, answer Dr. Hatch."

Dear Mother. I was back in the optometrist's office to be fitted for contacts. My goal: to take my glasses off my face. I wanted to smuggle my vision back into my body.

After reluctantly completing the eye test and leaving the exam chair, I sat in the back room for a brief eternity, first getting up the courage to move my finger against my instincts and directly into my eye, and then poking myself bloodshot for forty-five minutes until I finally got the lenses to cup right and stay put. Satisfied that I could reproduce this little experiment at home on my own, Hatch sent me away with an invisibility cloak in the form of a small cardboard box filled with tiny translucent saucers.

7

A drop of water made for the first microscope. Seneca, recognizing that vital fluid's magnificatory powers, used a glass globe filled with water to enlarge printed letters. Pushing the globe from left to right along a line, the words would scroll across the elementary marquee, fattening into bulbous view, immersing the reader in the text. This is reading as bathing in the thinking of another. This is why we love water, vision, and reading each: they bring the far world close.

8

When contact lenses adhere correctly, they do so in satisfaction of the supple eye's desire for wetness. This is a poetic construction of a brutish process: once one determines that the disk is right-side up on the index finger, one administers a drop of contact solution into the bowl and proceeds to jam it past one's pried eyelids. With luck, the drop of solution presses between the lens and the cornea, spreading across the disk's circumference in a blanket of hydrogen bonds that hug the saucer to the spherical organ. Vision is thereby restored.

But, restored? Is this the word? The name of that false water would suggest as much: if we invert "contact solution" we arrive at "separation problem." Surely my first bout with glasses made for a kind of separation problem: the frames newly disrupted my anonymity and opened my face to mockery; and surely the contact lenses, by rendering the technology of my vision unseeable once more, solved somewhat for this early site of embarrassment. I resent, however, the suggestion that the vision of my birth somehow made me inadequate to the visible, that my eyes were a problem. If you feel separated from the world, is this a deficiency of the body, or a failure of the world?

9

Whatever contact solution's metaphysical status, I never seemed to have it when I needed it. As a child, I was always calling home, asking my mother to ferry a bottle to a friend's house across town, and dopey adolescence amplified my forgetfulness. Only rarely could a small bottle of the stuff be found in the front pocket of my backpack. I regretted my neglect most when asked to stay out on certain special nights, either of the high school variety, up-til-the-small-hours on beer that someone's brother bought with Timmy and the Alexes, or the (un)planned amorous kind I learned as a young adult. Constantly I found myself trusting my vision to Dixie cups filled with two fingers of hard tap water, or else saying the hell with it and consenting to morning blindness, the two disks going brittle on the hardwood floor.

10

Sleeping in contact lenses increases your risk for nasty eye infections six- to eightfold. It's one of the most common and risky things teen and adult contact lens wearers do… "Just don't do it," said Dr. Steinemann. "That's what I stress to my patients. Don't sleep in your contact lenses. Don't even take a nap."

– Jennifer Churchill, "Why You Should Never Sleep in your Contact Lenses," American Academy of Ophthalmology, 2018

11

How is sight for sore eyes? Not very good. The cornea becomes an airy husk, the eyeball a desiccated onion.

12

For my forgetfulness, and for the annoyance of maintaining the contact lensed life, I considered glasses again. It was not until my first year of college that this became a viable option for me, psychically speaking. Only after high school was in the past, and only by virtue of being unknown again could I consider donning my third and fourth eyes. After hounding the glasses shops of the Northeast for many months, I settled on a pair of thin gold wire frames. One new site of contact, however, kept me in distant touch with old Dr. Hatch.

I began playing rugby my freshman year. It was a club team, named for an unimposing variety of salamander. Ours was a tiny Quaker school. The average height of the starting lineup, when we could field a full side, was approximately five eight. The lack of seriousness facilitated my interest in the sport, as did a pair of contact lenses, the ruck and maul bringing me close to the straining bodies around me, to the fresh-mown field behind the stadium, my face pressed into rough cotton, a shoulder, the earth.

13

Fight, fight, Inner Light,
Kill, Quakers, kill!
Knock 'em down, beat 'em senseless,
Do it 'til we reach consensus!

– Rugby fight song, origin unknown

14

I loved the physicality of rugby. I loved what part of myself sprinted to meet the hulking farm boys of Penn State's C side. I loved the bruises and the total exhaustion I felt after a match. These were honest reminders of my form. In a tackle, I felt the acknowledgement of the opposing player, and in this acknowledgement I felt respect. In the game of rugby, you are worthy of bringing down because, for a moment, sprinting the flank with the ball cradled into your side, you are above the fray. You are agentic, potent, beautiful. Playing in front of my teammates and what piddling crowd of spectators we could draw, I did not feel watched or looked at. I felt seen.

Opening myself to this physicality was not without its risks, however. Around the time I joined the team, I began worrying, for the first time in my life, about getting into a fight.

I had not gone to many parties in high school, and the kind of extravagant alcohol consumption that ruled college gatherings set my dog ears to rigid attention. Perhaps some aggression leeched from the rugby field and into my eyes, but everywhere I saw the potential for blows. This fear was a revival of that day in Smith's classroom: if someone were to call me out beyond the sanctioning bounds of sport, I would need a left hook this time around. No more sweet boy. No more counting change. Just my deep-seated desire to remain unobserved and a willingness to protect it. My fear was irrational, but it was sufficiently preoccupying to cause me to defer my decision to hide out behind a pair of frames on a given night. I figured one good knock and the glass would shatter, and dire blindness would render me helpless.

15

A beat-up Henry Bemis awakens on the floor of a bank vault. He is shaken, befuddled, and frightened. Next to him on the floor lies a creased copy of *David Copperfield* and the daily newspaper. Bemis remembers a horrific sound. "Why am I here?" The room does not answer.

Pressing his back to the lock boxes, he pushes himself to his feet, dusts off his disheveled gray suit. His coke-bottle spectacles hang from one ear across his face, the left lens covering his mouth. Too stunned as yet to right them, he pulls open the heavy door. Something is wrong, but exactly what is unclear.

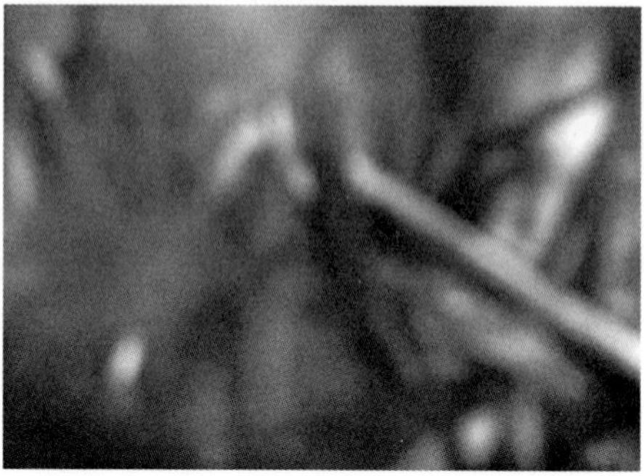

Heavy, broken lines appear where he remembers stairs. Rising dust takes body in the light. Silence prevails, and Bemis hesitates to disturb it. It is the refractory period after an accident, and so the world seems not to know how to be. Bemis lifts his hands to his glasses, bringing them up over his eyes.

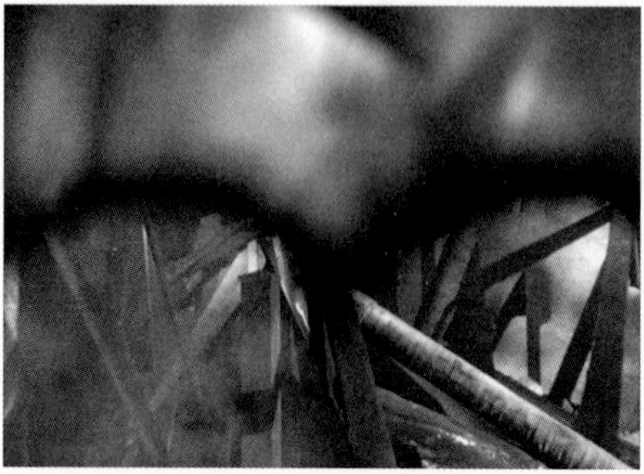

He raises the glasses slowly. They pan over the camera lens, the thick plastic frames clearing the debris like windshield wipers, organizing the chaos into definable shape. Bemis' fate, like the chalkboard that once spelled my ruin, focuses into crystalline view.

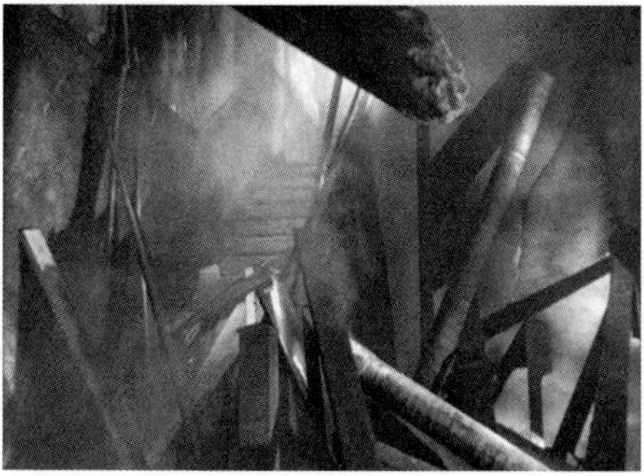

Henry Bemis has unwittingly survived the nuclear holocaust. A bank teller, he had escaped to the vault during his lunch break to read. Upon swinging shut the vault door and resuming his place in chapter three, the Germans dropped a bomb.

16

"What if the world ends tonight?" I asked the blurry visage.

I dragged the brush between my molars and my cheek, leaned in close. Ruby vessels meandered like the roots of a pothos plant. One jet black pupil receded from my gaze in the florescent light.

I pulled back slightly and returned my attention to the surface of the eye, to the place where I begin to call it mine, across the threshold over which that peculiar collection of derma, bone, blood, and water becomes my face. I gathered the toothpaste in my cheeks, looked down to the sink, spat, ran the faucet.

What if the world ends tonight? What if, after cleaning the blood from my split lip in the foul and bestickered bowl of a dive's bathroom sink, I stick my face under the hot-air hand dryer, then lean into the mirror to appraise the damage, decide I'm enough to return to the scene, slide the heavy bolt of the plywood door, and push it open, only to find that the world is gone?

"You Were Always on My Mind" plays into a hollow room. Not a soul's in sight. Light fixtures swing. Smell and feel of stuck beer. I walk through the hall and out into the street. Inexplicable daylight. No traffic—car, pedestrian, or otherwise. See a dog's leather collar still attached to the leash, flung in limp tableau on the lip of the curb. See clothing, like buildings, leveled. No trash blows, the air eerily windless. I stand in the aftermath of some unfathomable cataclysm.

In the bathroom of my dorm, about to put my contacts in, I would routinely entertain this anxiety dream, asking, what if the world ends tonight?

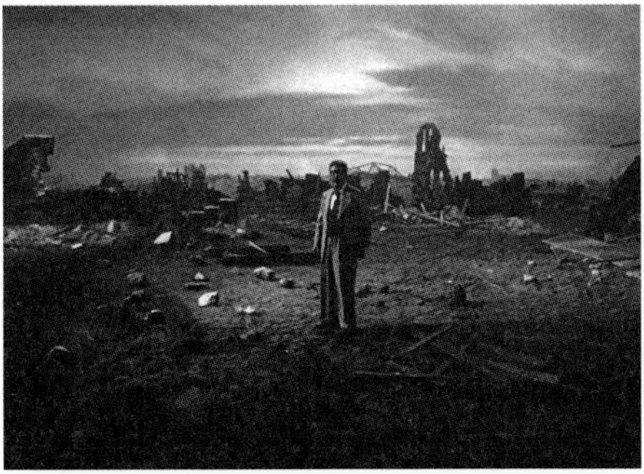

The barroom brawl, which of course never came, was always the precursor, the dress rehearsal, of a much greater fight: that for post-apocalyptic survival. And every time I had the dream, my first thought emerging onto the empty street, no people, no phone, dogs and birds absent, friends and family absent, only silent ruins to attest to the history of the human race: will the pharmacy door be shattered open so that I can acquire some contact solution? Because my eyes dry out easily enough and, well, if I'm to persist in the post-anthropocene, I'll just be terribly uncomfortable without a bottle of Opti Free.

17

Steve Huffman, the thirty-three-year-old co-founder and C.E.O. of Reddit, which is valued at six hundred million dollars, was nearsighted until November, 2015, when he arranged to have laser eye surgery. He underwent the procedure not for the sake of convenience or appearance but, rather, for a reason he doesn't usually talk much about: he hopes that it will improve his odds of surviving a disaster, whether natural or man-made. "If the world ends—and not even if the world ends, but if we have trouble—getting contacts or glasses is going to be a huge pain in the ass," he told me recently. "Without them, I'm fucked."

– Evan Osnos, "Doomsday Prep for the Super-rich," *The New Yorker*, 23 January 2017

18

Meet Henry Bemis: belittled husband, hapless employee, and the protagonist of episode eight, season one, of the mid-century American television classic, *The Twilight Zone*. Dubbed "a charter member in the fraternity of dreamers" by the show's disembodied voice-over, Bemis is an ardent bibliophile who hides between the covers to avoid his domineering wife, Helen, and his unrelenting boss, both of whom thwart his readerly intentions at every opportunity. Helen finds his copy of the Romantics in the kitchen cupboard and tears it to shreds; she makes certain that Melville, Eliot, and George Bernard Shaw all find their way to the curb. One night, with a sadism that puts Smith to shame, she asks Henry to read to her from his survey, *A Book of Modern Poetry*; an innocent and beaming Henry is delighted to oblige, only, when he opens the book to his favorite Wordsworth, he finds that Helen has scrawled in black crayon over every page, a savage, angular alphabet of diminishment, fury, and misanthropy.

When Bemis emerges from the vault to that voided and "smashed landscape," one can't but sympathize with his initial sense of relief. The dead cannot nag you back to the bank cage. This consolation, however, gives way, as it must, to loneliness. Bemis finds canned food enough for years and even a pack of cigarettes to help burn down the time, but the notion of waking up, eating to sustain himself, sleeping, and then repeating, without purpose or companionship, for an indeterminate forever soon becomes too much for him. He walks the desolate avenues to where he knows he can find a pistol. He closes his eyes and raises the barrel to his temple. Bemis is crying as he lifts his head for one last look, and through his tears, what does he see? The ruins of the library.

Salvation.

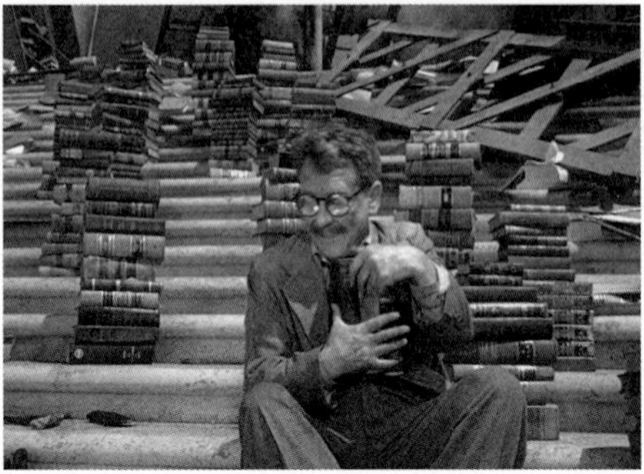

Bemis, who never found the quiet he sought in his working and domestic lives, can read unopposed into eternity. And he need not miss a soul: among the spines, he will never be alone. Wasting not a second, he sets about creating a calendar in stacks, one for January, one for February, March, April, with reading material enough to plot out years. The episode here gains its title: "Time Enough at Last."

Bemis stands up to proclaim his good fortune, puffing his chest, addressing the vanquished library clock, which rests at the foot of the building's steps. Elated, becalmed, Bemis breathes a triumphant sigh and returns to his seat. He reaches down to collect a copy of Dickens and begin the good work of living on, after all.

Bemis bends over. His fingers search across the concrete; the volume is just beyond his reach.

He leans further, his neck arching around the stopped clock. As he sends his gaze to meet his hand, his glasses fall off his ears. Bemis paws about: the paper pages, dust and ash, shards of glass, and then his empty frames. The lenses of his spectacles have shattered. Henry Bemis cannot see enough to read without them. "The best laid plans," quips the narrator. The reader Bemis is condemned, once again, and finally, to blurry desolation.

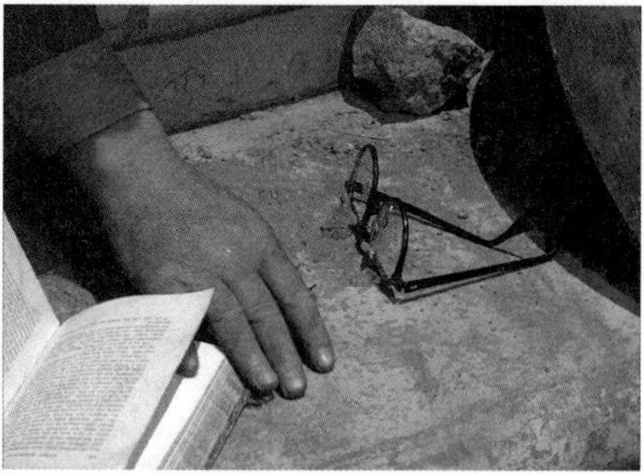

There was time now.

19

Without my glasses, I cannot drive or recognize faces from more than three feet away. This means no crossing the street without help. I can barely make it to the bathroom at night from my bedroom unassisted, much less leave the house. As such, there are certain jobs from which I am disqualified: I will never be your commercial airline pilot, nor will I fly for the military. I'm barred entirely from the state police, and it is unlikely that I'd be allowed to lifeguard. Technically I could, with my poor vision, become an optometrist like the good doctor Hatch, providing myself permanent access to the phoropter, that gorgeous machine, but I do not think the man-aflame necessarily makes the best firefighter.

There is, however, one utterly crucial skill I can manage without my glasses. I discovered this back in the second grade, just weeks after I first got those steely blue ovals: unlike poor Henry Bemis, I can read.

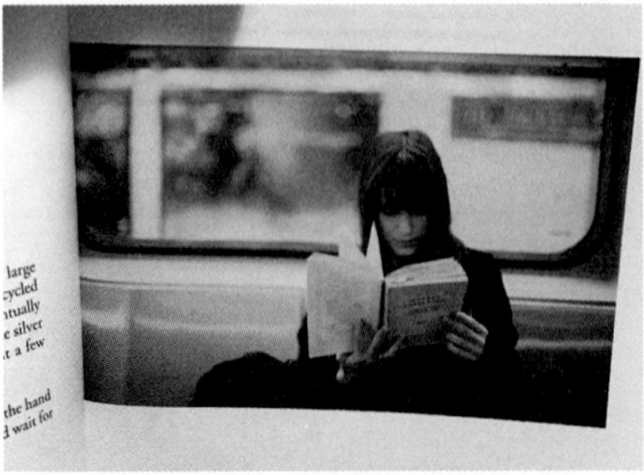

Burn the Diaries, Moyra Davey, 2014

20

When I lived in New York City, I rode the subway for at least two hours a day. I took the J to Bowery for work, the A/C to 86th for therapy, the 1/2/3 for my relationship and a friend who lived up in Harlem. I walked to the G for Milk & Roses in Greenpoint, and hopped on the L late night just to sit when my phone told me the only way home at three A.M. in thirty degrees was a bus in forty-five minutes.

Two daily hours of subway time makes for a sumptuous reading residency. Whether you find a seat or not, you have 120 minutes of public solitude to enjoy, the navigation and travel taken care of, the delays entirely out of your control. With luck, you'll have landed in a car with relative quiet, just a little earbud bleed to tune out, perhaps some chatter down a bench. Any reader will see that these are near ideal conditions (assuming one must leave the armchair-comfort of one's home). But you must know how best to take advantage of the time.

I take two sea-green foam cylinders out of my breast pocket. I roll them into tight spindles and slide them into my ears. The sound of their expansion moves to fill me, like a jet of tide rushing to fill a cave. I can hear my heart beat up my neck as the plugs spread to fill the vaulted recesses of my ear canal. Then I hear nothing, or nothing but the whooshing of a far-off train. Thirty-three decibel grade is best, but pharmacy-standard thirty-two will do. Then, I take off my glasses. I fold them into themselves, and hang them by an arm on my collar. The car fades. My book takes on a warm, gauzy halo, and all of my periphery goes to dewy oblivion. Finally, concentration. Time enough at last.

When I take off my glasses, I bid the world farewell for a while. This is why I will never surgically correct my vision. I will never forfeit this modality of refusal.

21

Consider, for example, another genre of images that, like female nudes, are representations of privacy par excellence: images of people reading. A book is a kind of daytime dream. Held in the hands, head bent low, the book is an exterior symbol of interiority, an objective correlative of the mindful, imaginative activity going on inside.

– Quinn Latimer, Room 3, "Interiors: Some Stanzas on the Pleasures of Privacy," *Like a Woman*, 2017

22

During a certain year in New York, over and over again, I read Moyra Davey's *Burn the Diaries*. It's a meditation on the relationship between a writer's life and their published work, on private living and public disclosure. Davey's text is interspersed with her photographs, many of which contain books or printed pages: the sun-faded blue and white cover of Violette Leduc's *La Bâtarde*; a stack of files and computer paper marked with handwritten labels in ballpoint. The collection opens and closes with images of a reader on the subway. It looks to me like the G train, with its diner-metal siding and inward-facing seats in orange, umber, faded maize. The book is a Gallimard edition, someone's *Oeuvres Complètes*.

Images of readers compel, fascinate, and comfort me. They drive me to think of the reader's mind for its embodiment in that familiar posture of concentration. Of the quiet subjects, I ask, *What are you reading? What are you thinking in there?* If I look long enough, I can almost start to see the lines of text register in the reader's gaze, the saccades moving from left to right in a choreographic index of that strange, inscrutable, whirring machinery we call the mind.

23

For one week every summer of my childhood, my family rented a small cottage by a lake in New Hampshire. The July after I graduated from Smith's second grade, my dignity folded tight like a paper football, worn and tearing at the edges, tucked into my back pocket, I couldn't wait for the chill dark of the lake water, for the familiar cool of the sheets in that musty bedroom that I briefly called mine.

I arrived at the water. My father had a cheerful vacation rule that we must swim each calendar day we were away. I was coated in SPF 45, the smell of Coppertone thick in my nose. The sun beat warmly. From the dock, I could see clear through to the sandy floor. A flicker of light meant a baby bass was passing. Mineral flecks shone, giving depth and body to the water. I wanted to join that body, to jump in with my own and feel it all around me. I wanted to sink to the bottom, to listen as the world went mute, to feel held by the pressure of the entire lake as it bore down firmly on my form. I lined my feet up to the edge of the splintering red boards. Just as I summoned the courage to leap, my mother called me from shore:

"Don't forget your glasses!"

The world had changed because my body had changed. No longer could I move freely from the dry to the wet, at least not without consideration for the hampering apparatus I wore on my face. Where I had known fluidity before, there was now an impasse, a site of conscious action. I ran back to shore and placed my glasses in a case. I approached the water timidly now.

I nursed my quiet summer despair for a few days. My parents were unaware. It was better that way. I left my glasses on a towel, on the deck, inside the house on the kitchen counter, always forgetting where I had left them, and feeling too blind to find them when I did. I hated this new interval.

Thursday was most miserable. The end of our time away was nigh, and I had yet to relax at all. I emerged from my required swim, dragging my feet through the sand like a depressed swamp thing. I slunk into a beach chair and picked up the book I was in, Jon Scieszka's *Your Mother was a Neanderthal*. The Time Warp Trio—Fred, Sam, and Joe—were trapped in front of a saber-toothed tiger. The Book that helped them apparate between ages could not be found, as writing had yet to be invented. My father called from the other side of the beach. I looked up. "Want a sandwich?" I could not see his grainy face. But I was reading.

24

If I couldn't see you approach, then you were not there. Perhaps you would call me, saying my name with a question mark or exclamation point. Assuming you were just shy or hesitant enough, or if your voice communicated any indifference at all,

I could ignore you, not unlike the way my mother, with perfect hearing but from whom I got my eyes, would studiously fail to hear my father.

When I removed my glasses, the world disappeared. In this way, my poor vision bestowed a new sight for me, and a new site of privacy. I would learn to instrumentalize this privacy over time, and I would learn how to defend it.

To quietly read among my family was to make them nervous. You became a sitting duck for conversation. Constantly they would approach with concerns and sudden interests in you, in how your school year had gone, whether or not you'd be playing such and such a town in soccer this year, etc. And they came in droves. Mine is a vast hoard, with twelve aunts and uncles *on each side*, and triple the number of first cousins. I think there was a panic at seeing someone silent and okay.

Reading dramatizes thinking. And this can be threatening in a tribe that prides itself on having forgotten its secret.

"When you think, do you think of me? And do you think well? Of me?"

25

...thinking's community is unquantifiable. Also, reading's topos, its place of agency, is invisible, and necessarily so. Reading resists being seen. This is not

to say that it has no effects on public life, but that those effects cannot be predetermined, cannot be conveniently mapped and often do not follow causal, or intentional, patterns. What I intend for reading is usually not where it takes me. Maybe whatever broader, worldly effects reading has could be modeled on the random agency of the Epicurean clinamen, that wide-open and troubling proposition of utterly uncaused and spontaneous material change. Reading does change the world, but usually not in the way one might wish it to, and perhaps not visibly. Its acts are clandestine. I make this unproblematic segue from thinking to reading because, for me, the two activities are completely implicated, folded into one another. I am only certain that I think insofar as I read.

– Lisa Robertson, "Lastingness: Réage, Lucrèce, Arendt," *Nilling*, 2012

26

When I see someone reading a book on the subway, especially one I have loved, or one I hope to love someday, I feel less lonely.

27

Over many years, she used figures of light and visibility in her accounts of what was necessary for there to be any substantive political life. For an individual to have political effectiveness, there needed to be a balance, a moving back and forth between the bright, even harsh exposure of public activity and the protected, shielded sphere of domestic or private life, of what she calls "the darkness of sheltered existence." Elsewhere she refers to "the twilight that suffuses our private and intimate lives." Without that space or time of privacy, away from the "implacable bright light of the constant presence of others on the public scene," there could be no possibility of the nurturing of the singularity of the self, a self that could make a substantive contribution to exchanges about the common good.

– Jonathan Crary, on Hannah Arendt, *24/7*, 2013

28

Temporarily refusing the world is, ultimately, a way to love it. Just as in my family, leaving the torpor of its community, taking time to read, though it registered as a kind of violence to the fabric of rapacious and outward-looking talk, was a way for me to be a better member of the kitchen table. I could be more calm, and I had more to say, having staked, for a spell, my place.

But if the family can be hostile to the site of reading, then the world can be triply so. A privacy that pays no heed to the importance of industry and pay makes a landlord nervous and an unhappy careerist insecure. *Why aren't you working?* Here, reading signifies not interiority, but idleness. And idleness needs be exploited.

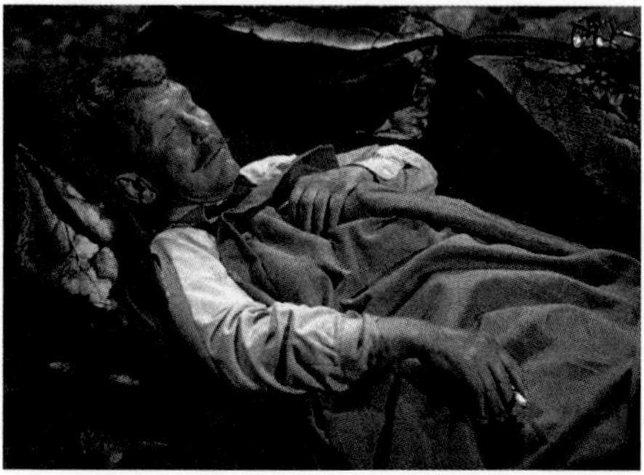

29

You, Mr. Bemis, do not function within the organization. You are neither an efficient bank teller nor a proficient employee. You, Mr. Bemis, are a reader.

– Bemis' Boss, "Time Enough at Last," *The Twilight Zone*, 1959

30

And it's not just lucre's terrible siren that keeps me from reading, from myself. As soon as my vision was brought to standard, the world crowded it with trash and horror. I remember the infomercials for Bowflex and the veiny palms of the Marlboro Man; I began collecting "Got Milk?" spreads from *Sports Illustrated*; I remember Ruthie's red soccer jersey from *Real World: Hawaii. Why?*

All the time, this desperate seduction, this clamor for attention. And the reaching arm of the world has only gotten stronger, more flexible, deft—from the moment of waking to the quietest part of the night, my bedside table, my pocket, my very hand shakes with its address. When the tremor becomes too much, I turn to the quiet spines lined up along my shelves.

31

Between my eye and the lens, I found a golden little seam. I can fill it with a book and disappear into the gutter between the pages, a fissure in the world. I reemerge later, better. But while reading is paramount among the ways I've come to be at home in the world, it is also the means by which I was first exiled from myself.

Do you remember the first time you were instructed to close one eye, place one little hand over it, and to look at a chart swinging from a nail on the door? Do you remember the poster, the text that you read? One large letter on top, an impossible word in smaller type just beneath, and then a cascade that grew more garrulous, minuscule, and nonsensical as it prattled on down the page. You were made to read until you failed, and exactly where you failed indexed the weakness of your vision.

Thus the message about what was wrong with me was delivered through the activity I held most dear. This is often how it happens: what you love is instrumentalized against you. The trick is to reclaim it, to love it again, to use it as a tool to carve out, however crudely, a little dwelling in the world.

Perhaps reading is the way for you, though it needn't be: whatever modality of interiority animates, amplifies your thinking life is the one to pursue. This is a social responsibility: per Arendt, as permutated by Crary, where there is no time or space for thinking, for privacy, there is no meaningful political life. Where there is no interior life, there is no resistance to what is outside us. And we need modes of resistance now, from the many forces anticipated by Debord and described by Crary.

32

There can be time enough again, but only if we make it.

33

The society of my spectacles is a mobile territory approximately ten inches in diameter. I am its little monarch. For its meager spatial claim, its temporal bounds are massive on the order of a conundrum: it contains multitudes. Various jetsam from the whole scope of printed matter have been known to pass through its realm, sometimes in sequence, sometimes in pell-mell-immediacy. This quiet society is cacophonous with ideas and opinions. It is my humble stay against the raging turpitude of the out-there. I go there to be alone, along with everyone who has written. I have written this to you that you might have known some time in it.

Christopher Potter

The Word is What

I can remember a time when I could not read, and I can remember a time when I began to read. What I can't quite get to is that precise moment of transcendence when a blur of symbols first resolved into meaning.

It was my mother who taught me. Not for her those alphabet books of pictures and nouns: carrot, duck, fox, tree. I do not know for certain if my mother had some kind of antipathy to primers but years later, when I was aged ten or so, and when I could in theory choose for myself whatever I might want to read, I seemed to have had an instinct about what books *not* to bring home from the public library. What stopped me from taking out anything by A.A. Milne, Kenneth Grahame, and Arthur Ransome? I was pretty sure that even our namesake Beatrix Potter would have been on my mother's unspoken and unwritten *Index Librorum Prohibitorum*. Enid Blyton I was certain was on the list, my mother would have deplored the quality of Blyton's writing, a criticism that could not, however, be leveled at the other writers. There was something else. My mother would have been suspicious of the social (not sufficiently Socialist!) world of all these authors. Not that that stopped me from secretly and guiltily devouring Blyton, but only as an adult have I found my way to Toad Hall and the Hundred Acre Wood. Looking back, I feel sure my mother would have had no such prohibitions, that this anecdote reveals more about me than it does about my mother.

One of my earliest memories is of being stirred from sleep by the sound of the paperboy as he attempted to push the folded newspaper through the letterbox. I lay there listening intently, hoping the paper would be pushed all the way through and land with a satisfying thud on the floorboards, not hang silently and frustratingly half in and half out. We took the *Guardian*, the *Manchester Guardian* as it was in those days. In Manchester was where we were living at the time, but the *Manchester Guardian* was popular across the whole of the North of England as a sort of left-wing counterpart to *The Times*, as suited the political and geographical divide that more sharply divided the country then than it does today. The paper was delivered very early every weekday morning, including Saturday, a half-day for my father as it was for many workers in the early 1960s. There was no time to read the paper at breakfast and my father took it with him to work. On weekdays I hoped I would still be up when he got home again. I particularly liked it when he was back in time to watch the *Magic Roundabout*, a five minute TV program purportedly for children that came on immediately before the six o'clock news. The droll script made my father laugh. I loved to hear him laugh. In the evening it would be my mother's turn to read the paper. I did not yet know how to read—I would have been four or five at the time—but I knew what reading looked like. Clumsily, I held the paper in front of me and attempted to turn the giant pages in a pretense of reading. Perhaps it was then that my mother came over and slowly ran her finger across one of the headlines, at the same time reading the words out loud: "Unnamed…man… helping…police…with…their…inquiries." The *Guardian* was to be my primer. I can remember living for a time in a twilight zone in which the words in the headlines flickered on the edges of existence while everything printed in smaller type was entirely lifeless. It was as if it were size itself that mattered, like those English tourists abroad who think that they can make themselves better understood if they speak more slowly and loudly than usual. I do not know how long this transitional period lasted, but gradually the symbols that were letters adhered into symbols that were words, which in turn attached to themselves some kind of meaning, and magically I could read.

By the time I got to school I could already read. I think there were just the two of us who could, me and a girl whose name I cannot now recall. The teacher directed us towards a cupboard that served as the school's library to choose something to read while the rest of the class endeavored to make the leap into abstraction that we had already made. I can still feel the embarrassment and curiosity at being singled out as different from the others. I can remember being in the cupboard, but I can't remember what book I chose. I do remember feeling like an impostor. There were books in there that I surely would never be able to read. The teacher, I was convinced, had mistaken my abilities. Was it my mother, I wonder, who had told her that I could already read? Had I claimed the ability for myself? Unlikely. Or had I been called upon and revealed some modest ability to the teacher, Miss Hughes? "Good Morning Class," she would say at the beginning of the day. "Good Morning Miss Shoes" we would chorus in reply, much to her annoyance. She would make us say it again, and again. Some of us would get the giggles. We wanted to say Miss Hughes but it was beyond our collective ability. No matter how hard we tried it always came out as Miss Shoes. Occasionally she would lock one of us in the cupboard as punishment, though never me. I learned early on how to avoid punishment, even at the cost of betrayal. I think I hated her.

When I turned six I was given as a birthday present an illustrated edition of *Hiawatha*. I don't suppose there was any causal connection between the two events, but as I began to read—

On the shores of Gitche Gumee,
Of the shining Big-Sea-Water,
Stood Nokomis, the old woman,
Pointing with her finger westward,
O'er the water pointing westward,
To the purple clouds of sunset…

—my nose started to bleed. How I loved the rhythm of the lines, the repetition, the individual words! The bloodstains became an emblem of the book's specialness, the book and I as one. I don't suppose I understood what I was reading any more than I had the headlines in the *Manchester Guardian*, and yet I wonder if I have ever again been quite so immersed in a poem as I was then.

I was about seven years old when I got taken up by the local rector and his wife, the Revd and Mrs. Archer, a childless couple. My mother must surely have disapproved of the church's High Anglicanism—bells and smells—but she liked the Archers. The rector became my godfather and at some point I joined the choir. I loved the hymns, particularly the evening hymns—"The day though gavest Lord is ended, the darkness falls at thy behest." Such strange incantatory words: gavest, behest, cleft, zeal, atonement, redeemeth. I was mesmerized too by the words—and the rhythms of the sentences—of the *Book of Common Prayer*:

> We have erred and strayed from thy ways like lost sheep. We have followed too much the devices and desires of our own hearts. We have left undone those things which we ought to have done; And we have done those things we ought not to have done; And there is no health in us.

At church, how kind Mr. Archer was, how beautiful the words and the music, but the sentiments behind the words! I could sense even then a severity and coldness in Christianity that the church building itself seemed to mirror.

At home I had become addicted to reading. I fantasized that I was really a foundling child. I was an alien from another world, the formless world of pre-birth. On endlessly ebbing and flowing waves I had non-existed until a moment nevertheless arrived when the wave swelled more than it ebbed and broke on the shore. I was frustrated, as children are, that my desires were huge but without form. Desire hung around me like a cloud, like the symbol of all possible desires. How I longed to have a desire that I could name, to hold as my own. There were days when I would wake up aching with nameless desire, both for the world I had woken to and the world I had left behind in dreaming. The pain of that childhood frustration has of course lessened over the decades since but it has never entirely gone away. I think even now I am still a little angry that I am here at all. As a child I resolutely faced the sea, my back to the shore. If I had to be here, then in imaginary worlds conjured out of symbols on a page was where I was most happy to exist. The real world was evanescent but the imaginary worlds conjured up by writers lived forever in symbols, requiring only a reciprocal act of conjuration on the part of the reader. Reading was a private act of magic enacted between magicians: the writer and the reader.

I continued to attend church all through my teenage years, even the repellant coldness and piousness of the suffering Christ was not enough to deter me. I had my own private theology that comforted me. Any of us might become Christ, I believed, just as anyone, so the old joke goes, might become President of the United States (and anyone usually does, boom boom). Only later did I discover that the belief I held was a heresy known as Arianism and had been brutally suppressed by the church. I turned my back on organized religion. Gradually I found comfort and other members of my tribe in literature. How could my heart not leap when I came across this passage in *Madame Bovary*?

> I have a religion, my religion, and I even have more than all these others with their mummeries and their juggling. I adore God...I believe in the Supreme Being, in a Creator, whatever he may be. I care little who has placed us here below to fulfil our duties as citizens and fathers of families; but I don't need to go to church to kiss silver plates, and fatten, out of my pocket, a lot of good-for-nothings who live better than we do. For one can know Him as well in a wood, in a field, or even contemplating the eternal vault like the ancients. My God! Mine is the God of Socrates, of Franklin, of Voltaire, and of Beranger!...I can't admit of an old boy of a God who takes walks in his garden with a cane in his hand, who lodges his friends in the belly of whales, dies uttering a cry, and rises again at the end of three days; things absurd in themselves, and completely opposed, moreover, to all physical laws, which prove to us, by the way, that priests have always wallowed in turpid ignorance, in which they would fain engulf the people with them.

Or to this from *Middlemarch*, when Dorothea exclaims:

> "I have a belief of my own, and it comforts me."
>
> "What is that?" said Will, rather jealous of the belief.
>
> "That by desiring what is perfectly good, even when we don't quite know what it is and cannot do what we would, we are part of the divine power against evil—widening the skirts of light and making the struggle with darkness narrower."
>
> "That is a beautiful mysticism—it is a—"
>
> "Please not to call it by any name," said Dorothea, putting out her hands entreatingly. "You will say it is Persian, or something else geographical. It is my life. I have found it out, and cannot part with it. I have always been finding out my religion since I was a little girl. I used to pray so much—now I hardly ever pray. I try not to have desires merely for myself, because they may not be good for others, and I have too much already. I only told you, that you might know quite well how my days go…

I used to think that I had gone on to live my life in large part in reaction to the miserableness of Anglicanism, but I look back now on those childhood days more lovingly. I now see that there was something else going on, something that has continued to compel me, even though I didn't realize what it was at the time. One of the Christmas readings began:

> In the beginning was the Word, and the Word was with God, and the Word was God. The same was in the beginning with God. All things were made by him; and without him was not any thing made that was made. In him was life; and the life was the light of men. And the light shineth in darkness; and the darkness comprehended it not.

What word? Was the word—the Word—a kind of short incantation that had conjured the world into existence? What did it mean that the Word—whatever that Word was—was *with* God? I was frustrated by my desire to get to the literal meaning behind the word "word." The verses made no sense, but beyond my frustration I also knew that whatever the gospel according to John was trying to tell me it was something I needed to understand, and indeed in some way already understood. I knew, too, that somehow these verses were also related to the opening sentences of the Old Testament, another Christmastide reading:

> In the beginning God created the heaven and the earth. And the earth was without

> form, and void; and darkness was upon the face of the deep. And the Spirit of God moved upon the face of the waters. And God said, Let there be light: and there was light. And God saw the light, that it was good: and God divided the light from the darkness. And God called the light Day, and the darkness he called Night. And the evening and the morning were the first day. And God said, Let there be a firmament in the midst of the waters, and let it divide the waters from the waters. And God made the firmament, and divided the waters which were under the firmament from the waters which were above the firmament: and it was so. And God called the firmament Heaven. And the evening and the morning were the second day.

God had made the world by naming things; this naming, I felt sure, must have some connection to the Word that John refers to. I could not have articulated the connection at the time but somewhere my body already *knew*.

I had always known, or so it seems in retrospect—I might better say that I suspect I had always known—that I would write *for a living*. I knew too, or suspect I knew too, that I would only write when I had something to say, and that I would probably be quite old by then.

Circles close as we get older, perhaps only so that we might move around them again. I learned that in the original Greek in which the book of John came down to us that the word Word is a translation of *logos*. I knew from my studies in philosophy that *logos* is one of those fluid Greek words that has many shades of meaning: *word*, *knowledge*, and *form* among them. From it we have, of course, the suffix *-ology*. While researching my first book I learned that according to an ancient philosophy promoted by Heraclitus and others, the universe had existed in a state not of nothingness but of chaos, a world without form. Bring form to chaos—the Greek word, transliterated, is *kaos*—and out of it comes order—*kosmos*. In the beginning was *logos*. The Word turned chaos into cosmos: the Creation. A universe of things emerged out of a state of no-thingness by being named. There had once been a seemingly timeless and eternal universe that was no thing but was not nothing, rather One Thing. And yet, even so, there was also a moment when—through the power of the Word—there came into being the world of things, among which things we might include ourselves. And as close as we can get to that moment between the two existences, we cannot get to the moment itself. There, there, we might cry, but there is no there there. In the gaps of transcendence there lies magic.

In his last days of life, living in a nursing home, Samuel Beckett wrote a poem called, "What is the Word." Not a question, a statement. The Word is What. Now what could that mean?

Mary Marge Locker

Forward, West

I was reading about people who were dirty and thirsty and lost.

I was warm, but not hot (these people were hot; their lips were chapped and caked with dust and if their mouths were full it was just with stones they were sucking), and I was well-fed (they had just finished the jerky of the most recently keeled-over ox), and the light was just right, soft and easy (their light was harsh and loud and their skin, if you could see it beneath all that tan and detritus, was peeling off in strips that probably reminded them too much of that jerky).

These people occupied a hundred-odd pages of H.W. Brands's definitive history of the Gold Rush, *The Age of Gold*. I read this book while wrapped in a blanket and bathed in that aforementioned easy light.

These people had beaten out cholera, raids, scams, and food shortages just to make it to Mormon country too late to try and forge ahead across the Rockies. So, too much adrenaline to stick around in Salt Lake, too much riding on the gold (so close, by this point, that they could probably feel their tools twitching in their pockets; clothes and heirlooms were laid to waste by the side of the wagon trail before things like picks or shovels or scales, hawked out of households in Missouri), they followed what began as a river—rumored to reach California—until it turned into a trickle that dripped straight back down into a sandy hole in the ground. And then they were surrounded by walls. Walls, and desert. They had inadvertently and so, so reluctantly, discovered what we now know as Death Valley. Clearly they were the ones to name it that. They were doomed. Lost. Hungry. Thirsty, more than anything. They were incredibly fucked.

(They weren't just wandering, though, we'd do well to remember. They were making a claim. To gold, yeah, but also to half the country.)

(It's easy to forget that darker context when we look at them from above, thirsty pinpricks in a desperate topography.)

(And I have to admit, too, that I have a soft spot for stranded pioneers.)

(I have a soft spot for stranded pioneers, because in this cataclysm of Westward expansion, their stories are the stories I first learned, and then mimicked at play in the bend of a river in the place where I grew up, panning fruitlessly for gold, and then mimicked further in the clicking and typing on a computer screen. In the reading, in the insertion of myself, I have considered every outcome and tried every trail.)

(And they really were fucked.)

And reading these hundred-odd pages, so far from stranded myself, practically its opposite in a little lit room with my feet propped up, I felt propelled, too, maybe not westward, but called, anyway, toward something, even if that something was just these people's own destinies, destinations, conclusions, deaths. I was moving forward in my own way, through that cinderblock of a book, westward ho, moving forth into territory that, yes, had been charted, but that had not been charted by me.

And how would I move to get there? Go overland, pack a trunk to be disposed of like all the others, risk the illness, the marauders, the nights so quiet on the prairie? Or charter a boat, like others, sail all the way south and around, hoping everything—the momentum, the ruckus, the gold—would still be there when I finally pulled into port? There is something to these choices we give ourselves, especially as readers, especially with this subject matter—because we only know this history in the context of choices. *Ford the river? Hire the ferryman? Caulk the wagon and float?*

(When you read something that moves, even when its metaphor isn't as obvious as that of the

Oregon Trail, you move with it. You fall in step, you wipe the sweat.)

But there is no active choice in reading about them, these stuck, dying people, other than to read about them at all. Thumb further pages, just like clicking through green text on an outdated computer screen. To read the history is to insert oneself, to hope there will still be something shining in the mill water for me; to know if there is, it's not my doing. It is an active choice to be passive, a lesson in acceptance of some kind. To choose option one, two, or three, and still watch one's whole wagon party die of cholera.

I wanted them to survive, there in Death Valley, but I knew they didn't survive—this is almost 200 years ago, they're all dead, even if they survived the canyons. But I still wished them safely to Sutter's Fort, wanted to stand beside them and see it for the first time, too. The smell of campstoves lit and hungry. The paintbrush sounds of the small creek behind the trees. I wasn't dirty or thirsty or lost, but I was there, really, I was. And I can't change their deaths, but I can read them, know them, can count a wake of vultures looming in the distance. A book its own trek toward something, something expansive and wild and not made for you, but ripe to be witnessed, explored, and changed (but whose story is changing? yours, or theirs? and can you change it for the better? do no harm? send a flare of some warning, pass along a full canteen?), a frontier flung open—not claimed and closed off or reeking of carrion—just by the fact of being read.

Liz Scheer

Red Room Wrap

Narrative forms, like the objects in a tool kit, build patterns, structures, and arrangements out of words. But while a hammer or fork operates "simply," we think of literature as being built with more opaque and complex tools—through metaphors and symbols—devices that are less "user-friendly."

To consider the functional properties of reading, this essay begins by borrowing two concepts from design theory: *affordances* and *constraints*. Donald Norman uses the term *affordance* to describe the potential uses or actions concealed in materials or designs.[1] Rubber affords flexibility and smoothness. Glass affords transparency. Clay affords malleability; and metal, durability. Specific designs make use of the affordances embedded in these materials: a cup affords scooping and containment; a knife affords not only sharpness, but also cutting, opening, and piercing. As Caroline Levine has noted, the affordances of designed things often extend beyond their intended function; we may hang clothing on the back of a chair, or use a kitchen utensil to pry open a lid.[2]

If affordances, as they have been so marked, refer to the capacities of a material or an object, constraints refer to its limitations. Glass can never be spongy; wool is not adhesive. The affordances and constraints of objects mediate our interactions with the outer-sense world, since it is through these properties that we ascertain our relation to the forms that make up our everyday experiences. Reading, reified as a "device," can be seen in these same functional terms. As a tool used to glean or gather data, reading affords the accrual of new information and insight. Despite its affordances, however, reading is often deemed to be "constrained" by the fact that it is, at root, a private enterprise. It is regarded as a wholly personal technology, a technology whose affordances apply to the individual and not to the common good.

Reading must be rescued from such misconceptions regarding its hermetic and cloistered "properties." To this end, it can be argued that the patterns and arrangements apparent in narrative texts are repeated in larger, more invisible ways in the social sphere. Indeed, this essay aligns itself with an emerging strand of New Formalism: one that contends that human relationships (both within and outside of narrative texts) can be conceived in the language of design theory, since the physical pressures that mediate the object world (tension, resistance, balance, and support, to name several) mediate the human world as well. We see this phenomenon in our everyday language; human relationships are already often concretized through spatial terms: we speak of being "distant" or "close" to one another; "attached" or "connected." In the political sphere, this kind of spatial language is hardly metaphoric, since power is quite literally organized in knowable arrangements and shapes; the hierarchies of government, the binaries of the electoral college, the totalizing wholes of bounded states and nations are all real and lived.

Indeed, reading involves both functional and social iterations of design theory, since it is a twofold activity, an object-oriented exercise involving reader and book, and a human-oriented exercise involving the reader, the writer, and the world that the story presents. Conceiving of reading in this way, that is, as a process that lies at the synapse between two different but related structural domains (the domain of the object and the domain of the social), the activity holds a unique set of affordances in its own right. Crucially, a distinction has been made here between the noun, "book," and the gerund, "reading." Invoked as it is in the singular ("a book"; "the book"), the former suggests a similarly singular user: "a reader," "the reader." In contrast, "reading" declares no subject. The reader could be alone in her study, or she could be reading in the company of others, with others. If "reading" were to be reified into a *thing*, therefore, what would that thing look like, and what affordances and constraints would it hold? Rendered as a tangible device, would "reading" be an apparatus intended for individual use, like a spoon or toothbrush, or would its functioning rely upon multiple bodies?

To grapple with these questions regarding form, function and the affordances of reading, let us consider a novel that takes up these very themes. Charlotte Bronte's *Jane Eyre* is, in essence, a bildungsroman, a novel where we see a woman being "built," not merely in spite of but rather *through* the various socio-historical pressures (economic, familial, marital, spiritual) that define and confine her. The novel, then, lends itself to design theory, since its central drama constellates around Jane's unwillingness to let the culture literally "objectify" her. At every juncture of her life, the protagonist is treated as a functional object; Jane-as-thing "affords" *inferiority* at Gateshead (the Reeds validate themselves through their subjugation of her), *instruction* at Lowood, and *intimacy* at Thornfield. Indeed, from the novel's very outset, Jane is treated as a passive object, a "noxious thing" without agency or interior life ("Her size is small: what is her age?" Mr. Brocklehurst asks Mrs. Reed at Jane's interview for the Lowood School, as though he is evaluating inanimate matter). Given the suffering that permeates Jane's early life, it would be easy to conclude that her "affordances" are the very source of her personal "constraints"; that is, in fulfilling her function for others, Jane is stymied in her own capacity for self-actualization. While this is undoubtedly true, it is also true that without Jane's tribulations there would be no novel, and no narrative material that the protagonist could wield to become the heroine of her own life. In a kind of narrative aporia, therefore, Jane's personal constraints are also her own affordances; in resisting the pressures of the world, Jane finds her place *in* the world.

It is *reading* and that activity's unique affordances that ultimately save Jane from being absorbed by the demands of a patriarchal culture. When John Reed hits Jane with a book at the beginning of the novel, that act of violence could be seen as a metaphor for all of the novel's subsequent abuses: the book is the answer to the difficulty of Jane's life. Indeed, at this crucial moment of the text, the material and immaterial affordances of reading are offered at a kind of moral crossroads. Reading, though tied to (afforded by, contingent upon) the material fact of the book, operates *beyond* the book: it speaks to the internalization of information, and thus, to a kind of psychical, even spiritual, form of apprehension. For John, the anti-reader, the book has nothing to do with reading; concerned only with its physical properties of weight and scale, John deploys the book as a mere projectile, inert matter to be tossed in violence. Jane, on the other hand, perceives the book as another kind of metaphoric projectile; the act of reading (afforded by the book) will "launch" her towards the life of the mind, an internal freedom distinct from the material exigencies of the world around her and its deadening pressures. Jane's arsenal, in other words, is literature; in it she discovers a newfound wellspring of audacity and pluck:

> "Wicked and cruel boy!" I said. "You are like a murderer—you are like a slave-driver—you are like the Roman emperors!"
>
> I had read Goldsmith's History of Rome, and had formed my opinion of Nero, Caligula, etc. Also I had drawn parallels in silence, which I never thought thus to have declared aloud.

The mimetic capacities of narrative, as they are apparent either in singular similes ("*like* a slave-driver"; "*like* the Roman emperor") or in whole patches of text (Jane's experience was *like* one to which the reader can relate) is perhaps the greatest affordance of reading a novel. It is through such constructions that the reader can operate as an individual interpretive agent, while simultaneously perceiving their ineluctable connection to the other: the other appearing, by these terms, as the writer, the character, or some other personage, real or imagined, in the world outside the text.

The outset of this essay considered the socio-political implications of affordances and constraints, and the ways in which the forms that populate our narratives and our object-worlds might also appear in larger regimes of power and authority. It may well behoove us, as citizens and as activists, to consider the political affordances embedded in narrative forms, since those structures might help to conceive new emancipatory forms through which to organize and arrange human experience.

* * *

1. See Donald Norman's *The Design of Everyday Things*. New York: Doubleday, 1990.
2. I am indebted to Caroline Levine's work on the intersections between aesthetic and political forms. See: *Forms: Whole, Rhythm, Hierarchy, Network*. Princeton: Princeton University Press, 2015. In particular, Levine's discussion of design theory, pages 6–10.

Michael Cunningham

Unsayable

Last fall, I went to Auschwitz. I was on a book tour in Kraków, which is an hour's drive from Auschwitz, I had a free morning…

[Already, we enter the real of the grotesque. I was in Kraków anyway, I had a free morning, so I went to Auschwitz…]

And yet I did have one free morning in Kraków. I didn't exactly want to go to Auschwitz but it seemed that I should (and, more complicatedly, it seemed that I should have wanted to go, whereas going there had more to do with my desire to be the kind of person who'd want to go to Auschwitz…).

I was driven there by Alicja Brus, a lovely young Polish woman who was my… minder, I suppose. Writers on book tours are inevitably minded by young people who are almost always women, whose job it is to make sure the hotel is all right and the interviews go reasonably well and the writer gets to the readings more or less on time and more or less sober.

Poor Alicja, however, got the writer who wanted her to take him to Auschwitz. She'd lived in Poland all her life, but had never gone there.

You often fall in love with these women, even if you're gay, there's really nothing like the intimacy of spending every day together, even if it's only a few days, and all the more so if that person knows the local language and customs, all the more so if that person gets you where you need to be on time, all the more so if that person sits through interview after interview listening to you give the same answers, tell the same jokes...

All the more so if that person borrows a car and drives you to Auschwitz when neither of you really wants to go but you, the writer, feel that you should.

And all the more so—this three-day romance, this miniature love affair—if you can joke with the person, if one of you for instance says, as you drive through the disconcertingly ordinary town that verges on Auschwitz, *What if we just had lunch and told everybody that we went to Auschwitz...*

But then, there you are. Alicja has arranged for a guide.

You start not in Auschwitz proper but in Birkenau, it's full name is Auschwitz-Birkenau but they're a short distance apart. Auschwitz was built first, meant primarily for Polish prisoners. Auschwitz is where the *Arbeit Macht Frei* sign is, Auschwitz is where you can see the displays of eyeglasses and shoes and suitcases, Auschwitz is full of tour groups...

Birkenau is the death star within the death star. Birkenau is where the train tracks ended. Birkenau is the site of the barracks and the gas chambers.

Birkenau is where the travelers were told to put their names on their suitcases so they could reclaim them after they'd rested and gotten themselves cleaned up; Birkenau is where doctors stood by, white-coated and attentive, prepared to do absolutely nothing, their only purpose being the appearance of normality; Birkenau is where the gas canisters were kept in ambulances; all to prevent panic, to convey the idea that people were being cared for, people were on their way to work on farms...

All the effort that went into convincing people that this was just a stop along the way...

Birkenau is largely unvisited, whereas Auschwitz attracts hoards of tourists. Birkenau is a vast green plain (though it was all mud, not grass, when it was functioning). It is possessed of a profound silence. It is ringed by forest. Birkenau might strike you as beautiful, if you didn't know what had happened there.

I fell apart almost immediately. Alicja did not. Our guide was in his mid-thirties, respectful and respectable, a kind-eyed and decent man who might have worked just about anywhere.

He was more devoted to facts than emotion, which seemed appropriate. Facts, after all, lead us someplace, whereas emotion just leads us back to ourselves.

I learned that our guide was one member of a staff of 600 people who work constantly to preserve that which was shoddy at its inception. Imagine curating something built quickly and carelessly, out of the spare parts salvaged from the village that had been leveled to make room for the camp. Imagine maintaining indifferently-made buildings, preserving their slapdash qualities—buildings that, if not constantly repaired, would have collapsed decades ago.

Our guide showed us around with… what? A sense of compassionate distance, I suppose. Both he and Alicja were restrained and dignified; I was not. I wept when we walked across the grounds and wept in the barracks and wept in the showers… I couldn't seem to care if I was being the standard-issue sentimental tourist. It seemed to me that part of the point of visiting Birkenau was the notion that so many of us believe we're tourists, just passing through.

When we were finished at Birkenau, when our guide walked us to the gate, I had a final question (I'd had many).

"I feel funny asking you this. I don't really believe in ghosts, but if anywhere on earth is haunted…"

"Of course we are asked this question," he said. "I will tell you. I have been here alone, at midnight. And I have felt no fear, no presences, nothing."

After Alicja and I had left him, as we made our way to Auschwitz, I said to her, "Do you think even their ghosts were extinguished?"

She answered, "Who would want to come back to this place in any form?"

Auschwitz was as crowded as Birkenau was empty. Student groups were marshaled along by their teachers, who spoke to them in Polish through megaphones. Tourists with backpacks consulted maps. The general emotional atmosphere was illegible, I can only call it mild curiosity, and I lasted there less than ten minutes, until we saw a young girl posing, smiling, under the *Arbeit Macht Frei* sign, for a picture being taken by her boyfriend with his iPhone. I told Alicja that we had to leave. She was more than willing.

We didn't speak on the drive back to Kraków. We had another two days together, but we never referred, not once, to Auschwitz-Birkenau.

What, after all, was there for us to say?

I thought then, and I think now, that language stopped at Auschwitz-Birkenau. It stopped for me, at any rate. I can find no way to speak or write about it, and of what I've just written, nothing truly important has been said; nothing essential; nothing that conveys the actual experience. I can tell you about the exteriors. I can't tell you, not really, about the effects they had. Or—maybe more truthfully—I can't tell you about those effects without feeling fraudulent, self-dramatizing, and ridiculous.

In fact, the very idea that going to a concentration camp caused me to be traumatized by an encounter with language's limits, that I'd found for the first time (I, who have given most of my life to language) an experience I could not put into language... the very idea that I was troubled by my own sense of inadequacy at Auschwitz-Birkenau strikes me as fraudulent, self-dramatizing, and ridiculous.

I did, however, recently have a chance to sit silently by myself in a room devoted to reading and writing in solitude. I read *Man's Search for Meaning* by Viktor Frankl, who was in the camp, and whose language did not fail him.

I can tell you that Frankl survived the camp, and wrote:

> ...for the first time in my life I saw the truth as it is set into song by so many poets, proclaimed as the final wisdom by so many thinkers. The truth—that love is the ultimate and the highest goal to which man can aspire. Then I grasped

> the meaning of the greatest secret that human poetry and human thought and belief have to impart: *The salvation of man is through love and in love.*

I can tell you that he wrote:

> What is demanded of man is not, as some existential philosophers teach, to endure the meaninglessness of life, but rather to bear his incapacity to grasp its unconditional meaningfulness in rational terms.

There is no hysteria in Frankl's book. It is, if anything, possessed of the clear-eyed rationality of someone who has survived the unspeakable.

After reading *Man's Search for Meaning*, I wrote down all my feelings, everything I could recall, about a trip I'd made, by car, on the single free morning I had in Kraków, after which I returned to Kraków, signed books, did a few more interviews, met people for dinner in a nice restaurant. I didn't worry about the tininess of my own distress. I didn't veer away from self-pity or self-indulgence. I was like a baby, fussing. I didn't care about the needs of others, any more than a baby does. I wrote furiously, shamelessly, about how that trip to the concentration camp had made me feel, like, really, really bad. I permitted myself to write about Auschwitz-Birkenau as something that had happened to me (even that phrase is painful to write).

After I'd left the room, I immediately deleted everything I'd written. Writing it had mattered to me, but it had no other purpose.

After all, not everything we create is meant to live beyond its most immediate usefulness. If I needed to write about having gone to Auschwitz-Birkenau, I not only didn't need anyone to read it, I wanted it obliterated, as if I'd never written it at all, in more or less the way you'd try to forget about some embarrassing lapse, some public humiliation you'd brought upon yourself.

I'm not romantic enough to say I was cleansed by the writing and the subsequent deletion, but I can say that something had been... if not laid to rest, at least deprived of its ability to haunt in quite the way it had.

There are, after all, places, and experiences, that murder even their own ghosts.

Jennie Uleman

Dissertation Notes,

c. 1993

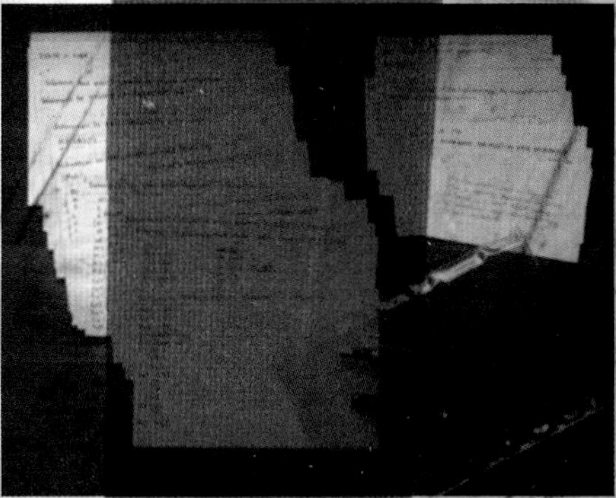

Which summers did I spend in Athens exactly? At least two between 1992 and 1994, during graduate school, but which? I lived there with a boyfriend in an apartment in a neighborhood named after milk, or after the galaxy, at least in my mind—the galaxy being, after all, the milky way: the neighborhood was called Galatsi. The apartment was in a small modern building, built on a corner in a mainly residential area. There was a paint store on the ground floor the summers I was there. The apartments were on the second and third floors. My boyfriend's family owned the building and occupied the three third-floor apartments. The building was made from cement, metal, and marble; the windows were good quality and all had lace curtains. Balconies wrapped around and looked out over the street and a small garden.

My boyfriend's sister, her husband, and their two daughters lived in one of the third-floor apartments (or were they all on a fourth floor?), and furnished their apartment with heavy carved wood furniture. My boyfriend's parents lived in another third-floor apartment with more upholstered and delicate furniture; my boyfriend and his sister had grown up in that apartment. (Now I am remembering the elevator—maybe there were four floors.) My boyfriend lived in a third small apartment, and had furnished it mainly with books and records. The apartment had a bedroom, a small unfinished kitchen, a bathroom, a living area, and a balcony. It would eventually become his mother's, after his father died and my boyfriend—by then my ex-boyfriend—moved into the larger apartment in which he had grown up. The summers I was there, we ate all our meals with his family in one of the other apartments. We spent the rest of our days in his apartment, making coffees, rolling cigarettes, and reading philosophy. At night, we'd listen to records and maybe friends would come over for drinks and to hang out and talk.

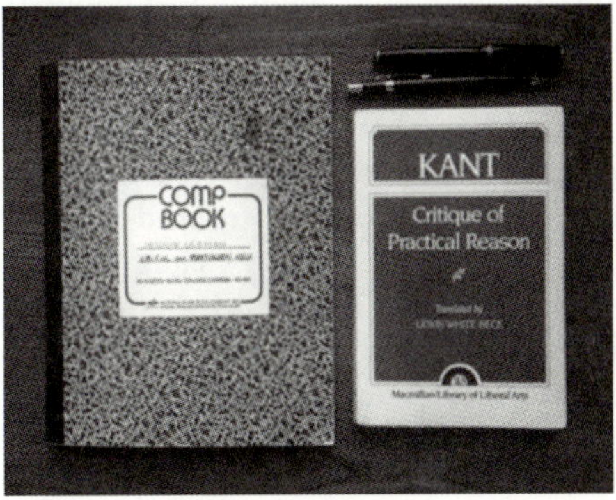

These notebooks, one for each of the major texts informing my dissertation, along with these index cards, used for tracking references, were often spread out on the small apartment's kitchen table, which I think had aluminum legs and a Formica top. The unfinished kitchen was my office; my boyfriend worked in the other room. The tabletop was covered with a patterned plastic tablecloth, maybe flowers, maybe calico patches, maybe both, something like that. The air was dry and the windows were always open. The air smelled like sun, dust, marble, plants being watered on balconies, exhaust, and, as the day wore on, cooking olive oil. I read and took notes nervously. Kant and I were not exactly on the same page, and I was often pulled apart, wanting to both understand him and undermine him. Faithful copying out of significant passages satisfied both impulses. I could get inside a passage, learn its rhythms and structure, learn Kant's mind, at the same time that I could capture it, pin it down, in order possibly to hold it up as evidence against Kant. I sat in a chair at the table in that kitchen reading and writing / copying in a way that was jittery and intense. It was hot; I mostly sat in sleeveless t-shirts and cut-offs, or a short denim skirt I had made in high school from very faded black jeans and some scraps of purplish maroon corduroy.

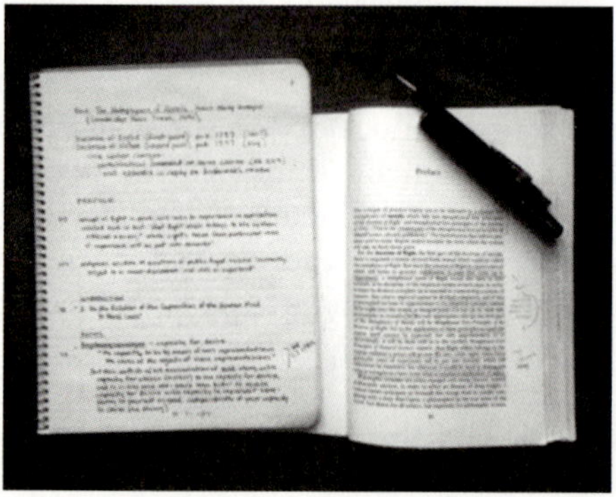

For making notes in the books themselves, I used a Pentel mechanical pencil, black or maroon (the maroon ones are rare), with 0.5mm HB leads. I always had a Staedtler eraser nearby. For the notebooks, I used a fountain pen I bought in the 1980s in a fountain pen shop in Park Slope, or that I anyway had had rehabbed and repaired there, at least once—I can't remember now exactly, but I think, yes, now that I think of it, I must have bought the pen someplace, a thrift shop or flea market, and it didn't work, so I took it to the shop. I remember liking to spend time in that shop; it was on the second floor of a corner building on Seventh Ave not far from Union St., maybe at President. This was before graduate school. The man who ran the shop loved pens, and showed me how mine worked. They were all different. Mine had a kind of balloon inkwell. He showed me the best way to refill it, pumping bubbles into the ink jar itself. My favorite ink was blue-black. I can picture the bottle of the kind I used, squat and dark, but I can't think of the brand now. Because my pen would blob when it got close to empty, there was always a folded up paper towel on my writing / reading table, polka-dotted with different size ink spots. I once saw a pen identical to mine in photos accompanying a piece on Collette's home in *The New York Times Magazine*. Besides the pencil and pen, I had a lined piece of oaktag which had originally come with a calligraphy pad. I used it under the unlined sketchbook pages so my lines would be straight. I think my handwriting hasn't changed much.

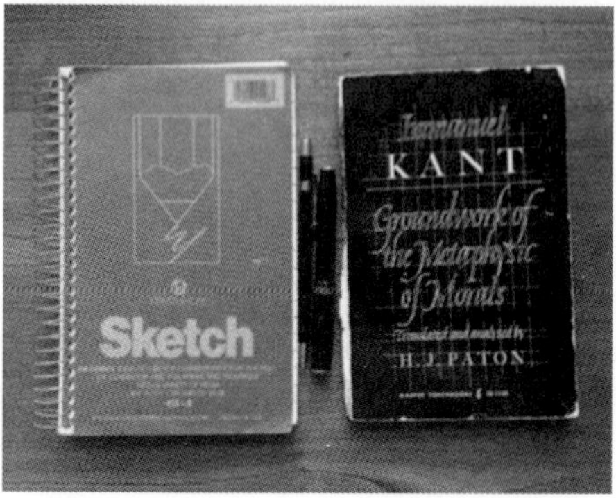

(Why weren't you on the same page with Kant? Trenelle asks. I was not on the same page with Kant because of something about the way things, for Kant, are supposed to stay put. It isn't the dualisms, I want to tell her—I have no problem with dualisms, *per se*—but how static they are that bothers me. Things—ideas, actions, truths, objects, whatever—are supposed for Kant to stay in one place, to stay rational or natural, phenomenal or noumenal, *a priori* or *a posteriori*, analytic or synthetic, free or determined, and even if, like human beings, they are on Kant's account mixed things, they are mixed like oil and vinegar are mixed in a salad dressing, one without egg or anything else to emulsify them.)

* * *

I was in love. I was far from home. I was in graduate school. I hadn't started to learn modern Greek and, even though some of my boyfriend's friends spoke English, I was mostly alone with the language in which I was working and in which I thought, which wasn't even Kant's language. The name of the neighborhood, Galatsi, *Γαλάτσι*, may come from Symeon Galakis, a "squire" (Wikipedia's word), who bought a lot of the land that is now Galatsi about fifty years after Kant died. In Athens, at that time, his name would have been pronounced "Galatsis." But it's possible that Galatsi was named for milk; according also to Wikipedia, "Galatsi" may derive "from *gala*, the Greek word for the *milk* that the shepherds of the area's rangelands yelled hovering around in order to sell their products." *Gala*, γάλα, milk, was one of the first words I picked up, since I liked my Greek coffee frappes *me gala*, με γάλα, with milk. I liked saying it; *me gala* always sounded to me like a feminine version of "megalo," as in the first syllables of "megalomaniac." You could not often see the milky way from the balcony in Galatsi, but I read Kant there, my own pen, pencil, notebooks, and notecards in place on that one table in the galaxy.

Randall Szott

Reading as an Experiment in Democracy

...democracy is concerned not with freaks or geniuses or heroes or divine leaders but with associated individuals in which each by intercourse with others somehow make the life of each more distinctive.

– John Dewey,
"Philosophy and Democracy," 1919

This is, to say the least, a precarious moment for democracy. In many ways, the sort of democracy Dewey advocated has only existed in small pockets—grandmothers sharing recipes with their grandchildren, neighbors arguing over property lines, children improvising rules on the playground, *quinceañera* parties, community potlucks, neighborhood meetings about gentrification, or even gathering to read in Manhattan.

Recently, I have taken particular care in deciding what to read. That is the alchemical power of the Dewey's conception of democracy, it transforms the atomization of reading into one of associated life. It has been impossible for me to ignore the political context of my reading choices, given that liberal democracy's empty proceduralism has made millions even more vulnerable.

If ever there were a time to vigorously pursue Dewey's vision of democracy as experience, it is now. For too long liberals have pinned their hopes on facts and policies, treating democracy as an epistemological problem. #alternativefacts is an acid that has dissolved the basis for this hope. The crisis of *meaning*, not knowledge, should be our central concern if we hope to achieve democracy. Thus, we should cultivate in ourselves and others the sensitivity, grace, and inventiveness that only aesthetic approaches to democratic life can bring.

In this spirit, I re-read *John Dewey's Ethics: Democracy as Experience* by Gregory Pappas. It is a remarkable book with far too much wisdom to share with a ready summary. I am happy to have revisited it, and to have this opportunity to direct others to it. To join in collective reading, thinking and discussion of it would embody the very heart of democratic practice. As Dewey says:

> I am inclined to believe that the heart and final guarantee of democracy is in free gatherings of neighbors on the street corner...and in gatherings of friends in the living rooms of houses and apartments.

Alan Huck

The Mute Testimony
(Excerpt)

the space of a single minute [1]
the negation of chronology [2]
the site of a gap, a sublime breach between the sensible and the intelligible, between copy and reality, between a memory and a hope [3]
a plagiarism of nature [4]
a prophecy of the glorious body [5]
a secret about a secret [6]
like images in the memory of a total stranger [7]
like a quotation, or a maxim or proverb [8]
a free and familiar coinage of meaning [9]
a message without a code [10]
a language that names what it describes [11]
a language that is guided and interrupted by the desire for the very thing that, always lost, and never comprehended, remains to be mourned [12]
a consoling object [13]
an act of love [14]
a memento from a life being lived [15]
like flies in amber [16]
like a footprint or a death mask [17]

the tomb of the real [18]
a kind of deposit of the real itself [19]
an hallucination that is also a fact [20]
a concrete kind of fiction [21]
a certificate of presence [22]
a scientific performance [23]
an immobile and silent surface [24]
the absolute Particular, the sovereign Contingency [25]
the simultaneous recognition, in a fraction of a second, of the significance of an event [26]
a species of alchemy [27]
the great, the incredible instrument of symbolic actuality [28]
the central instrument of our time [29]
a building block in a larger structure [30]
a universe of dots [31]
the golden key opening the door to the wonders of the external universe [32]
the name of the destruction of any consciousness of identity [33]
the product of complete alienation [34]
the prophecy of a human memory yet to be socially and politically achieved [35]
some marvel of a fairy tale or delusion of necromancy [36]
possible contributions to history [37]
fragile and slippery carriers of meaning [38]
loose leaves which can be passed from hand to hand [39]
signs, half-truths, cripples, fictions that live only by moments and know only the surface of things [40]

inadequate and overwhelming thing, poor compensation, impossible testimony [41]
just a picture [42]
an utterance of some sort [43]

* * *

The Mute Testimony is a permanently expanding index of phrases that attempt to define or describe the practice of photography. The phrases are extracted from the readings of the artist Alan Huck, with their original authors cited below.

1. William Henry Fox Talbot
2. Geoff Dyer
3. Giorgio Agamben
4. Alphonse de Lamartine
5. Giorgio Agamben
6. Diane Arbus
7. John Berger
8. Susan Sontag
9. Victor Burgin
10. Roland Barthes
11. Tod Papageorge
12. Eduardo Cadava
13. Thierry de Duve
14. Hervé Guibert
15. John Berger
16. Peter Wollen
17. Susan Sontag
18. John Tagg
19. Rosalind Krauss
20. André Bazin
21. John Szarkowski
22. Roland Barthes
23. Henry Peach Robinson
24. Vilém Flusser
25. Roland Barthes
26. Henri Cartier-Bresson
27. Susan Sontag
28. Walker Evans
29. James Agee

30. Abigail Solomon-Godeau
31. Don DeLillo
32. László Moholy-Nagy
33. Eduardo Cadava
34. Siegfried Kracauer
35. John Berger
36. Author Unknown, via Geoffrey Batchen
37. John Berger
38. Gerry Badger
39. Vilém Flusser
40. Tod Papageorge
41. John Tagg
42. Tod Papageorge
43. Allan Sekula

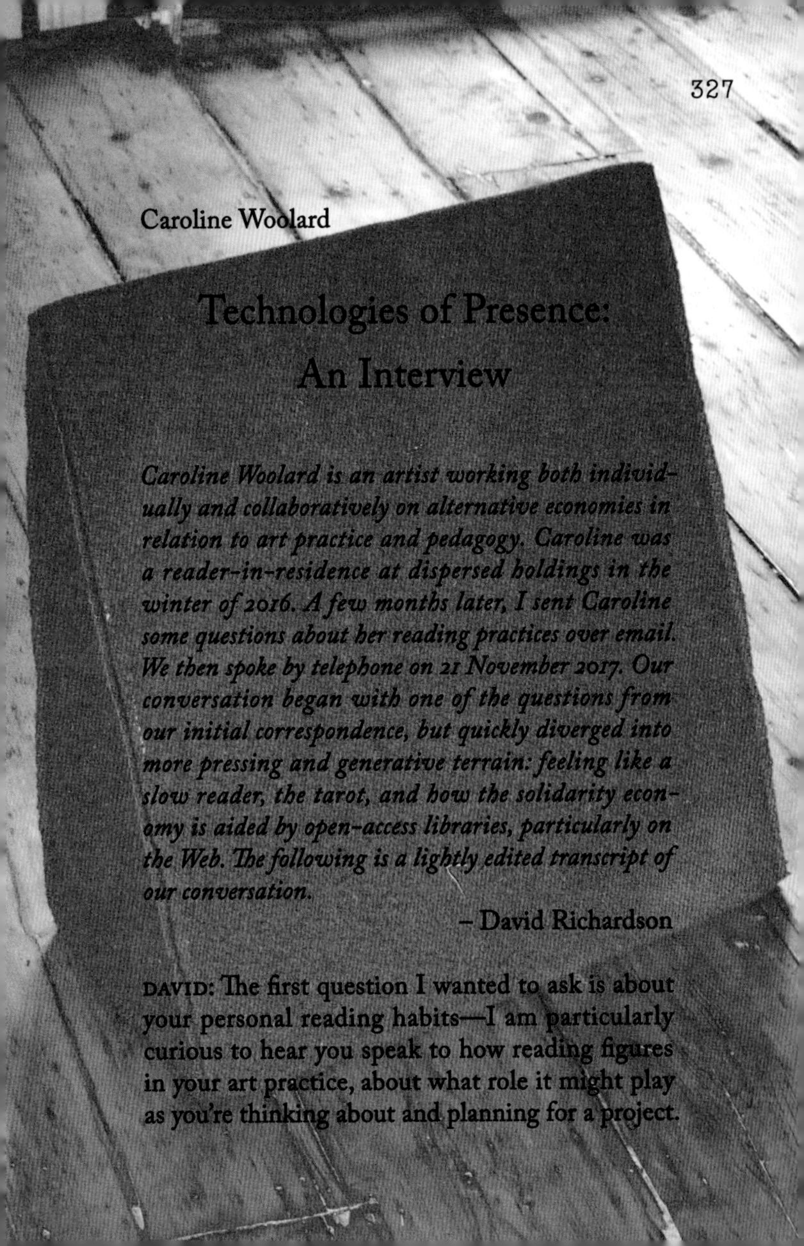

Caroline Woolard

Technologies of Presence: An Interview

Caroline Woolard is an artist working both individually and collaboratively on alternative economies in relation to art practice and pedagogy. Caroline was a reader-in-residence at dispersed holdings in the winter of 2016. A few months later, I sent Caroline some questions about her reading practices over email. We then spoke by telephone on 21 November 2017. Our conversation began with one of the questions from our initial correspondence, but quickly diverged into more pressing and generative terrain: feeling like a slow reader, the tarot, and how the solidarity economy is aided by open-access libraries, particularly on the Web. The following is a lightly edited transcript of our conversation.

– David Richardson

DAVID: The first question I wanted to ask is about your personal reading habits—I am particularly curious to hear you speak to how reading figures in your art practice, about what role it might play as you're thinking about and planning for a project.

CAROLINE: This question, at first, to be honest, terrified me. I thought, "Oh no, I don't think I read enough. How am I supposed to balance my practice of making, and convening, and being in collaboration with people, and teaching, and making money with the reading that I always want to do." So I imagined all the books that I've purchased and then never read—they sit around like little friends waiting to have dinner. I see my bookshelf and I think, "I'm so sorry I still haven't gotten to you." So I think that's why it took me some time to feel like I could have this conversation.

But then, I remembered that the way that I actually read is in groups. I tend to read with Susan Jahoda, and sometimes also with Emilio Martinez Poppe. We all realized that we are all relatively slow readers—in many ways, we probably ended up in the art classroom because we were unconventional learners. I think we are all somewhat dyslexic, and probably much more interested in embodied knowledge and different modes of haptic learning that weren't available in our schools growing up, so we were put in the art classroom because we needed to do something with our bodies. The three of us have talked a lot about feeling shame around being slow readers. We were able to begin moving past that when we realized that because we read out loud as slowly or quickly as we read to ourselves, respectively, we actually love to read together. So that's what we've been doing lately; it's in many ways how we did the research for the book that we're writing together. And we are writing that book in a very visual way. I think it connects in that way to the work of dispersed holdings, which is in part about reading together, about the social and relational sides of reading.

DAVID: Yes—that is a really good formulation of some of dispersed's concerns. When you read socially, in groups, do you read out loud to each other, or do you each tuck away, do your reading, and then come back and discuss? Or perhaps it's a combination of both?

CAROLINE: Mostly we read together, out loud. But we also read individually—we give each other reading assignments, actually. For example, right now, Susan and I have given each other an assignment to understand the influence that the Bauhaus has had on our current approaches to pedagogy, and we are both doing similar readings and then reporting back to each other.

DAVID: Then you have a meet-up about a particular topic?

CAROLINE: Yeah, in our slow times we meet once a week, and in our best times—usually the summer and the winter, when we're not teaching—we'll meet every morning, either in person or virtually, for three or four hours.

DAVID: Could you speak to the difference of reading aloud in terms of something like comprehension, or a different feeling around reading? What is different when the text is being embodied by your voice?

CAROLINE: Well I think it's different for each of us, but I think that for me, I cannot take it in as well when I'm reading silently, but if I'm looking at the words and hearing them at the same time, it's really helpful. And the way we tend to read, we rotate, passing the text whenever we feel like we've had enough, or like we don't want to read anymore. Then we tend to underline different things that are confusing or exciting. We use this same process, actually, when editing our own writing as well.

One thing we noticed as a group is that there's this tendency to jump on a section or a word and never finish an article or our own chapter that we're proofreading because we just fall into a rabbit hole based on one small phrase, or one word, or one footnote, and so we have a new rule that we've established over the past year: we each underline something that we know we want to come back to and talk about, or we make a comment (as we are often working in a Google Doc) if we need to remember what we were thinking, and then we make ourselves get through the whole text. And each of us has to read some part of it so that by the end, we were all both listeners and readers, and underliners. That takes, say, half-an-hour, and then the next hour is spent going over all of the underlines to get clarity and see if we agree on the different adjustments that we each want to make.

DAVID: I imagine that you have some interesting reading protocols beyond the "reading rule" you just mentioned. Can you think of other readerly "rules" you might have together in the group?

CAROLINE: There are probably many, but they're likely so ingrained that I don't even think of them. I guess one thing that we have been trying to do, though it's difficult to enact when we are each teaching (so let's say in the winter and in the summer), we try to do some breathing together, or some kind of stretching, before we start. It allows us to sync up. An encounter with the text is always an encounter with yourself, and often we bring our own agitation from the day and from life generally into our dialogue. We felt that if we did different things, like the Simone Fortier breathing protocol, or even just a little humming together or stretching, it helps us notice and be sensitive to the other parts of the day that are maybe inhibiting us.

Lately we have been doing a tarot card reading where we each draw one card. That card figures as our individual thing to respond to for the day. Also, because we are a group of three, we are able to represent the past, present, and future for the day of the group. The card we draw is also meant to speak to the time we are assigned. So, for example, if I get the Sun of Pentacles, I am both that right now, and whatever I have to say will reveal something about how I'm doing presently, but the Sun of Pentacles will also speak to the past of the group. So the card I draw says something about me and the group at the same time. And whatever we say really helps the group know where we are at, like, "I'm having a really bad day," or, "I'm very anxious today about my health," or whatever it is, so that we can try to be more tender with each other when we're debating something. You just try and notice how much you might be defending your knowledge, for instance. There are these power dynamics at play when we are wanting to think through an idea together—we have been working together for maybe four years, Susan and I, and Emilio has been in the group for two years now, so we are getting more and more conscious of these weird emergent power struggles around certain areas, places where one of us might feel the need to claim, "I know," to feel like an idea is valued. So these tarot card readings and the breathing exercises have helped us.

DAVID: The notion of reading espoused by the practice with the tarot cards is not one we explore elsewhere in *Reading Room*. It's nice to be reminded that there are so many different forms of reading, that "reading" stands in for so many different activities.

CAROLINE: The card deck we use is from an artist I know named Kim Krans. The deck is called *The Wild Unknown*, and all the characters are animals. It's nice to see Kim's interpretations. We just look at the card and read it visually to understand it before we read the guide book.

DAVID: When did you start reading tarot?

CAROLINE: Not a long time ago—in fact, it's very recent for me. Someone I was working for introduced me to it. I was helping her edit a book, and we went on a writing retreat, and she gave me this deck. Her name is Jodie Evans, she founded the feminist anti-war organization Code Pink. Jodie gave me the deck and we read them together everyday, and then I brought that reading practice back to the collective because it was such a useful way to set the tone—I found that it allowed sideways inspiration to enter, like the breeze or the sun, just other modes of understanding. It's amazing what you find. With Jodie's work and my work we would always be the opposite of each other, and with Emilio and Susan we have very different readings, but amazing patterns recur, especially around Pentacles.

DAVID: I am not very familiar with reading tarot, but over the course of our work at dispersed holdings, Sal and I have often read the *I Ching* together. I have found the *I Ching* to be a great presencing tool. If we are very busy, or otherwise stressed or anxious, it's a nice way to arrive in the room. Perhaps every reading practice is in some way a technology of presence.

To speak to the other side of reading practice, could you talk about the book you are writing right now?

CAROLINE: Sure! It has been in the works for about three years. It came on the heels of a report I made with the collective BFAMFAPhD, called *Artists Report Back*, where we looked at inequity in art school education along race, ethnicity, and gender. We came to realize that while we could try to be policy advisors—and we were successful in small ways and big ways, like being cited by the NEA, and I gave a keynote at their anniversary—we were still struggling in the classroom. We thought, "That's where we are all the time, why not try to imagine a new textbook or series of pedagogical tools for arts educators like us who don't know what to do given this cultural inequity, which is often reflected in the material that's being taught and in the way that people approach learning?

All that's to say, the book is called *Ways of Being*, like John Berger's *Ways of Seeing*, only less perceptual or ocular—one might argue that a perceptual or ocular focus is a kind of ableist approach. Instead, it's about sensing and bringing the social and emotional intelligences that are necessary for collaboration and interdisciplinary work into the classroom. It includes very, very basic activities that help people think about how they're working with one another. What we see is that there's been a big focus on the phase of the life of any artwork that we call "the encounter." You spend all this time, as an artist, making something, you obsess over how it's encountered, how it's seen, how it's perceived, and how it communicates. But if you imagine that your whole life and the whole process of making the work is as important as that final encounter, which in our fantasies is with a stranger, potentially in a white cube, if you imagine all these other phases are equally important, then we have to think through different kinds of activities and teaching tools that allow people to focus on how they source materials, or how they work with each other, how they copyright their work, how they exchange with people, how they support themselves and each other, and how the materials finally depart, ready for a new life cycle where they can become source materials for someone else.

We have been developing very basic tools, such as the social-ecological model, where you have to ask yourself, for example, "If your new project has to focus on labor and how you work with other people, what are your existing beliefs about your capacity to work with other people? How about the importance of working with other people as a visual artist?" And if you look at the social-ecological model for public health, you have to do things like ask, "What are the messages you've received already, from your friends and family, about labor or work as an artist, especially a visual artist? And then how does that change when you get messages from your community? And then from institutions around you? And then from larger historical forces? And then influences beyond that, what we call earth, mystery, and spirit?" You use these questions to track this scale of influence, all the while trying to become more aware of your blind spots and your biases—your socio-cultural positionality, essentially, so that you don't just assume that your perspective hasn't been shaped by these other factors. We are coming to terms with this legacy of the modernist genius and the autonomous work.

So the book is a textbook—it'll be very basic, and we have videos and a card game, different ways to learn that are not just reading in the traditional sense.

DAVID: The disparity between the time of making and the time of encounter for visual art is interesting. I have been thinking about the same paradigm in terms of writing. It takes so much longer to write a book than it does to read it! And of course a book requests your attention in an entirely different way than a visual work might—the purely visual encounter tends to be much shorter. I like how *Ways of Being* expands the notion of reading by introducing different kinds of readerly engagement—card games and the like—thereby affecting the temporality of the readerly encounter.

CAROLINE: Yes, it's true. It's a challenge—sometimes I say to Susan, "Would we be able to read our own book? Let's make sure that we edit it well!" It'll be like Berger's *Ways of Seeing* in that it will be really beautifully illustrated and designed so that words get a lot of space. You can take it on in whatever order you want. We are trying to allow the labor of reading to be playful in the same way that our reading practice tries to be.

DAVID: Are you designing it yourselves?

CAROLINE: Susan and I are co-authors, and Emilio is designing it. They are involved in the conversations around editing, and life beyond, so we hope that in general the concepts we discuss as a group are somehow infused, embossed, set into the text and the design.

DAVID: What is the book's relationship to the Study Center for Group Work, an artist collective begun in 2016 with a focus on collaborative methods?

CAROLINE: The Study Center just happens to be overlapping, time-wise. I am just really interested in artist's methods for collaboration and listening, and I think more and more visual artists want to learn how to be with each other in groups. There is a possibility that we'll ask some of the artists in the Study Center for Group Work to contribute to the book itself. It's kind of an ongoing question for us as to what constitutes "the book" because it's an epistemological project that takes many forms. If, for example, it's a website and cards and videos and printed matter, it needs to be constantly updated online as PDFs, and what needs to be in print and for how long is unclear. For better or worse, many people still think of books like photographs—when you read a book you don't always think, "Oh, this is a picture of an ongoing conversation from just one moment—there will be more." But it takes so much work to finish a book. First we had thought there would be a different book every month, and readers could just print it out and think of it as a kind of snapshot. But then when we realized how much work it is to design and print it, and then to work with our publisher, we decided that there will be one definitive book, and other things will go online. And the online things might be collaborations from the study group site.

DAVID: You are hoping the book lands in classrooms, I gather, but are you also hoping to send it out to libraries? Does the Study Center for Group Work have its own library?

CAROLINE: Two things: one, this book, *Ways of Being*, has a somewhat traditional publisher, and they will do the work of getting it in the Library of Congress and all that. It's called Punctum Books. They really support open-source, open-access distribution. They are totally happy to have excerpts available before the book comes out, which we've already done, and to make some of it free as a PDF.

And second, in terms of the Study Center for Group Work, yes, I think of it as a library that is open-access in that it's a working document that is always changing. Anyone can add a PDF to the library, but as a physical space, it was open at Cooper Union in 2016 from October to November, and we have had different workshops in different spaces including the Brooklyn Commons and the New York Public Library.

Actually, I was thinking of a story that might be interesting, one that maybe shaped a lot of how I think about reading and making PDFs available. It's quick. Can I tell you?

DAVID: Yes! Please!

CAROLINE: I was thinking that a lot of this, for me, comes back to when I was twenty-two, and I had just graduated from school, and I was working at night, from ten P.M. to six A.M., and I was kind of a night guard, so I just had to walk through this building every hour—it took me about ten minutes—and take down whoever was there, make sure nothing was going wrong, and then I had nothing else to do. So I ended up searching the internet a lot. I eventually found this website called the Community Economies Collective—communityeconomies.org. I just stumbled upon it. I had never heard of the concept of a solidarity or community economy, and I was so excited because at the time I had been bartering with a lot of people, and the CEC just framed things so well for me. I remember seeing this iceberg image of labor in a firm, with wage labor being the thing that you see above the water. Underwater, there are all these other things that make up this huge mass of the iceberg, like gift-giving and bartering and mutual aid. And they had tons of PDFs for free on the website, so I read all the PDFs at night while I was at work, and then when I ran out of PDFs to read, I emailed their general email and this person wrote back. This is right after Julie Graham (from J.K. Gibson-Graham) had passed away. It was her writing partner, Katherine Gibson, who was saying, "We are so overwhelmed, we don't know the future of the collective, but maybe this person, Ethan Miller, cc'd, can help you." And then for a few years, Ethan Miller, living in Australia, sent me readings. It was through that that my thinking evolved, and I met him, and he eventually introduced me to this guy who lived in an intentional community where they share money in

Staten Island called Ganas. I got involved in the Solidarity Economy group in New York, and I helped them make media and websites. Eventually it connected me to a big community of living practice, where learning fed our action, and vice versa. Because of that, and because I was so isolated and lonely after school, working at night, feeling like no one cared about ideas or visual art or anything, really—I think it's because of that that I've been so dedicated to building online websites for people who can't meet in person, either because of ability or geography or personality, anything. I do have this real excitement about virtual libraries and reading access, as much as it can feed into in-person community and action, that's great too.

DAVID: What an amazing story.

CAROLINE: Yeah! I was thinking, "That's why I care about websites!" No one ever seems to care, but my thinking is that I'm gonna build that website and put PDFs on it because I don't know where the twenty-two-year-old me is. Someone out there wants this.

DAVID: Are there other virtual libraries you can think of that either have played an important role in your reading life or that you think are doing good work?

CAROLINE: Well there is AAAAAAARG.org. You can't not love AAAAAAARG. There is also this library called Temporary Services, put together by Brett Bloom and Marc Fisher, and one called the Library of Radiant Optimism, put together by Brett Bloom and Bonnie Fortune. It's amazing—it's full of PDF versions of sixties and seventies radical pamphlets and zines about how to make your own geodesic dome, and Black Power, and healing, and self-care. They often turn them into printed zines that you can buy from their Half Letter Press website. And then the basic ones like UbuWeb, you know. I think it's interesting that there are artists behind UbuWeb and AAAAAAARG, and that they understand that the economy of the arts is the commons—it wants to be free, it wants to be distributed, and it can't be held by proprietary regulations that maybe institutions supportive of the arts want to use to control distribution. With UbuWeb, for instance, Kenneth Goldsmith doesn't ask for copyright from anybody—UbuWeb doesn't care.

DAVID: Every library, a dispersed holdings. Thank you so much for the conversation!

CAROLINE: Thank you!

John Muse

Now and Then Contemporary: "I will write to her!"

...as if resurrection always occurred alongside *the thing expressed: role of the Phantom, of the Shadow.*
– Roland Barthes, "Deliberation," 1979

Enthusiastically reading an essay by scholar Mary Lydon entitled "Amplification: Barthes, Freud, and Paranoia," I land here:

> Is it not curious, first of all, that Barthes, who declared "I have a disease, I *see* language," the writer of such texts as *s/z*, and the essays on Erté's alphabet and Cy Twombly's singularly graphic art, who consistently privileged the letter throughout his career, should choose to *hear* photography, an intrinsically visual artistic practice—arguably the most uncompromisingly visible language, since it is inscribed by light itself? "Hence, strangely, the only thing that I tolerate, that I like, that is familiar to me, when I am photographed, is the sound of the

> camera.” Note that what Barthes pleasurably hears is the sound of the camera itself in the act of taking a picture, and a picture, furthermore, of himself. And is it not a further coincidence that he should then so readily associate the noise of the camera with the noise of Time, hence with clocks? “For me the noise of Time is not sad: I love bells, clocks, watches... cameras, in short, were clocks for seeing.”

Reading and rereading this paragraph, I luxuriate in Lydon’s language, in the jaunty series of nonrestrictive clauses that buoy the long first sentence, in the prick of the em dash after “practice,” which amplifies the meaning of the two adverbs, “insistently” and “uncompromisingly,” in the Roland Barthes she cites, in his *Camera Lucida* aka *La chambre claire*, my very favorite, in her knowing mentions of Erté and Twombly, in her chatty if leading opening: “Is it not curious...?” Yes, it is curious, all the more so because Lydon adopts the idiom she is writing about, Edgar Allen Poe’s idiom, Dupin’s idiom, the idiom of detection and revelation and paranoia: “Is it not curious...” is the way one begins when either suspicions are to be confirmed or delusions tested. I luxuriate too in being offered an imperative: “Note that what Barthes hears...” Noted. Which curiously and coincidentally reiterates the subtitle of *La chambre claire: Note sur la photographie*. I am curious with her, and I am noting what she notes and how she notes it; the present tense of "It *is* curious..." and "...*is* it not a further coincidence...," these tenses hold me to the time of the reading, the seeing and hearing of language crossed with photography.

There's so much more to say about Lydon's paranoia, about the coincidence of clocks and cameras, which links Barthes to the Freud Lydon writes about, thus, there's so much to say about the other woman, Freud's patient, who hears the click of a hidden camera but is told by her lover, no, that's the ticking of a clock, and by Freud, no, that's the throbbing of your clitoris projected "as a perception of an external object." Lydon maps Barthes to this woman, his body to hers, her throbbing to his, her projection to his deflection, her anxious relation to noise, voyeurism, and pleasure to Barthes' approving, desirous relation to the photographer's body and its mechanical prostheses. Lydon argues for and enacts a criticism that multiplies rather than reduces projections, stealing all her lines from Poe and her article's epigraph: "It will be understood that I speak of coincidences and no more."

Or so I say now, but at the time, a few weeks ago, I only felt the blossoming of an impulse, which took the form of, "I will write to her!" The scene of reading, of holding a book, touching a page, even lingering over the crystalline glow of screen and the handwork of scrolling through texts: the scene drifts, the flats change, the one writing becomes someone writing to me, and then I become the one who must respond and who wants a response, who deserves a response, who is and always will be the addressee. The one writing becomes the one who can't live without my reply, my recognition, my appreciation. Only I will understand her, hear her, see her—and thus do I supplant her; my reading takes over the writing. I fill the scene with myself; what will begin as a "thank you" will end not with a "you're welcome" but with gifts and laurels and even more luxury, even more light.

Having been moved to write Lydon, I discover through a search that she taught at the University of Wisconsin, Madison: Emerita she is. No email address on the webpage. And then in a book I don't know, about a theorist, Jean-François Lyotard, whose work I know too little, I find this:

> The speakers at the Irvine event also included Mary Lydon, who was to have completed her translation of Lyotard's *Discourse, Figure*. Sadly, she subsequently also passed away just before the twenty-fifth annual IAPL conference in May 2001.

Lydon. Dead. "...also passed away." Also? Lyotard died in 1998. The Irvine event was a memorial for

Lyotard; Lydon was there—yes, I see the scramble of letters, the shared capital "L" and the "Y," the "O" and the "D"; coincidences that make one death of several, make death expand, letter by letter. "Is it not curious?" as she might ask, might have asked of these letters? The passage walks through and over one event ("...also included...") to anticipate another that didn't come to pass ("...was to have completed...") to mark yet another ("...she subsequently also passed away...") that fails to arrive at yet another ("...just before..."). Weaving tenses, the passage enacts the staccato interruptions that death, that passing is—thinking now of trains, planes, and automobiles, vehicles that pass each other, some speeding along as others fall behind, Lydon passing Lyotard passing Hugh J. Silverman; the latter authored the above paragraph. He also dies, sometime later, in 2013. Who can keep up, find their place, know their place and time relative to the times and passages and places of writing and reading? Not me. Or precisely me passing, someday soon enough.

I share my blip of panic, my seventeen years of belated surprise, on Facebook. Having written there as I write here, "I discover that Professor Lydon died some time ago," I ask,

> Is that really some time ago? Or yesterday? Or never, because when reading this 1989 essay, I feel that it's still to

> come; that she is still to come. Thank you, Professor Lydon.

A friend writes in response:

> Amazing to see this! You know Mary was a close friend of my Mother, and she first introduced me to Barthes, Foucault, and much other French critical and feminist theory of that time—when I was a badly educated art student and critical theory had not yet hit the art school curricula. Deeply shaping. She was Irish and also wrote stunningly on Beckett and other Modernist writers. Her book *Skirting the Issue: Essays in Literary Theory* was a deeply felt and observed exploration of literary aesthetics when such things were still discussed. I often wonder what she would make of the current intellectual and cultural climate of the academy today, sigh. But how wonderful she is rediscovered and recognized by deep divers like you! Still, she is becoming.

Skirting the Issue is next to me; within it, the essay on Barthes, Poe, and Freud. We were to have been contemporaries. And now? Whenever that was or is or will be? I stumble around the names and markers: the dates of publication, the dates of death and commemoration, the dates of social media posts—the deeply shaping and deeply felt meeting me, the deep diver—feeling the turbulence caused by the churn of what my friend above calls the "current climate" with my blossomings and impulses: how to live with work that invites and ruins reply, that tells me that I will necessarily fail all tests of synchronization, that teaches me that I am late and only appreciative of the vanquished and *démodé*? Above I offered the hyperbole that Lydon "cannot live without my reply"; neither will she live with it, on it, or for it. Which is wrong, because, as my friend writes, loosely quoting me, "Still, she is becoming." And to quote Barthes, who, when writing about a photograph of his recently deceased mother as a young girl in a winter garden, which Lydon calls instead the *light room*, echoing the French title of the book, *la chambre claire*—about this photograph Barthes gives us the mad and pained superimposition of three tenses, "There she is!" And "She is dead." And "She is going to die." I've always loved the order of these brief sentences, or rather, I love their being out of order, out of chronological order: "she is *going to die*" comes after "she is dead." As though the "going to" were both reprieve and executioner's song, a loop both vicious and to die for. So too must I write about this encounter with Lydon, insofar as her name, in its oh-so-literal inscription, letter by letter, both refers to and fails to refer to this unique being, to Lydon herself, her singularity and singular quality. I never knew her and know very well this not-knowing, this intimate distance.

But here I'm only rediscovering what Lydon, her contemporaries, my mentors, and my beloved Roland Barthes have taught and exemplified, not only in *Camera Lucida*, but also famously in the opening paragraph of "The Death of the Author":

> ...[W]riting is the destruction of every voice, of every point of origin. Writing is that neutral, composite, oblique space where our subject slips away, the negative where all identity is lost, starting with the very identity of the body writing.

How to fall for this destruction, welcome it, write for it, read with it, enact it, and endure it—as death sentence and enabling constraint—knowing that the punctual gathering of origin, of voice, of identity isn't even to be renounced, having never been possible? "I will write to her!" makes all the mistakes, is failure itself and fantasy's very durability. And yet, the death of the author is still the time of your life: the destruction sustains the same pathos, the same panicked lost and found and lost again. "There she is! She is dead. She is going to die." Or rather, in my case: first, "Here she is, in this text, speaking to me now! I will write to her!" and then, "She has slipped away such that she was never there at all, not an origin but an effect, a tissue of quotations, dismembered as she is remembered. The text is always already death; to write is to have died, always already." Finally, "She is going to slip away, will recede and drift and come apart, perpetually, a flicker, a flash, an afterimage, a mirage." The reader who follows this writing, this dizzying invitation both to get over it and hold on to everything, is all echo and no voice.

As a matter of due diligence, and many days after beginning this brief text, I search my own files and am surprised and not surprised to discover Mary Lydon yet again. She was the opening plenary speaker at a conference I attended in early October of 2000, "The Dreams of Interpretation / *The Interpretation of Dreams*," held at the University of Minnesota to commemorate the centennial of Sigmund Freud's dream book. I presented a paper there and no doubt heard her, saw her, perhaps talked to her, shook her hand, touched the hand that writes. Her paper began thusly:

> Thank you very much, John, and I have an impulse before I begin to remember a late dear friend of ours who is always associated for me with the University of Minnesota, who is George Bauer, who is professor of French here for a number of years. [Pause, exhale.]

"Thank you very much, John..." I am not this John, but of course I am addressed, particularly in my desire to be so recognized, in my desire to here share impulses of my own—yes, I wrote "blossoming of an impulse" above *before* I rediscovered Lydon's "I have an impulse." I am called inside out for having prematurely accepted a call—John!—that wasn't meant for me but to which I nonetheless have already answered. This other John, John Mowitt, one of the book's editors, introduced Lydon at the 2000 conference and does so again in the 2007 book that gathers together many of the conference papers. His introduction to her text, which is entitled "Such Stuff as Dreams Are Made of: Freud, Life, and Literature," opens with the above thank you note as an epigraph; Mowitt then narrates their friendship and resuscitates the occasion. After a few pages, he breaks off his commemoration and lets her essay have and be the last word. And, strangely, he and the editors reiterate her extemporaneous framing, this time truncated, polished, and subtly transformed:

> I have an impulse before I begin to remember a late, dear friend of ours, who is always associated for me with the University of Minnesota, who is George Bauer, who was a professor of French for a great number of years.

"[Pause, exhale]" has been dropped, and there are a few additional commas; "John" too has been lost. These are perhaps trivial and expected edits given that Lydon's published text need no longer reference the moment of its public performance. But is it merely coincidental that the repetition of "who is...who is...who is..." in Mowitt's first citation becomes, "who is...who is...who *was*..." in his second? I read and reread these two passages hoping to discover my mistake, but finding John's instead, his not mine. Or someone's. Someone gives me both "*is* a professor..." and "*was* a professor," because melancholia demands one thing ("There she is!") and mourning another ("She is dead."), and I answer to these demands, mixing George and Mary and Lyotard and all the others. The ambiguity neutralizes tense—again—and protests against the rule of either fiction: on the one hand, the fictive literary present, on the other, the fictive simple past.

"There she is! I will write to her!" This declaration not only indexes a contemporary impulse but an older one as well. Curiously, my deep dive into Lydon, into my motives and points of contact, was commanded by Lydon herself, by the encrypted and still echoing voice of one recollecting a dearly departed friend, by one commanded by some-thing to repeat "who is...who is...who is..." And further, always further, when I presented my paper at this conference, a paper on Freud and Hamlet and ghosts, near its end, long after Lydon's plenary, having hidden myself away to write, thus skipping the bulk of the panels and papers, meeting no one, skulking idiotically, unable to join the timely conversations about that untimely thing known as Sigmund Freud, scribbling as though the point were to make my not-even-perfectible paper the enemy of the occasion, which should have been a celebration, a pleasure—when I presented this paper, I forgot to thank my teacher, who was in the room with me, seated right in front of me, beaming and giving all the good graces. She noticed and noted my lapse, asking me later, generously and in private, to account for my oversight, teaching me protocols and kindness as much as registering surprise. And if this returns to me now—resurrected *alongside* the more durable inscriptions—it's precisely because I didn't write to her, didn't acknowledge her in the moment. The timely word failed me and failed us, failing her. And so, it is both curious and no surprise that I would say to myself, "I will write to her!" when feeling at home in the interests of another because I had felt similarly at home on this earlier occasion, treating my teacher as a setting rather than an auditor, a unique being, as a space to fill up with myself rather than as a friend and mentor. If I don't name her here, it's to avoid covering myself with her glories, the spectacle of my circuitous retrieval of good enough conscience being bad enough.

Doubly commanded to write to her, both by Lydon herself and by the above broken promise, my text articulates this command, seeks to follow it dutifully, and even styles itself according to its affection for coincidences. And so, here's the last one. At the end of Mowitt's epigraph I find "[Pause, exhale.]" The bracketed phrase is a closed caption, the two words separated by a comma doing their best to tell me what I would hear were I to listen, as Mowitt presumably has, to a recording of Lydon's opening remarks. I would hear her pause; I would hear her exhale. Or so I imagine and have to imagine. First, a silence, then a breath. But a silence that is a pause, an interval, a hiatus, not an end. And only the breathing out; as though speaking of death and the "great number of years," measure of greatness and attachment, were exhausting and have taken their physical and psychic tolls. Lydon's body, pausing and exhaling, relaxing its grip, letting go, is here noted, that is to say, *notated*, scored; hers is a speaking body performing in excess of its speaking, breaking its pose if only barely: a pause, an exhalation. Mowitt shows something graphically, words and brackets, that give me something to read now about something he heard then. There she is, breathing! I hear her! I see only the brackets, and yet I also hear the brackets. Am I hearing things? I hear their gentle expansion and contraction, or rather, their opening and closing, a soft but pointed click, like the lid of a box snapping shut. In *Camera Lucida* Barthes mentions such a box, a compact, *un poudrier*; it belonged to his mother: "I loved the sound of its lid."

Lydon too loves the sound of this lid, bringing the latter into the mixtape of her essay: the clocks, the two cameras, their ticking and clicking, heard both by Freud's patient and by Barthes—and a few throbbing organs, the ones that share their beatings with and through these devices. The Barthes she quotes above in the passage that moved me to write and that I will quote now in turn comes from the beginning and end of a longer passage. Lydon brackets—as in "put aside temporarily"—the middle, which reads:

> For me, the Photographer's organ is not his eye (which terrifies me) but his finger: what is linked to the trigger of the lens [*ce qui est lié au déclic de l'objectif*], to the metallic shifting of the plates (when the camera still has such things). I love these mechanical sounds in an almost voluptuous way, as if, in the Photograph, they were the very thing—and the only thing—to which my desire clings, their abrupt

> click [*claquement*] breaking through the mortiferous layer of the Pose.

For me, for him, for her, the click is both there and not there, is heard *because* and *as* it is projected, desire clinging and ringing, clanging all these otherwise obdurate bodies, inside and out. The click is less a singular point than a point on a loop, audible now for having been audible before, again and again, the rhythm of a beat, making time as it breaks through the Pose, touching the body under the body. This body, a tender and shaggy thing, exposed, a delicate fabric—this is the bracketed body, which pauses and exhales, commanding me to do the same as I write, as I write to her, my fingers typing these words and touching these sounds. But that would be writing, the writing I've here sought to celebrate, remember, and care for. Mary Lydon, writing.

* * *

Barthes, Roland. *Camera Lucida: Reflections on Photography*. 1st American ed. New York: Hill and Wang, 1981.

Barthes, Roland. *La Chambre Claire: Note Sur La Photographie*. Cahiers Du CinéMa Gallimard. Paris: Gallimard, 1980.

Lydon, Mary. *Skirting the Issue: Essays in Literary Theory*. Madison, Wis.: University of Wisconsin Press, 1995.

Lydon, Mary. “Such Stuff as Dreams Are Made of: Freud, Life, and Literature.” In *The Dreams of Interpretation*. A Century Down the Royal Road, 357–66: University of Minnesota Press, 2007.

Silverman, Hugh J. *Lyotard: Philosophy, Politics, and the Sublime*. Continental Philosophy. New York: Routledge, 2002.

Walker Rutter-Bowman

My *Jernigan*

My copy of *Jernigan* is the Vintage Contemporaries paperback edition. The back cover has a matrix of dots in the top right corner, a black-and-white author photo of David Gates holding his face, his pinkie sneaking under his octagonal glasses. The blurry front cover shows a man. The sleeves of his white oxford are rolled up; his arms are crossed. Unfortunately, the cover does not have one of those lurid Rick Lovell illustrations, like the cover of *Taking Care* with its palm-tree covered in snow, or the wonderfully trippy cover of *Airships* with a giant jet-winged saxophone screaming across the sky. If put to the task, Lovell would've had a field day with *Jernigan*. A tipped-over gin bottle in the foreground, clear spirits soaking into a tufty lawn? A rabbit hutch with a pistol resting on a wooden crate? A little cabin in the snow, flames shooting from the roof—and in an upstairs window, two heedless teens making love? In the background, faintly, the Manhattan skyline, etched against a sunset blazing like a smashed peach?

I know my copy of *Jernigan* well. Its interior gives off a sweet almond-y smell with a sour, yogurt-like finish. The pages are yellowing near the edges at their oxidized border. A dozen or so shadowy mold-speckles dot the top. The pages, once crisp and white, are faded and coarse. These Vintage Contemporaries books have laminated covers to give them a nice sheen, and when they are handled too much, like my *Jernigan*, the laminate starts to ruffle and curl at the corners, and little parallel ridge-lines form along the edge in a fringe of wrinkling plastic. There are small punctures from the few times I held the book between my teeth.

Like all books, it bears the impressions and damages inflicted by its readers. Books like *Jernigan* are battered witnesses to the ungentle act of reading. For me, most books do not go quietly—do not broadcast themselves, whole and immaculate, to my ready mind. Reading requires the body's participation. It is an exertion, an extraction, and its physical circumstances are consequential. Just as *Jernigan*, a vulnerable paperback, is susceptible to physical changes, so am I, the reader, at the mercy of physical factors. Peter Jernigan, the novel's protagonist, is at their mercy, too. As a reader, Jernigan strives to sit in the right chair, be the right temperature, drink the right amount of coffee, the right amount of gin. For him, reading can be calm and sedentary, but not passive. It requires fine-tuning, active calibration. I too am that kind of restless reader, trying to find the fortuitous harmony of circumstances that will make me my best version.

I read *Jernigan* on my grey couch, its arms pilling where my cat has thrashed them. I read *Jernigan* amid a bout of back pain, between fistfuls of ibuprofen—like Peter Jernigan himself, who gulps down his girlfriend's Pamprins to quell the pain from his hangover and self-induced bullet wound. I read *Jernigan* with coffee, always coffee. I read *Jernigan* on the Amtrak, the Lake Shore Limited, letting my gaze slide off the page and onto the passing scenery: the Palisades and the Hudson River, the grey blocks of West Point, the red brick Hudson-Athens lighthouse, the knitted metal Hudson walkway, the arching white Kingston-Rhinecliff Bridge; the brittle trees, the steely water, the foamy clouds. I read Jernigan at my girlfriend's uncle's house, in Vermont, on the couch by the window where the jade plant explodes, with a smelly lab lying on my feet like a Chicago overcoat. I read *Jernigan* in my attic apartment in Syracuse, now and then peeping between the pines that scrape the windows to watch students drive their cars like Hot Wheels up and down the Clarendon hill. Then once more back to the grey couch, the bad cat, and my scratchy blanket—not unlike a blanket Jernigan might drape over his legs on a winter night, reading his Wodehouse by the dying fire, the stove growing cold.

Jernigan is so much about reading and what happens when one is attentive—or, more appropriately, inattentive—to the surrounding world. Peter Jernigan thinks of himself as a keen observer and an intelligent interpreter of his surroundings. And he can be. But Peter Jernigan is an unreliable reader. He is blindered, unfocused, cavalier. He misreads the extent of his grief, the authoritarian grip of his addiction, and the emotional needs of others. He tries to read people: his son, his girlfriend, himself. He tries to read a book: Wodehouse. In fact, my favorite scene in the novel is Jernigan's late-night communion with *Leave It to Psmith*. It begins when Martha, Jernigan's girlfriend, comes home from work and tells him that the forecast calls for an overnight frost. They'll lose the tomatoes if they don't harvest them now. Jernigan decides he needs coffee before he can harvest anything. "Isn't it going to keep you awake?" asks Martha, but Jernigan ignores her. He reheats some coffee, splashes in some cream, guzzles it down, and joins Martha among the tomatoes. That night, Martha sleeps easily; Jernigan, caffeinated, lies awake. His mind races. He'll be up all night unless he does something about it—and Jernigan is a man of action. He goes downstairs with his Wodehouse. To make himself drowsy he decides to tuck into the gin, sipping straight from the bottle rather than "doling it out...by the mingy glassful." Inching his way down the bottle, he starts to get a little drowsy. But now the Wodehouse has gotten good. He doesn't want to stop reading. He finishes off what's left of the reheated coffee and makes a fresh pot. He sips from the gin and coffee in competing measures. His mind dilates and contracts; his senses soften, sharpen. He believes he can perfectly calibrate his mental states: a little languor from alcohol, some buzzy focus from caffeine. Now he can happily follow Freddie Threepwood and Psmith. The Wodehouse takes hold. Really, the Wodehouse is just a flimsy cover for a discrete bender: in the morning he's drunk, raving. Struck by a fatherly impulse, he tries to lecture the kids on responsibility before they go to school, saying things like, "Let's see if we can't agree on what the nature of our contract actually is." Martha can tell he's utterly pickled. She steps in: "You're not making very much sense," she says.

Perhaps I found this scene so penetrating because I read it while furiously trying to calibrate my own stimulant package. Later in the book, the narrator looks at himself as "Jernigan micromanaging his consciousness"—that rings so true to my reading self. While the novel presents a portrait of addiction—the hunger, the self-manipulation, the tricks to skirt or short-circuit the better powers of reason—it also shows the lengths a reader might go to be his or her best thinking self. For some, the unaccompanied story is good enough; for others, some chemical aid paves the way. Jernigan hopes he can ping-pong between upper and downer and land at last on a golden mean, a state of attention worthy of Wodehouse. It is a quest to find the ur-reader within, an earnest search for the traces of his true reader—the most acute, most present, and most attentive.

The reading scene in *Jernigan* is, like most good fiction, set on the physical plane. But reading is difficult to dramatize. Drama is born of action, or a series of actions, or a failure to act. Reading is an action, but a largely hidden one. Movies, for instance, struggle to capture reading's potency; they opt to over-spice the drama with an implausible big sigh, sharp gasp, or chilling cry. In *Jernigan*, Gates presents the circumstances of reading, its bells and whistles, as far more interesting than the content of the reading material. He doesn't really tell us what Jernigan thinks of Wodehouse, opting instead to create a scene alive and rich with sensory detail and attention to the body. I like to think the scene's antecedent is Isabel Archer's fireside vigil in *The Portrait of a Lady*. Like Jernigan, Isabel stays awake to read, though not a book. Instead, she reads her cruel and calculating husband, Osmond, whom she has misjudged: "she had not read him right." In a silent drawing room Isabel leans back in her chair. The fire smolders, the candles gutter. She thinks of Osmond, who does not love her, and Ralph, who does. Even though we follow Isabel's mind as it tours the wreckage of her marriage, we never lose our physical bearings: a chilly, spacious drawing room, the rigid chair, the dying fire flicking its heat and orange-red light across the dark floor, a beautiful woman hunched before the glow, skirts bunched around her legs, face pale and drawn with agitation, motionless but for her mind, spinning like a top.

In *Jernigan* the physical landscape is just as vividly realized: a worn couch with a rough throw; the clang of a saucepan as Jernigan makes a fresh pot of coffee; the sappy zing of gin; the feel of the wood slats on the Morris chair; the yellow glow from the lamp; the orb of heat from the woodstove; and, eventually, "branchy webs of frost on the windowpanes." Like Isabel's, his mind is restless, violent in its roving. Both scenes present moments of heightened perception and uncommon emotional fervor. For her, it is that fever of agitation: "Her mind, assailed by visions, was in a state of extraordinary activity." Jernigan, too, is haunted, assailed by specters of self-hatred, urging him towards self destruction:

> Now, probably at the same time I was up reading P.G. Wodehouse in the Morris chair, some rock-and-roll star in New York was speedballing coke and heroin and getting sucked off, as flunkies stuck needles into both arms, by a groupie in a leather skirt. Okay. But who's to say I wasn't as close to my edge as he to his?

I am not them—not Isabel Archer, Peter Jernigan, Henry James, or David Gates. My scene of reading *Jernigan* underwhelms, though I too strive to draw out my best reader within. I choose and scale the stimulants that will prime me to read: I drink a cup of coffee and read seventeen pages, then decide another cup of coffee is in order. I drink another cup of coffee and read thirty-one pages, then decide another cup of coffee is in order. I drink another cup of coffee and read four pages. But now I've had too much. My hands are shaking. My stomach whimpers. I can feel every filling, the backs of my eyelids, my heart blasting away like field artillery. I should eat something, I decide, so I prepare breakfast. I think of drunk Jernigan marveling at "the springy snap of the toaster's lever." I eat too much toast. Now I feel drowsy, too. I consider a post-toast cup of coffee. I return to *Jernigan*.

The drama is minimal: I am just a man on a couch, legs crossed, one leg slowly going numb.

He holds the book in his hands: the thumb and pinkie of his left hand contacting the splayed pages, his three other fingers bracing the front cover, spine, back cover. His right arm is crossed over his torso, his right hand cupping his left elbow in a show of support. He is sleepy, but he keeps reading. He reads a passage and, barely awake, has a small dream, a mini-explosion in which his mind conflates the fiction with itself. He sits up straighter. He takes a sip of water. Some water dribbles down his lip and onto his shirt, forming a wet mark shaped like Florida. He remembers going to Florida once. Sanibel, Captiva. Then another time: Jupiter, Tampa, whatever's in between. Thinking of Florida, he's read several paragraphs without processing the words. He backtracks. He finds a familiar sentence, swings around it to resume the forward trudge. He has to focus. He has to pee. The need to pee will help him focus. He runs his fingers through his tangled hair. He rolls a loose hair into a tight hairball, places it on the arm of the couch, watches it roll off like a tumbleweed. Finally, he gets to turn a page.

My fidgety reading habits are symptoms of the same hope Jernigan harbors: that, arranged properly, the physical factors will yield a more direct channel to the reading mind. As readers, we hope for reading to show its transporting power, for a book to flip its alchemical switch: a rectangular stack of paper and glue becomes a peopled, detailed world. Readers remember their most engrossing reading experiences: another world appears, the real world fades. When it does, the physical trappings of reading fade, too. The experience of the mind overshadows the experience of the body. The mind announces its achievement: I have read a book! I have been exalted, changed! It takes all the credit. The dutiful body stays quiet, makes no claims to what it has endured at the hands of the novel. But I would like to give credit where credit is due. I do not want to forget what my body did for *Jernigan*, and I think *Jernigan* wants to give credit to bodies. It wants its readers to honor the physical toil of reading. It wants them to remember what it has impressed upon the flesh: the contortions in chair or chaise or recliner; the beverages, hot and cold; the naps, voluntary or not; the sedentary discomforts, and all the consequent wiggles and stretches, crackings and cranings, massagings and pickings and itchings. If nothing else, let this essay testify to what books have wrought on bodies. My body. By the smallest increments, reading *Jernigan* has made me older, shorter, less flexible. More blind. More stooped, arthritic. But I am glad it bears the stamp of *Jernigan*. So, I say, thank you, body. Let it be known that this essay is a space to honor you, to value the work you do, to lament the damage done to you by books, and to warn you: there may still be danger ahead.

* * *

One morning, when I finish *Jernigan*, read that final line of grudging pride—"I stand up and say: Jernigan"—I think of standing to announce my name. I stand up and say: Rutter-Bowman. I stand up and say: Walker. I stand up and say: thank you. Gratitude is perhaps the best note to end on—gratitude towards Peter Jernigan and David Gates; gratitude towards my patient body; gratitude towards coffee beans, couches, cats. I would like the feeling to last, to linger, to suffuse me with a rare new energy, driving me back to the book's beginning: the blurry man on the cover, the first line, "I ended up driving all night." I'll end up reading all morning, all day. I'll re-read, taken by the title's sonic suggestion: *journey again, journey begin*. I'll blitz through it, this book Heller called "a sizzler of a novel." But sizzle or no, the feeling fades. My back hurts, my coffee is gone, my cat demands attention. It has started to rain, and all my windows are open. Peter Jernigan has experienced a major life event: despite his best efforts, he has survived. And I have too. I have read another book.

Luc Rioual

As Sand Itself

For years I have been preoccupied with beginnings and lineage: with pedigrees. Appropriately, I will depart from and return to this.

First, I would like to talk about the opening of Harold Brodkey's novel, *The Runaway Soul.* Like a fugitive friend or foe, a truant lover, a sibling lost—to difference, to distance, to spite—it has haunted me since I first took stabs at its wily heft and the life of Wiley Silenowicz, the narrator who bears no small resemblance to the late Brodkey himself.

Some requisite accounting: on 25 October 1930, Harold Brodkey was born Aaron Roy Weintraub, in (either) Staunton or Alton, Illinois, later adopted by his junkie father's second-cousins, Joseph and Doris Brodkey of University City, IL, after the death of his birth-mother, Ceil, when he was two. When Harold was nine, Joseph had a heart attack—or stroke (the documentation is unclear)—and was an invalid until his death five years later, one year after Doris came down with cancer. Harold went on to Harvard at sixteen, later landed his first story in *The New*

Yorker—where he was even later on staff, writing essays and *Talk of the Town* bits while he and his novel in-progress were a talk of the town themselves—and then went on to endure a long, complicated life of (arguably) intermittent publication, confusing prestige, and never-ending rumor, eventually dying of AIDS on 26 January 1996, in New York. One could contend his life—so thoroughly reduced and ordered here, by me, into biographical fragments like the bits and bobs of a written-down war—was a series of placements, displacements, and replacements—genetic, familial, religious, geographical, social, educational, sexual, cultural, so on and on—only secured ("fixed or fastened," "protected against attack or other criminal activity") by well-built habits of reading and writing: drilled means of intellection: decades of discipline: procedures of orientation like practicing somersaults for gym class; writing and reading: these acts are—like that wire, unnecessary for normal operation, but whose third point of connectivity provides safety from hazardous shock—grounding.

"I was slapped and hurried along in the private applause of birth—I think I remember this. Well, I imagine it anyway—" is how the book begins: an act of placement and its instantaneous, vital disruption. It continues: "—the blind boy's rose-and-milk-walled (and salty) aquarium, the aquarium overthrown, the uproar in the woman-barn..." where now, not memory, but metaphor is overturned, the Ceiling of maternal water broken, the boy subjected to the irrevocable, wooden landscape of man, "...the awful contamination of actual light. I think I remember the breath crouched in me and then leaping out yowlingly: this uncancellable sort of beginning." ("I long to be free—desperately free. Free as the stillborn are free," said Emil Cioran, Romanian philosopher writing in French, in 1973.)

The Runaway Soul is also the namesake of what it designates: the particulars of its own genesis: published in 1991, it emerged from the weighty breadths of *A Party of Animals*, once called *The Animal Corner*—what writer and editor Gordon Lish has called a superior book to its mostly maligned and neglected progeny, not to leave out major praise from Harold Bloom, Denis Donoghue, Don DeLillo, Susan Sontag, and countless other authorial hands—in what amounted to several-thousand pages of manuscript, and thirty-years of labor, aborted. A 1986 *Washington Post* profile of Brodkey by (current) *New Yorker* editor David Remnick, cites the opening lines as then being: "I remember crawling naively and being slapped and hurried and rolled along in the private applause of birth—the applause was that of my mother. Do I remember this?" or—Brodkey had not yet decided—"Imagine a mind shaped like a person." Even then, twenty-some-odd years deep into the weight of memory and manner—recall or performance—he had not determined which should come first: the body, or the mind: Harold the orphan, or Harold the Harvard Boy? And is this not the distinction on our hands: the contrast between the furrows of one's bloodline or birthright, and their refined, daily being? between the given and the chosen?

Let's put down one H for another: let us consider Helen DeWitt—another writer for whom my preoccupation has no known limits—and her first (published) novel, *The Last Samurai*, a book she wanted to call (and was denied doing so by her publishers), after the Kurosawa film featured so prominently in her book and the lives of its characters', *Seven Samurai*. DeWitt's parents were diplomats, and she spent much of her youth scattered about Central America. She attended Smith College where she dropped out twice, eventually finishing her undergraduate degree and D.Phil at Oxford. *Samurai* (or "Opus 101" as she has apparently taken to calling it) began—or began to emerge as we have it—from a phone conversation with her father wherein he "harangued" her, and DeWitt found herself feeling: "We don't pick our parents." "If I had picked a father, I wouldn't have picked somebody like you." This, in a way, maps for us the trajectory of the novel: single-mother Sibylla (a loose reference to the epigraph in Eliot's *The Wasteland*, from Petronius' *Satyricon*: "Sibyl, what do you want?" "άπσΘνειν Θελω": I want to die) raises Ludo by herself under the auspices of J.S. Mill's nineteenth-century education—ancient Greek at three!—and the masculine influence of *Seven Samurai*. Ancient Greek lives in the book, and the film embeds itself in the characters' lives, providing through its plot a methodology, a framework by which her son Ludo performs DeWitt's preliminary question—the germ, by way of Henry James, of her novel—searching out and scrutinizing potential fathers, hoping to elect the one best suited for him. "If we fought with real swords I would kill you," time and again, he finds.

We can even add to this register William H. Gass—another thirty-year-novel St. Louis man, son to a loudmouth racist and fierce drunk—and his more crass articulation of these troubles: "I decided, as one of my characters says, to pick another cunt to come from."

I, myself, spent the better part of a year writing an essay I envisioned and intended as a *Preface to All Future Work*. It was concerned with these questions—this query into pedigree: into the personal: into our collective, communal topic: reading, but also writing—but more of their underlying tenor and tremor: my ambition, and its interwoven woes of guilt and shame. My pedigree—the ironies of my formal education, the years that laurel my name, not lost on me—has never felt up to snuff.

I thought, recently, to write about the lists I keep: as I read, I write down words that strike me sonically, logically, visually, associatively, words I don't know and words I do, on the reverse side of grocery store and library receipts, against bad habits of processed-sugar, procrastination, and forgetfulness: attempts at rounding up my holdings all dispersed. I (re)write them to rewrite them, once again, later.

From Rick Moody's book—principally concerned with these questions of *whence I come* and its countless honorifics, his own title taken from Nathaniel Hawthorne—*The Black Veil*, or what little of it I've read, there are these: wrench (v.), eccentricities, school (v.), refold, acronym, purveyor, inheritance, peregrination, motor function, cellophane, rebellion, portfolio, anthem, ballad, milestone, indomitable, pension, curfew, shoptalk. I did not write down the word *patrimony* from page eleven, but it was with that word and its appetites that I began this essay (v.).

I work through other's words, poaching with adoration and intent: it is from their scraps I feed. This process of criminal transcription is my private "assay of bias": a phrase filched from *Hamlet*, brought to my life by poet Arthur Freeman chanced on two-years ago who knows how, but whose lines "But conquest is as sand itself, which slips / from fist to fist and remains sand" have never left. I do not hold the lines and the words so much as they, too, move between my fists.

Hugh Kenner quoting Yeats in his *The Elsewhere Community*:

...Better go down upon your-marrow
 bones
And scrub a kitchen pavement, or break
 stones
Like an old pauper, in all kinds of weather;
For to articulate sweet sounds together
Is to work harder than all these, and yet
Be thought an idler by the noisy set
Of bankers, schoolmasters, and clergymen
The martyrs call the world.

I wanted the essay, the preface, to be an announcement of my arrival, of my (re)birth: a forewarning of my presence at the dinner table whose hierarchy I (still) intend to climb—or, better: dispel the illusion thereof—but also a detachment from my cast(e): a way of shedding (or covering) skin: of dropping off my cross: of showing I had left *there*, and I belong *here*; I felt a need to brandish my new documentation: to flash, against the moon shine, my phony passport and its homemade stamps of approval.

The question is: why have I decided that my means of entry—that my folded wallet papers—must be fraudulent? would be perceived as an imitation? that I would never be granted a sanctioned entrance? kosher, halal, organic documentation?

The answer is complicated and, to some degree, immaterial; however, in short: a life of the mind is a dramatic deviation both from the key-print of my pedigree—immigrant, blue-collar, boozy, and timid—and its lofty aspirations for me: I was, like so many, to relinquish the heavy drapes of poverty and foul labor to become a doctor or a lawyer, windfalls and waysides of my poor handwriting and weakness for combative reasoning (not to discount the possible profit sharing for the brood). They would never themselves say this, but that is how it felt. I even followed the requisite routes—a New England Liberal Arts School and an Ivy League, a process which has flooded me with ever-swelling debt, more than $200,000 worth invested in "my invisible house," as I once read fellow nose-dive debtor, ivory-alumna, and interloper Tupelo Hassman call it—but, in truth, I, the boy who once forged his mother's signature all across the dotted lines of his Cub Scout handbook, had already wandered off the reservation and stolen himself into another land where he now—here—roams. There: here: he has no job, no prospects, no clear providence, and little money: only words are in wealth.

It would be foolish to overlook the implications of these writer's upbringings and my (at first unrelated) admiration of them: these matters are as clearly entwined as their lives are in their work. They were—and are—by some measure, constellations from which to pull stars and reshape the sky, assembling new orders with the borrowed pieces; they are connective tissues: comrades in encroachment: partners in provocation: guideposts by which to walk in this open dark.

In a way, it has felt like a problem of hunger: I outgrew my terracotta pot. All the same, it was and is a larger matter of perspective: years of fear aside, I have never once had to go without food. (I have only ever chosen to.) But my taste has also changed. I ate my first grape at twenty. Twelve friends of varying emotional proximity stood around me. They asked me what it tasted like, and I told them, "Like an apple."

"I was supposed to have been a rich boy in some better world," said Michael Silverblatt in a 1991 interview with Brodkey, who responded, "Me too." I often wonder, myself, what this would be like: to not live under the heavy thumb of missed fortune.

In 1986, Harold was asked, "How did you get by all those years?" How did he get by without the grandeur and paying press of the (real) Great Male Narcissists™? His response? "I am an incredibly good dinner guest."

"Me too," I say.

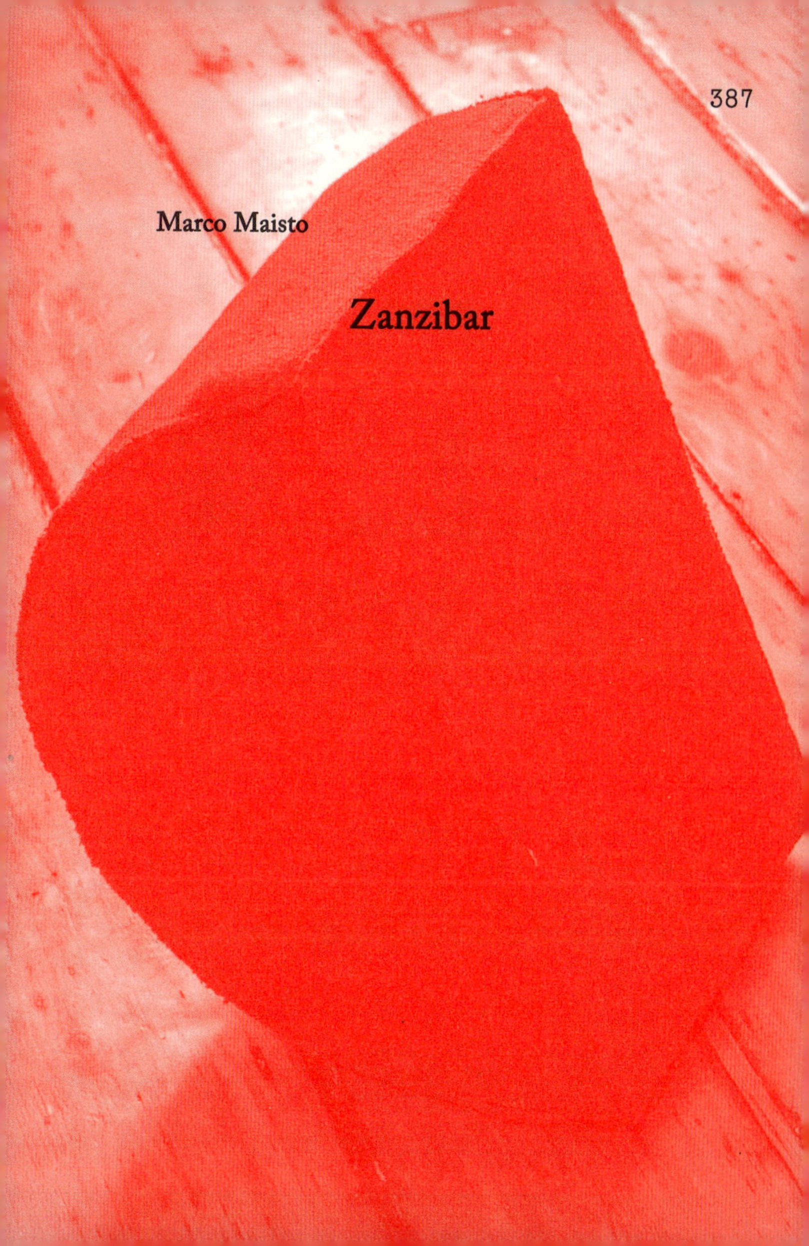

Marco Maisto

Zanzibar

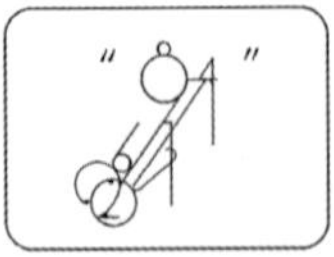

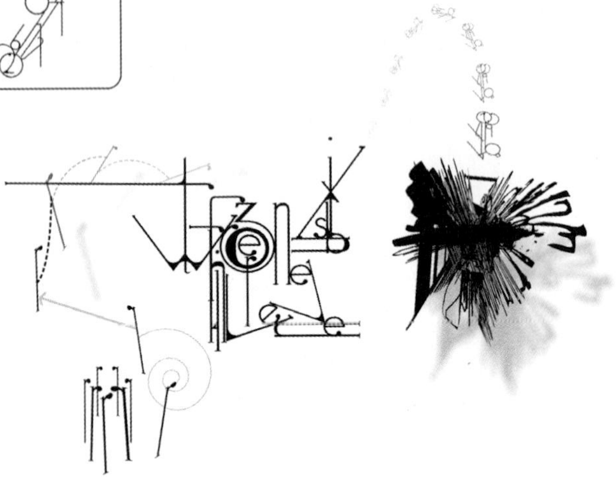

Desire and Counting ("0=10" + "0=10") In the machine above, a reader is represented by the Fibonacci spiral seducing anerrant letter /r/.

(/r/ = the author, or, in this case, the mechanic.)

Drones stare at me all the time. I can't wait for 25 years to go by.

Z A N Z I B A R

In my experience this engagement in ambient reading is (not was, because in recounting it I reenact it) about space, ontology, engagement, emotion and escape. In other words, the world. These notes ought to be outfitted with a narrative or some expository glue that would translate my experience to the reader, for sure. Perhaps that's a follow-up project.

Instead, I'm reconstructing some of what surfaced that night and leaving things there, hoping that the re-reader will find or assemble whichever story she pleases. In fact, since my experience at the reading room was ultimately a creative, rhizomatic, personal and alien one (almost pushing reading itself to the periphery), I think that the fragments, little things, and captured ((re-)stolen) holdings that follow are the most appropriate gift I can give-forward : some-things that I happily relinquish ownership of, that some-one may make with them.

Like I said, this experience is about space. For me at least. And it's my hope that by linking some aspects of conceptual space (the space of book, the escape-space of a note book, the almost-living spaces of a storm and a dying (?) relationship, the space designed to contain and power all possible spaces (that room)) to my personal experience, it will somehow depersonalize that experience. These intensely particular and yet wildly disparate (dispersed?) items have been made strange enough so they can be yours. I hope you enjoy the quick read that is this unfinished map or mathless diagram. May it be, for the reader, an othering space; a heterotopia (I read Foucault that night) of proto-sequential (I read Matt Kindt and Deleuze & Guattari too) space made out of soft subversions, foul weather, loss, art (I drew) and a dreamless sleep at which point I will have been long gone leaving you to figure out what comes next. Let me know how it turns out.
From a place of love,
--MM

Did you ever have a dream that was like a story?

And at the end of the dream there's a twist ending?

How can your mind do that to you?

You're creating the dream.

How can you surprise yourself?

("Mind MGMNT")

It's pouring. And cold. I'm wet; I should cancel.

I brought too many books. I always do. How is it I remembered to make MIND MGMNT one of—what?—7 or 8 things I took in my bag?

I bring vol 1., because I'm finally at vol 6., but need to reread something from an earliert time.
Away from home: 2 weeks.

There hasn't been weather—any—for weeks.

Books, diagrams, notes of every kind are things you can use to introduce a surprise ending as your body and you move forward in time. There's a knock on the door.

Ghost-town.
Heartland.
Heart room,
Heart blooms.

Returning to a ~~familiar story~~ story you have read before because that world is still how you left it. It's still raining on page 27. It's pouring outside this tiny, perfect alcove. He turns to page 40. It's sunny there.

~~Everyone goes to Zanzibar to live in permanent amnesia.~~
This is the ultimate witness protection program.

It's pouring. And cold. I'm wet; I should cancel.

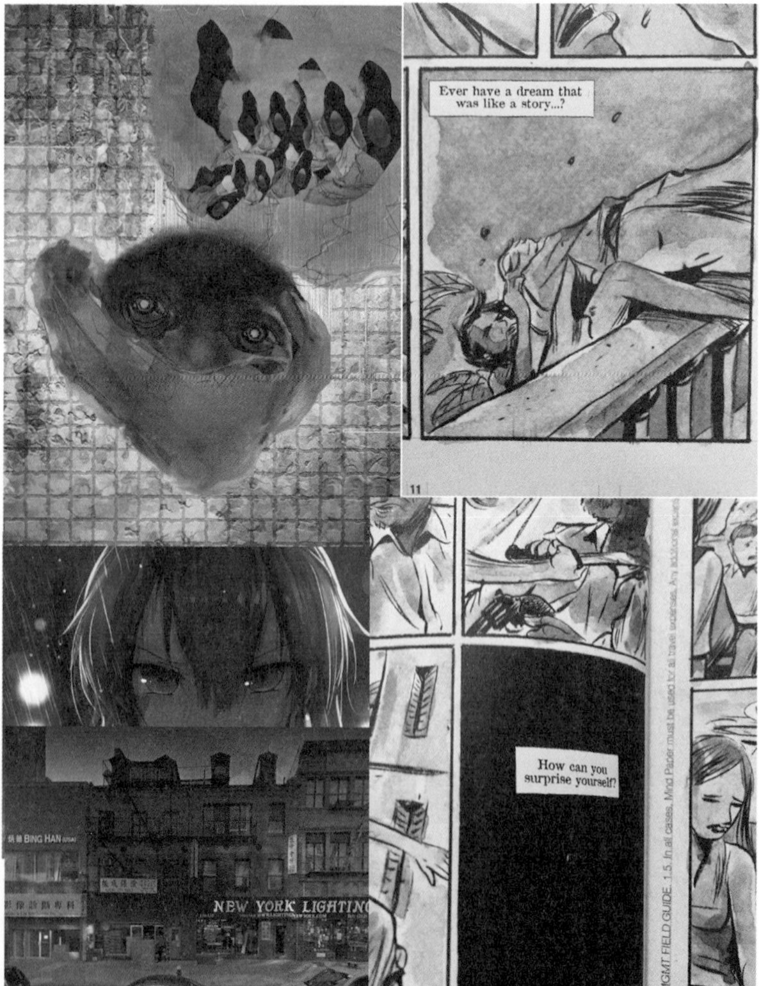
Ever have a dream that was like a story...?
11
BING HAN
NEW YORK LIGHTIN
How can you surprise yourself?
MIND MGMT FIELD GUIDE 1.5. In all cases, Mind Paper must be used for all travel expenses.

This room is designed to stop the body, (but not erase it) so that the mind can move at whatever speed it wants to.

We stopped living four years ago and forgot everything everything everything so we could live together; our

I've never left the apartment because of a fight before now. Certainly never agreed to sleep at a hotel instead. I'm going to be tired. Can a lover

hearts were heavy, sunburned, dripping wet bookmarks we used to stop each others' story dead in its tracks.

There's no weather in the mind in Zen meditation, and a forgotten body is the meterological precondition of satori. But this room is a low-pressure system of all previous and future minds, and while the body is elsewhere, it is an elsewhere too far for sitting zazen. When you thought there could be nothing more holy than a zendo, you find yourself here.

slow down so I can catch you

slow down so I can catch you

Every handmade cushion is a miniature zendo; together they are a poem to the room. My heartbeat is a metrical assemblage, a refrain, a communication, a battery, a wife, or no, a bride.

further dimensionalizes the act of reading. Reading and heterotopia.

oh god, let's go.

We might as well be Tibet, reading a travel guide to Zanzibar that running out of disappearing ink.

Foucault’s heterotopia, Deleuze & Guattari’s refrain and more, Baudrillard’s grandfather clock, my lover, across town making changes to an entirely different book than mine.

HETEROTOPIA : THE RAIN BECAME AN OCEAN

A READING ROOM :: THE OCEAN

THIS READING ROOM : THE ABSENCE OF ALL ROOMS.

It’s pouring. And cold. I’m wet;
I should cancel.

It’s pouring. And cold. I’m wet;
I should cancel.

“In civilizations without ships, dreams dry up; espionage takes the place of adventure, the police that of corsairs.”–MF

It’s pouring. And cold. I’m wet;
I should cancel.

It’s pouring. And cold. I’m wet;
I should cancel.

The unnatural energy
found in books.

I’m trying.
Baby.

Foucault’s ocean is the standing wave of ink
you’ve drown the city in. I draw “the city in.”

Here, reading is more than an escape from the here and now.
Here, the novel space novelizes the reading material.

Fallingasleepfunny in a
runawaystory.

Slow down.
Hey, slow. . .

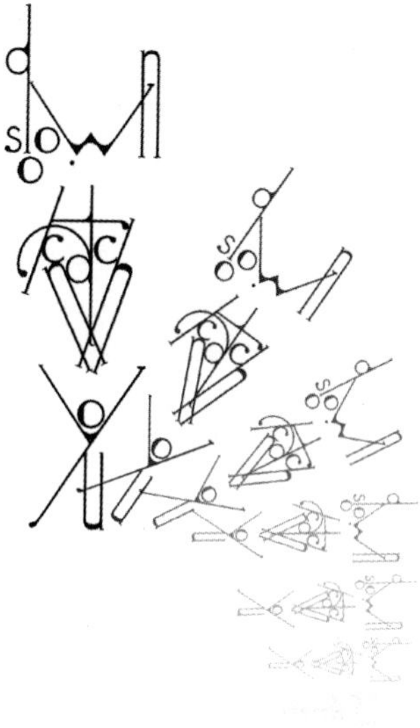

Something less than a knock, more than a bird vocalization: Sal’s home.

~~*DOES ANYTHING REALLY END?*~~

I haven't gone home in 6 months. I draw that. Six months silent in rain. Longer, in these texts, longer lost in some tender textiles sewn above the Chinese light shop.

Returning to a ~~familiar story~~ story you have read before because that world is still how you left it. It's still raining on page 27. It's pouring outside this tiny, perfect alcove. He turns to page 40. It's sunny there.

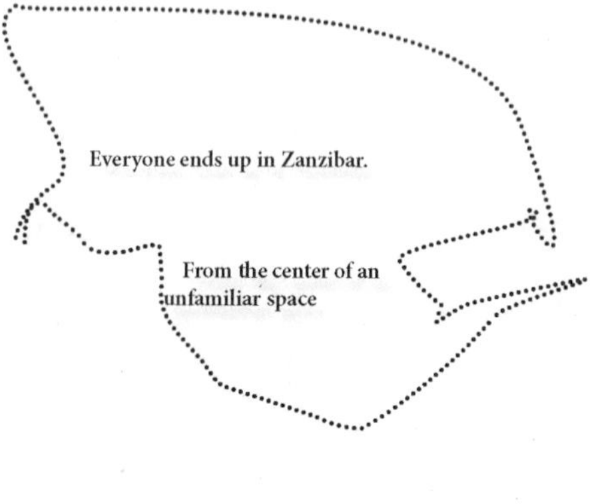

Eva Barbarossa

Reading Adelphi

Reading has always been for me a sort of practical cartography.

– Alberto Manguel, *A History of Reading*, 2014

Reading is a morning activity. I begin an hour or so before dawn. The sky is still dark, no hint yet of the blue morning to come. I make a coffee, then I choose what suits me, what author and which book, then I sit down on the flat's threadbare red sofa.

Rarely is there a book to complete, one I left unfinished yesterday. I prefer to read books in a single sitting; I like to swallow them whole. But the books themselves, stacked on every surface, closed or even open, are not enough on their own. I want to live with their contents, and with their authors' lives, in multiple ways.

Across the room from me is an eight-foot-wide wall I painted with chalkboard paint. The wall allows words, some of them, to escape their pages, to hover, to keep their eye on me as I keep my eye on them. It enables me to *see* what I read in a space where I can think outside myself. The wall collects fragments, ideas, and tangents, anything I want to consider and reconsider.

At the base of the wall, in that odd way of old NYC tenement spaces, is a storage locker. Three feet high, it presents as a stage. I step up to engage with my chalkboard, I climb off and step back a pace or two for a view of the whole.

The chalkboard seems to have its own ideas, and a will too. I often find myself standing on the locker, chalk in hand but nothing particular in mind; suddenly I write out a passage from a book, something that has stuck with me. I map a timeline or network graph. I list books I need to buy. I translate words I want to hold in two or three or four languages at once. I draw maps of former worlds. I hang photos of authors, usually long dead.

The wall is an extension, a prosthesis. It is my mind outside my mind.

The wall, always present, its content, always changing, makes reading happen outside of me, not just on the page or in my mind. The experience is spatial and temporal; always shifting, malleable.

Over the first year, I cover and re-cover the wall. In February, while I read the thirty-seven Russian authors in the catalog, I fill its space with historical timelines, from Ivan the Great to the present day. I list every key Russian author—not just those in the catalog. I note their dates of birth and death, their causes of death. I add notes on dissidents, acts of violence, ignored authors. Using chalk of a different color, I map the gulags where many of these writers found themselves. With each book the wall changes, asking new questions, adding new data. A Russian friend puts up the Cyrillic alphabet; now I can see the shape of the letters, and imagine how the names were written. I doubt I get them right; my mistakes do not diminish the pleasure I take in making the shapes and sounds.

Sometimes I fall asleep on the stage below the wall. When I awake I find the bottom few lines of notes have rubbed off on my leg. I rewrite them from the chalk ghosts they've left. As I begin to sleep beneath the words more frequently, instead of in my bed, I take care not to write all the way to the bottom of the wall. Then, instead, I begin leaving notes on that part of the wall that I wish to absorb through my skin—beautiful words, meaningful words, invading my thoughts and dreams through my eyes and ears, and through my flesh as well.

I begin to read the books out loud and find I want to read them in more than one language. How does the sound of the language change the meaning of the book? How is Simenon different in English, in Italian, from the original French? I want to read the Russians in French as well as

English. And what of the translations? I want to read more than one English translation of a given book, to experience the subtle mysteries captured as a work shifts from author to translator and among multiple translators into a single language.

One night I copy a poem onto the wall. In the act of copying a poem or a bit of a book to this large-scale format, I discover a different type of reading: that of ingestion, and, at times, performance. I copy the poem in translation, in English, not Italian, and I begin to imagine and map what the Italian would look like. I attempt to reverse engineer what was in the mind of the translator. I attempt to recreate an atomic view of this project, small to large; words, phrases, paragraphs, each building to the next. It is the same as what I am attempting with this project; to recreate a history of this creation, by author, by translator, by publisher. First, each constellation; then, a cosmos.

This cosmos is a spiritual landscape. What, I ask myself, is the essence that holds these books together? How do they combine and recombine to create stories which intertwine? With each book not just the story of the author, but the story of the emergence of the book, of the event or series of events which drove the author to its creation. Each question I ask myself is a thread to more questions, and, being in no rush, I pull all the threads and wade slowly through these books.

The existence of this catalog, and its structure, presents me with a mystery. What was the vision of the publisher? How did he choose these books? How did he decide their order? What meaning does he create with his choices? I think, perhaps if I read each one, in the order in which they were published, I might find I understand what he is trying to say, to tell us. I might have a vision not only of the mysteries of his view, but of my own internal mysteries as well. I wish to follow his path, to see what the view is from mine. The path that, as I continue to read, I am certain is not a path, but a mosaic of some as yet unseen constellation.

This reading project began with a small book called *The Art of Publishing*, in which Roberto Calasso speaks of the creation of the Adelphi publishing house, and of this series in particular. (I am not without a guide in my quest.) The Adelphi publishing house and Calasso were known to me. Calasso has long been a scholar and author whom I admire, whose books I read. But it was this book which handed me a mystery I wanted to solve. And so I decided to compress sixty-four years of publishing into what I initially thought would be two years of reading. Now, of course, I understand it will never really end. There is no time frame for completion. The path has changed me, and this project will never be complete. I am half done; I will always be half done.

With each book I add to my map, my constellation. But there is always another dimension, another view of history, a different geography of creation. Layer after layer. At its simplest, a history of the house and of the publisher, but it continues into the depths. As I look at how the authors intertwined in the world: who knew whom, where they wrote their books, who took their coffee in the same cafe, who sat on the same hill, it becomes personal to each of them, as well. So what becomes a personal cartography for me, wrapped into history, is also the map of an outsider, one peering into the perspective of another, one who can never know.

In two years I have read 371 books, most in several versions. In a reading project of 700 books, reading each one two or three times, it becomes clear why there is no end in sight. To read like this for the rest of my life, however, is not a complaint, it is a gift. I haven't yet a map or a constellation to offer. I have hazy visions and shadows, a taste of meaning. But I can't tell you yet. In the meantime, may I offer you a book?

Charles Perry

Laughing and Reading

A light disturbance is witnessed on the face of the reader, but its origin is difficult to determine. Perhaps its source is the air entering and exiting the nostrils, whistling as it passes through fine hairs. The reader engages in an act that resembles breathing, but it's of an irregular sort: pace quickened, they draw in short pulls of oxygen that would probably lead to suffocation if repeated without pause, without the punctuation of a deeper, calmer breath; it is a pulmonary exercise that never actually brings oxygen to lung; it borders on hyperventilation—or it might be just a single, stuttered exhalation, the breath catching against the back of the tongue, then issuing forth in a string of tiny coughs. In a more aggravated case, it comes through the mouth, which hangs just open enough to shape the sound of silent air into the slightest of vocal gestures: the empty wind sliding over the front teeth and against a tightened lip and whispering with their interference as it exits the body. Or the voice may enter the act; it may say something like "hum" or "huh" come forth as a single grand harumph that, in a different context, would probably indicate concern. Then again, perhaps the reader will just do a laugh in its most streamlined, familiar form: a sustained, guttural bellow that swings upward in pitch, or a rollicking, properly projected "Ha! Ha!" occurring continuously until the internal cause of the response grows calmed as the reflex ceases to respond to a stimulus that has either grown dull or departed...

Few reactions have the power to combine an effusive feeling of uncontrollable joy with the sudden awareness of the utter solitude of existence as does the unexpected occurrence of laughter experienced while reading. Just before, the reader was engaged in the most silent of practices—their brow furrowed, their concentration focused, their hands carefully gripping the edges of the page exposed before them. As eyes moved across a mid-page line, the reader became dimly aware of a funny feeling welling up from behind the words, a silliness underlying the rhythm, and a current of poignant jocularity drawing them secretly and swiftly towards the inevitability of laughter. They read and let the voice of the text wash over them; they let it engulf them completely; the words echoed through their quiet mind, and, taking their place therein, developed a linear logic. Those words were saying something, almost like how these ones are, spreading themselves across the page, saying perhaps whatever comes to the mind of the writer, or—just as likely—saying things that are the result of days or years of intense thought. Now, as the reader continues, reflecting without reflection, caught up in the intoxicating rhythm of the line that will, and must, conclude, their knowledge-consuming eyes look forward only to the period at its end that will seal the thought for good, making it complete and, just as quickly, devoured; the reader’s thoughts are immersed, in this way, in the text, and quite without realizing it until it is far too late, their greedy eyes consume too much. Unthinkingly, the reader follows the sentence too far in the direction of its latent humor; whatever tickles them about the text is tickling them now even more, until they are tickled to the tickling’s pinnacle, its ultimate conclusion—“Oh, damn it all, I’m going to laugh!” And the reader does laugh; a deep belly-laugh that explodes into the crowded subway car. Their fellow passengers, who are also reading, look up from their pamphlets or their notebooks or their phones or their paperbacks and give a jealous yet perturbed glance at the reader who has so rudely corrupted this transitional sanctuary. Fellow passengers bring their presence to bear on the outlier: If you see something, say something—and yet, instead they say nothing, and in their saying nothing speak volumes with their chastening glares… Now reading eyes become censuring eyes; now they become fleeting eyes that connect at random with others around them; for a few more moments it feels like anything might happen, and anything does—potentially anything, but really just one thing, a hushed act that falls like a blanket across the car: they all lower their eyes again and settle back down into the individual texts before them.

As for those eyes that squinted, moments earlier, with laughter, they too settle down and return to the page. The reader won't laugh again... or will they? Somehow the text proves irresistible; the reader flirts with the possibility of once more subjecting those nearby to the annoying sound of laughter. Like a masochist pushing on a bruise, thrilling at the memories flooding through its sore pain, the laughing reader revisits the funny part again and again, until eventually the line unceremoniously loses the ability to produce actual laughter—likely due to the gradual dulling of the surprise necessary to jolt the reader into physical response. Reading the passage becomes, through repetition, something like a mantra, or a habit. The reader grows bored. But even as this funny sentence or line or paragraph becomes absorbed by the mind, transcending a physical boundary and persisting as an intangible learned entity, the actual element that caused the laughter remains unclear. Try as he or she might to locate the precise word that spurred the reflex, the reader is faced with only a series of cold, dead symbols.

The situation is one much like that which once occasioned notable humorist E.B. White to remark: “You can dissect a joke like you dissect a frog, but both humor and frog-life will die in the process.” Only, perhaps the issue has implications far broader than White’s frog simile would lead one to believe. The difficulty faced by inquiry into the source of humor in the text is not simply an issue of understanding what makes things funny; instead, it requires a complex and sophisticated grasp of how meaning itself—enshrouded in a humorous tone—occurs or is made to occur. For as the line is dismantled by eyes roaming from word to word, the bonds forged by semantics and by word order and by simple proximity all become frayed and thinned. Each word is denuded and alone, signifying its own significance in isolation. Logically speaking, if one begins with the untethered presence of these words, it is incredibly difficult to hypothesize the likelihood of them being placed one beside another. The probability that the words would end up so perfectly arranged on the page such that their meanings would be limited, by grammar, from the infinite set of potential combinations and made to suit a single set of intentions—or, beyond even that, a single set of *humorous* intentions capable of communicating laughter from creator to consumer—is all but impossible. Yet remarkably, this conceptual difficulty isn't enough to deter people from constantly using language in their attempts to forge meaningful bonds with others, craft personal perspectives, or reflect on the world around them. Speakers babble at length through language and frequently manage to conjure laughter from one another using only words. Meaning is a curse, the joke a spell unleashed by calculated juxtaposition, and one writes as if chanting over a stirred cauldron. The spirit of laughter comes not through the words but through their connections: the invisible tissue that holds them together, the rhythm of their proximity to one another, that pounding of syllables that overtakes the mind of the subway-riding reader and corrupts their steadfast demeanor, unsettling it with the impulse to make a joyful sound...

Often, the elements of a written text most likely to move one to laughter are not put forth in the typical structure of a joke; in contrast to the audience of orally-delivered humor, a reader isn't likely to laugh at a punchline. Rather, the laughter-causing center of the line is usually qualified as such due to its unexpected nature, perhaps an ironic turn or a single, crucial word that contradicts or unsettles the preceding bits of the sentence and throws it into a humorously topsy-turvy realm. This deliciously unanticipated jocularity interrupts the reader's heightened attention; its effectiveness requires a focused reading, of the sort that allows the participant to truly hear the author’s voice in their own mind. In my personal experience, funny moments are missed completely in an inattentive gloss of the text; they are subtle, direct, and precise. At times, the humor might even be missed if the text is read attentively but with the wrong set of expectations, without an openness to laughter. The very same register can appear both solemn and absurd. Furthermore, textual humor can take many different forms, and produce drastically different kinds of laughter. Observational humor will likely give the reader a delightful burst, followed by a moment of poignant reflection. Absurdist humor triggers a sound that begins with surprise and trails off in a thoughtful puzzlement. There are also those writers whose humor lays bare the despairing vanity of the human condition, in response to which the laughing reader emits a grievous cry of anguish as if barking in the faces of wild dogs.

Humor is deeply personal and idiosyncratic, and those jokes encountered in a read text push this quality to its furthest limit, testing the reader’s taste and its alignment with that of the author. For this reason, laughter experienced while reading is the act in its purest form, unadulterated by the social pressure, often present in other humorous scenarios, to join in with one’s peers and laugh with them. Instead, the reading laugher experiences their humor alone, facing it head on. They may even be startled by the fact of their having found something funny enough to laugh at, and afterwards may find themselves reflecting on why, exactly, they enjoy the things they do. This, though, would prove easier in theory than in action—the reader would have to work at untangling threads of trauma, love, power, and pain that inform their general outlook on the world: no easy feat. A person's humor is the amalgamation of an entire life's worth of experiences, each one shaping the laughing reaction, each one qualifying and adjusting the interval of funniness. Your humor is constantly being realigned. Sometimes you may feel disappointed to learn that you no longer enjoy something that once made you chortle uncontrollably, and, at other times, you may feel a sense of embarrassment at having experienced that chortling at all. But this also means that a reader might revisit a text later in life and discover that the further development of their humor has unlocked new joys in moments that had never caused laughter before. How incredible, then, that one might find laughter in a text written hundreds or thousands of years before, in a moment of intense intimacy with a long-dead author. Their newly discovered kinship highlights the greatest goals of culture, and the preservational power of literature (though the results of preservation may not always be so fortunate as this). In the harmony of these two far-flung lives, author and reader, we glimpse life's deepest mysteries; and with a discerning ear, one senses the shrieks of their maddening cackle echoing just beneath the surface.

V. After Reading

Find yourself in a comfortable position – with your back supported, your feet on the ground.

Once you've settled, your whole body should feel supported.

What do you notice? Where do you feel most supported? Where does your body contact the floor, the chair? The back of the chair?

What do you notice in your sensation of your back, your chest, neck, jaw, and face?

When you're ready, close your eyes and just feel what it's like to sit with your eyes closed. Does closing your eyes give you any different sense of yourself?

Hello again. Scoot forward away from the wall or the back of the chair and locate some sense of your sits bones. You can rock a little bit from left to right if it helps to locate these two bony places of contact with the surface you're sitting on.

Now, if you can, allow your skeleton, the vertebrae of your spine, your shoulders, neck, and head to stack up one on top of the other. Feel supported from your sits bones to the top of your head. No need to strain or force yourself to "sit up," just notice the connection from your pelvis all the way up through your head.

Notice the effect this way of sitting has on your breathing. Breathe as fully or as deeply as you need to in order to sit in this way, towards the edge of the chair, legs uncrossed, both of your feet in contact with the ground if possible.

You might place the palms of your hands on your thighs. Whatever you do with your hands, make sure your arms are comfortable.

Now bring your attention to your breath again.

There’s a small space after you exhale before you inhale. See if you can rest there after exhaling, and before inhaling. Spend a little time there in that space after your exhalation before your inhalation begins.

Great.

Now take your tongue to the back of your right back molar, or the farthest back tooth on the right side of your mouth, where the tooth and gum meet, and slowly run your tongue along the back of your top teeth.

Take your time, moving tooth by tooth, gently touching and sensing each tooth with your tongue.

What do you feel? What do you notice? Continuing towards the front of the mouth, in back of the right front tooth and left front tooth, slowly sensing the back of the teeth on the left side.

Eventually, you’ll make your way around to the farthest top tooth on the left. When you get there, bring your tongue to the front surface of that last tooth, to the *front* of your top teeth. Make your way, tooth by tooth, slowly, back to the right. Running your tongue along the front of your top teeth, between your teeth and your cheek or the flesh above your lip.

You can allow your mouth to open as you do this or you can keep your mouth gently closed. Notice how much space there is for your tongue between your teeth, your gums, and the flesh of your face. Notice how happy or spacious your cheek and lip feel separating from your teeth, softening.

Once you make your way back around the front of your teeth, bring your tongue down to your bottom farthest tooth on the right, where the gum and tooth meet, and continue with your tongue along the back of your *bottom* teeth. Take your time, explore each tooth – the sometimes curvy, sometimes flat *back* surfaces of your bottom teeth.

Now, when you’ve come all the way around the back of your bottom teeth, bring your tongue to the front of your left back molar, or the farthest back tooth on the *left* side of your mouth, and run your tongue along the front of your bottom teeth, between your teeth and your cheek, the flesh below your lip.

You might open your mouth, or you might see what it feels like to keep your mouth closed, your lips gently touching.

Again, take your time to feel each tooth. Feel your teeth and cheek and lip separating. Sense all of the space between your teeth and gums and the flesh of your face.

You might try *imagining* running your finger between your teeth and cheek, the way you have been running your tongue. You might find more space between your teeth and the flesh of your face this way. Go ahead – rest your tongue and just imagine your index finger running between your bottom teeth and your cheek. *Imagine* slowly sweeping your finger along your teeth and gums on one side of your mouth.

And then on the other side of your mouth.

How does that feel?

Okay, forget all that, and lean back again in your chair, your feet flat on the ground, eyes closed. What do you notice? Where do you feel most supported? Where does your body contact the floor, the back of the chair?

What do you notice in your sensation of your back, your chest, neck, jaw, and face, your head? Your breathing?

And return to your tongue. Bring your tongue to the front of the roof of your mouth and gently rest it against the back of your front top teeth.

Run your tongue back along the roof of your mouth from the front to the back, exploring the contours of the roof of your mouth. Is the ridge of the roof hard and bony? Is there a point at which it gets softer? Where does the soft palette begin?

Now go ahead and run your tongue back in the other direction, forward along the roof of your mouth, eventually coming to the back of your top front teeth.

And then bring your tongue down along your teeth so that it comes to rest at the back of your *bottom* teeth. Begin running your tongue back along the bottom of your mouth cavity.

Explore the bottom of your mouth, the skin, bone, muscle.

Now, continuing to run your tongue along the bottom and top of your mouth, bend your arm at the elbow, and have your palm and fingers – relaxed, gently curled – facing your body.

Bring the top or back of your hand and fingers up to your throat and run the tops of your fingers lightly up your neck and under your chin, as if you were Italian. But instead of flicking someone off or emphasizing your point, just rest the tops of your fingers there under your chin, in this triangle between your jaw bones.

Stay there, and feel this place with the back of your hand as you continue exploring your mouth with your tongue.

Feel, notice when the movement of the tongue causes a little bulge in this place under your chin. See if you can explore the roof of your mouth, the ridge, the bottom of the mouth cavity. Do it with your tongue, *without* causing any bulge or change under your chin.

How can you keep this little triangle quiet? Can you?

How can you keep the gentle, sensitive movement of the tongue quiet inside your mouth? How can you relax your jaw *and* relax your tongue *and* move your tongue?

Can you press more softly with your tongue – against the back of your teeth, along the ridge of your mouth, between your teeth and your cheeks – maintaining a sense of the space and softness of your mouth?

How can you let go of your tongue in order to use your tongue? Now let go of everything. Sit back in your chair or against the wall.

What do you notice? Where do you feel most supported? Where does your body contact the floor, the chair?

What do you notice in your sensation of your chest, your neck and jaw, cheeks, face? Your breathing?

You are now ready to read.

* * *

Body Mapping the Mouth Cavity is a Feldenkrais Awareness Through Movement adaptation by Madelyn Kent and Helen Singh Miller designed to help relax the tongue for reading.

Appendix B, "A Sort of Practical Cartography" 426

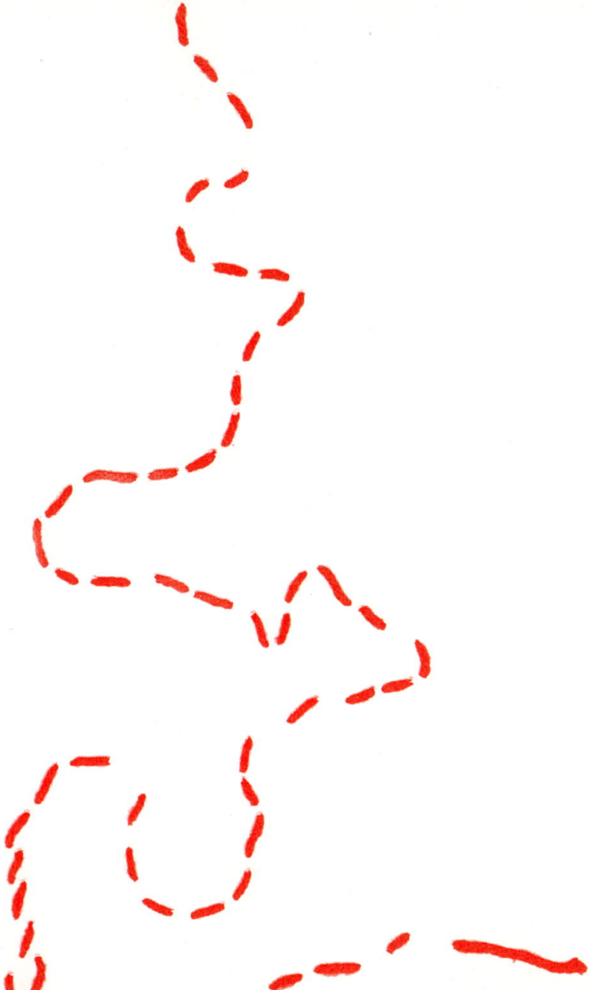

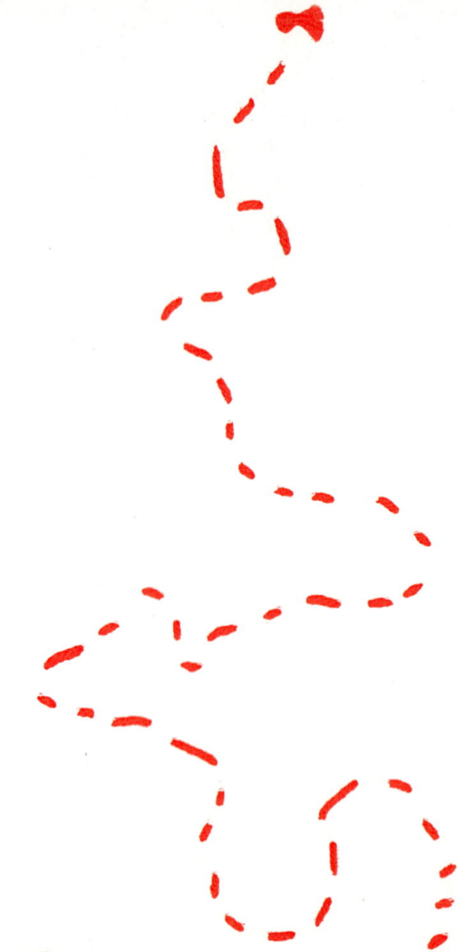

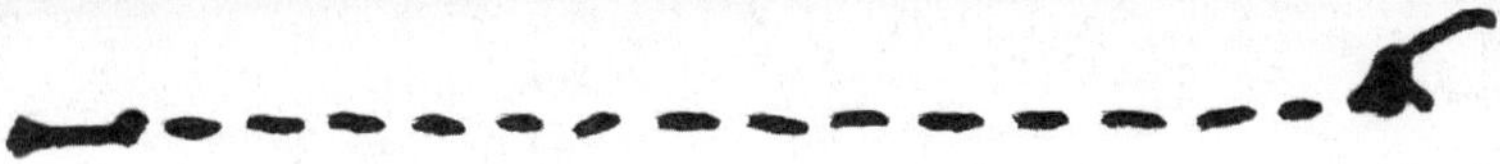